Beginner's Guide
to
Archaeology

Beginner's Guide
to
Archaeology

**The modern digger's
step-by-step introduction
to the expert ways
of unearthing the past**

Louis A. Brennan

Stackpole Books

BEGINNER'S GUIDE TO ARCHAEOLOGY

Copyright © 1973 by
THE STACKPOLE COMPANY

Published by
STACKPOLE BOOKS
Cameron and Kelker Streets
Harrisburg, Pa. 17105

Printed in U.S.A.

Library of Congress Cataloging in Publication Data

Brennan, Louis A
   Beginner's guide to archaeology.

   Includes bibliographical references.
   1. Indians of North America—Antiquities.
2. Archaeology—Methodology. 3. North America—Antiquities. I. Title.
E77.9.B73   913'.031   73-4193
ISBN 0-8117-0418-1

Contents

Contents (cont.)

Contents (cont.)

Contents (cont.)

Acknowledgments

THE AUTHOR WISHES to thank the persons, institutions, and publications listed below for permission to reprint material in this book:

Joffre Coe and the American Philosophical Society for the diagrams on pp. 27 and 28, which originally appeared in J. Coe, "Formative Cultures of the Carolina Piedmont," *Transactions of the American Philosophical Society,* Vol. 54, Pt. 5 (1964); Bettye Broyles and the West Virginia Geological and Economic Survey, Report of Archeological Investigations Series, for the diagrams on pp. 30-31, which were reproduced from Bettye Broyles' "Second Preliminary Report: The St. Albans Site, Kanawha County, West Virginia"; Melvin Fowler for the diagram on p. 33, reproduced by permission of the Society for American Archaeology from *American Antiquity* 24 (3), 1959; Waldo R. Wedel and Dr. Harold McCracken, Director, Buffalo Bill Historical Center of Cody, Wyoming, for the diagram on p. 34; *Pennsylvania Archaeologist* for the diagram on p. 133, which is reproduced from the April 1965 issue; Dr. James L. Swauger for the directions for recording petroglyphs on pp. 133-134; Stuart Struever for the excerpt from his article "Flotation Techniques for the Recovery of Small-Scale Archaeological Remains" on pp. 134-135, reproduced by permission of the Society for American Archaeology from *American Antiquity* 33: 354-355, 1968; Edward J. Kaeser for "The Ceramic Study" on pp. 202-205, reprinted from the New York State Archaeological Society *Bulletin* of November 1969; Robert L. Stephenson and the Museum of Anthropology of the University of Michigan for the type description and illustrations of vessel and rim profiles of Moyaone Cord Impressed pottery on pp. 205-207, which originally appeared in "The Accokeek Creek Site: A Middle Atlantic Seaboard Culture Sequence," *Anthropological Papers,* No. 20, Museum of Anthropology, University of Michigan, Ann Arbor; Gordon B. Willey, Philip Phillips, and the University of Chicago Press for the diagram on p. 216, which appeared in the above authors' *Method and Theory in American Archaeology,* published in 1958; Paul L. Weinman and Thomas P. Weinman for their report, "The Moonshine Rockshelter," on pp. 233-238, reprinted from the New York State Archaeological Society *Bulletin* of July 1969; and Herbert C. Kraft and the Seton Hall University Museum for the report, "The Miller Field Site in New Jersey and Its Influence upon the Terminal Archaic and Transitional Stages in New York State and Long Island," on pp. 240-258, reprinted from the New York State Archaeological Society *Bulletin* of March 1970.

Foreword

ARCHAEOLOGY is a science to which the nonprofessional can (and frequently does) contribute as much as does the professional. How and why this thesis is true will become apparent as you read this book. Most archaeological sites are found and worked (at least initially!) by nonprofessionals. The history of American archaeology is replete with the contributions made by nonprofessionals, and the roster of nationally known, prestigious archaeologists who were not formally trained in the subject is substantial and impressive.

There is no mystery to archaeology. Anyone with common sense, average mental and physical abilities, and an attitude of respect for the data can master the science. Whether one gets paid for doing it is really unimportant. In fact, with the relative scarcity of paying positions open in the field (as contrasted with the *need* for working archaeologists), paid archaeologists are greatly outnumbered by people who do *good* archaeology, but who earn their livings at some other trade or profession. Further, most paid archaeologists are limited in the amount of field research they can do, because of teaching or administrative loads they must carry. There are quite a few nonprofessionals who do more field and laboratory research and writing for publication than does the average professional archaeologist. These are some of the present-day "facts of life," and no criticism is implied or intended.

Because of this rather unique situation in the field of archaeology, especially in the United States, the role of the nonprofessional, or citizen, archaeologist is crucial. Naturally, the quality of the archaeological product, whether raw data or a finished publication, depends entirely on the knowledge, training, and motivation brought to the subject by the archaeologist. Fortunately, most nonprofessionals (as opposed to the vandals called "pot hunters") are seriously motivated, fairly well-read in the subject, and equipped with the personal qualities required. Many also bring to the work the skills they have acquired and use in their normal vocations. In many instances—such as in photography, surveying, drafting, use of hand or powered tools, creative writing, etc.—their skills exceed those of the average professional archaeologist.

Once we accept these truths, we can set out to improve ourselves and to help the practicing citizen archaeologist to become even better at his chosen avocation. While there are numerous "how-to" books on the subject of archaeology, very few stress these all-important points. Louis A. Brennan not only emphasizes these aspects of archaeology, but does so with the fervor, knowledge, and practicality which comes from a lifelong participation in archaeology. To his recipe for *doing* archaeology, he adds his personal philosophy, including a touch of humor, and he explains the rationale behind what he prescribes.

As Dr. Charles R. McGimsey has pointed out in numerous articles and one book, there is today a great and growing need for archaeological field work. With the accelerated destruction of archaeological sites, the only way we can hope to keep abreast is to involve more and more people in the work and to increase productivity in as many ways as possible. While it would be ideal if we could train and support more professionals in the field, this is probably too much to ask. With the limited funds available for archaeology, it is highly unlikely that there will ever be sufficient professionals to meet the need. Accordingly, the role of the nonprofessional needs to be enlarged and his productivity enhanced.

Several ways come to mind whereby we might accomplish these aims. We can induce more and more young people to pursue the hobby of scientific archaeology; some of these might well go into the field professionally. We can encourage the participation of collectors as volunteer workers on professionally run projects, so as to teach them the basic techniques of excavation and the types of records to maintain. Where possible, we can work with the active pot hunter, in order to redirect his efforts into constructive archaeology. In many instances, the pot hunter is one only because no one has taken the time and trouble to reach out to him and teach him. It is becoming obvious that we can no longer afford to stand aside, wringing our hands, and deploring his activities. We need to get to know him better, to gain his confidence, and to work with him, even if only to salvage what data we can from his work. In doing so, though, we can demonstrate to him how much more gratifying it is to recover the information which makes meaningful the artifacts he has been amassing. The writer has followed such a course in Virginia for several years and can attest to the successes which result from this approach. Lastly, on any project, professional archaeologists should welcome the services of anyone willing to contribute his/her time, labor, skills, political influence, or financial help. To turn away such help is to lessen our own output, both in research and in the educational aspect of archaeology as a science.

An important tool for the beginning archaeologist is a well-written, lucid, and detailed guide, such as Louis A. Brennan has here authored. By reading this book attentively, anyone with a serious interest in archaeology can acquire the fundamentals. Coupling this reading with practical work under an experienced supervisor-teacher, the beginner can before long become a qualified citizen archaeologist, a role he can fill with pride and satisfaction.

As one who has come into professional archaeology via the nonprofessional route, the writer commends Mr. Brennan for this work. Would that there had been something like it thirty years ago!

HOWARD A. MACCORD, SR.
Archaeologist, Virginia State Library, Richmond, Virginia

chapter 1

Ensuring a Future for the Past

ARCHAEOLOGY APPEALS TO many kinds of people, to those of scientific bent, to those with detective and problem-solving instincts, to the conservationist and ecologist, to the historian and the ancestor-minded, to the treasure hunter, and to those who are merely looking for a wholesome outdoor hobby that is at once not too financially demanding and yet genially social.

Any and all of the above types can be stimulated by reading this book, and other archaeological literature, to engage in what is now being called "public archaeology." By committing himself to the archaeological recovery of the remains of American prehistory the nonprofessional or public archaeologist contributes as much to the public good as those who join action groups for the preservation of a wildlife refuge, the depollution of a stream, or the abolition of strip mining. The heritage of America's prehistoric past is one with all these, and in a special way. Whereas the damage done to the environment can often be repaired or reversed, the destruction of a prehistoric site is permanent. Like Humpty Dumpty, it cannot be reassembled.

THE DESTRUCTION OF THE PAST

The limited corps of professional archaeologists cannot cope with the accelerating rate of destruction of archaeological sites, both prehistoric and historic, as millions of acres are bulldozed for new land uses each year and whole valleys are inundated in a season for reservoirs and recreation lakes. Archaeology, especially prehistoric archaeology in the United States, has always been stingily funded; when the economy is under any kind of stress—depression or inflation or both—it is the first activity to be dropped from the subsidy list. Nor does it, as the excavation of local sites without architectural ruins or the likelihood of producing *objets d'art,* excite the benefactions of affluent patrons. To them and to many professionals as well, it is backyard archaeology, as compared with the digging of Mayan temples and Inca cities. Meanwhile those backyard sites, with their irreplaceable information about 30,000 years of Stone Age habitation, remain in private hands unprotected by law or public awareness of their value.

In an article entitled "Is There a Future for the Past?" in the magazine *Archaeology,* October 1971, Hester A. Davis of the Arkansas Archaeological Survey and chairman of the Committee on Public Understanding of Archaeology of the Society for American Archaeology summed up the grim picture of site erasure. After pointing out the need of farmers, trailer parks, and shopping centers for level land, the author observed that "all the actions about which conservationists are so voluble today are just as destructive to the non-renewable archaeological resources as they are to the natural portions of the environment, except that the destruction of archaeological resources is more permanent. You can't grow a new Indian site."

In short, the face of the American land is being changed so rapidly that within the lifetime of many of us there will hardly remain a usable square foot unplowed, unbulldozed, uninundated, or unpaved. Wiped out utterly will be the record of achievement of American aborigines who are believed to have had no achievements because the record has been wiped out. It is almost like burning the Iliad and the Odyssey.

RESCUE MISSION OF THE ARCHAEOLOGIST

Some of this may be saved by a conservationist recognition that our prehistory is one of the natural elements of environment, as worthy of protection as flora, fauna, and the run of a brook. Amerinds, the American aborigines, lived within the natural environment as adjusted members of its ecosystem, in an intimacy that has lessons for modern man. In consequence of this ecological harmony, the more than 30,000 years of human habitation of this hemisphere have left cultural remains strewn along every stream valley and lake shore, present and extinct.

Obviously, the only way to "save" the past is to get to the sites before the earthmovers do. If the sites are to be destroyed, let them be destroyed by those who take scientific pains to recover the physical material and the anthropological facts they contain. Digging, however scientific, it should be acknowledged, does destroy a site even more thoroughly than bulldozing, but it destroys it for a purpose: the preservation of its record. Given the paucity of professionals, the scarcity of funds, and the inadequate legal protection for American archaeology, for both prehistoric and historical sites, a scientific tragedy can be averted only by the enlistment of citizens and amateur archaeologists in the campaign of preservation.

TEAMWORK OF NONPROFESSIONAL AND PROFESSIONAL ARCHAEOLOGISTS

Who is a public archaeologist? He is anybody who wants to do archaeology and is willing to learn and abide by the rules. He is anybody from seven to seventy—and these age extremes are doing useful work in the field—who plies a trowel or shovel knowledgeably and with sober archaeological intent. In order to make some clarifying distinctions, nonprofessional archaeologists may be divided into two groups, the citizen archaeologists and the amateurs. The former, adhering to professional standards and aspiring to a professional breadth of knowledge, conduct independent investigations with the intent of making new and original contributions to knowledge. The amateur is a knowing and disciplined digger who is aware of what he is digging and who records and reports it properly but who leaves the interpretation and analysis to others. There is no implication of difference in rank in these terms. The difference lies only in experience, in the intensity of interest, and in the time and effort spent in research. Both groups are avocational archaeologists who associate or affiliate with the organizations formed to foster the study of American prehistory.

Almost alone among the scientific disciplines American archaeology regularly brings together professionals and nonprofessionals in conferences of societies at which the principal business is to present reports on current investigations and studies. Nonprofessionals are freely accepted into the Society for American Archaeology, the organization to which 99 percent of professional American archaeologists belong, and they may attend the SAA annual conferences, though these are so crowded with papers from professionals and graduate students that it is doubtful that a contribution from a nonprofessional could ever make the program. But it is the state societies, consisting of alliances of local chapters, that give the nonprofessionals their sense of belonging in the field of archaeology, and their forum for reporting and discussion of their work. Here they will outnumber the professionals nine to one, but the professionals by contributing heavily to the annual conference's programs of papers, holding office, influencing policy, and setting standards give the state societies respectable scientific standing. The commingling is profitable to both groups.

In the eastern United States there functions, at the level above the state societies, the Eastern States Archaeological Federation, a consortium of state societies which follows the pattern of organization and annual conferences of SAA and the state societies. The professionals dominate this organization by the weight of what they have to contribute; after all, archaeology is their life's work. Attendance often is, however, 75 percent nonprofessional, for it is to the ESAF conference that the nonprofessionals come for updating and continuing education. In addition there are regional conferences, usually invitational and not organizationally structured, such as the Southeastern Archaeological Conference, the Ohio Valley Archaeological Conference, and the Middle Atlantic Seaboard States Conference, where the emphasis is on the synthesis of ongoing work and there is no caste system among those invited.

There is no Western States Archaeological Conference like the ESAF for state societies west of the Mississippi, and regional conferences, such as the Plains Archaeological Conference and the Southwest Anthropological Conference, meet sporadically and unpredictably. The result or, perhaps, the cause, is strained relationships between professionals and nonprofessionals as a result of site looting by piratical "pot hunters" interested in possessing prize artifacts.

THE ABOMINABLE POT HUNTERS

It is a conservative estimate that there are 5000 grave-robbing, site-gouging pot hunters in the state of Oregon alone who are doing more damage to the prehistoric record than 5000 bulldozers. After all, it is not the malicious intention of land developers to destroy sites; the destruction is incidental to another purpose. But the archaeological pirate is interested only in finding and looting sites, and he searches them out like Jack Horner probing for plums in his pie. In the Southwest the looters, who include casual tourists, number twice 5000. In the Midwest—particularly in Arkansas, Missouri, Illinois, Indiana, and Ohio, archaeologically rich territory—site looting is a long-established tradition going back before there was an American archaeology, and it has the same status in the public view as rabbit- and squirrel-hunting. The eastern states escape the worst ravages of looters only because sites are harder to find and often buried or are in remote places, and because the region is heavily populated and has been plowed over and under for centuries.

Pot hunters are as much to be pitied as scorned, more to be cured than cursed. When they steal from the American past, they also rob themselves. Just as jewels are more valuable in their settings as bracelets or necklaces, so artifacts (spearheads, stone axes, pottery, etc.) are more exciting to find, more satisfying to own, and more completely owned when they are recovered with the total assemblage and within the cultural context to which they belonged in the life of their makers and users. By themselves, artifacts are mere trinkets and curiosities. It is the scientific information about them, acquired by proper digging, that gives them their sheen of value, though in the flea market of artifact trading some items have high dollar values often because rich collectors have taken a fancy to a specific kind of artifact and pay well for what they covet. This stimulates the fakers and counterfeiters who should, perhaps, be encouraged to increase their production. Such faking and counterfeiting is not illegal and it feeds the acquisitiveness of the collector without requiring site looting.

THE REWARDS OF AMATEUR ARCHAEOLOGY

The citizen and amateur archaeologist, then, is not only a worker whose aim is to excavate so that he recovers artifacts within their association but a member of a scientific community committed to standards of ethics and performance. Instead of incurring the bad name of the pot hunter he may well earn a modest reputation for his work; if the site he digs happens to be one of high importance, his name may achieve a permanent place in the literature. In any case he will have the pleasure of confirming or adding to somebody else's work, or of making an original discovery.

A word of caution: there is no double standard of work for the professional and the nonprofessional, at whatever level the work is being done. What the nonprofessional does is to his credit or his discredit, as though it were a picture he had painted or a book he had authored. It becomes a contribution, *his* contribution, to knowledge about the past; and it behooves him not to introduce error by reason of carelessness or ineptitude. All excavation should be approached with a sense of obligation to the work and an anticipation of the opportunity lying ahead. Every site is important to a greater or lesser degree, but only painstaking archaeology will reveal its full record and story.

That each site tells a unique story, regardless of how many other sites appear to be similar, cannot be overstressed. Each represents a location where a group of individual human beings, with personal names and private personalities, with blood ties or community relations with one another, lived days of their lives or performed activities necessary to their existence, in fear or joy, in hunger or the repletion of good times, loving and hating, and hoping. There never was such a person as Paleo-man or Archaic man, terms applied in

American archaeology to the people who lived during the periods so designated. There were brothers and sisters, fathers, mothers, connubial mates, children, grandparents, the infirm and the healthy, the lucky and the unlucky, the talented and the dolts, the kind and the bitter. The excavator will feel this one day when he picks up a potsherd with the thumbprint of the potter who marked it. He will then realize he is figuratively touching hands with a woman dead 2,000 years who might have been known as Pocohantas or Sacajawea or the equivalent in the dialect of the district. Archaeology is for the imaginative and the humanist as well as the scientific. It is not just a way of spending leisure time; it is a form of personal enrichment.

chapter 2

How Archaeologists Work

THE WIDESPREAD IMPRESSION is that doing archaeology is going digging, in a place where artifactual goodies have been discovered lying beneath the surface of the ground, and harvesting them like spading up potatoes. True, the recovery of artifacts, cultural material, and data from their earthy matrix is indispensable to archaeology; but digging is only one of the labors that must be undertaken to achieve the objectives of archaeology.

STEPS IN THE ARCHAEOLOGICAL PROCESS

Archaeology, to offer a definition by function, is a process of several steps by which the nonverbal, material remains of the past are converted into knowledge about prehistory and prehistoric anthropology. Prehistory is the chronological succession of human events as man adjusted, invented, schemed, and fought to survive and improve his lot in the environments with which he had to contend. It is simply the history of times for which there are no contemporary written records—about 99.99 percent of human existence—since language writing, as distinguished from account keeping, is only about 5000 years old in the Old World and less than 2000 years old in America and even now the writing of American civilizations has been only partially deciphered. Prehistoric anthropology is the record of human sociocultural behavior, deduced from material remains and by analogy with known human patterns of behavior, in man's making his living, governing his communities, worshipping his gods, and burying his dead.

The first step of the process is survey. Since human activities were confined in time and place, the location of those activities must be found before evidence of them can be excavated. The second step is the excavation, controlled and recorded. Step three is the study and analysis of the material and data recovered and its assembling into meaningful cultural classes and combinations of information. The results of excavation and the results of study and analysis are incorporated in a report. This fourth step is followed by step five, publication of the report, the culmination of the process. When the report is in print, it becomes an addition to the body of knowledge we call archaeology.

The steps in the process may be listed thus:

1. Discovery through physical survey or research.
2. Excavation according to plan and recording of recoveries.
3. Study: identification, classification, tabulations, analysis.
4. Report: account of excavation, results of study-analysis, interpretation, conclusions.
5. Publication: entrance of the work into archaeological literature, where it becomes available for reference to other workers.

Survey

Physical survey may have either of two objectives: first, the discovery of all discoverable sites within a given area and a preliminary testing of these to ascertain their nature, in which case it is an archaeological project in itself; and, second, the discovery of a site, any site, to dig, or the location of a special site producing evidence of a specific culture because information about that culture is lacking or incomplete. Physical survey means land exploration afoot, walking fields, stream valleys, the hills in cave country, etc., with head down for the glint of flint chips or cracked rock or other clues to prehistoric activity. But sites can be, and more often than not are, discovered by other means: by inquiry of landowners, especially farmers; by consulting local histories and historical societies, by questioning known collectors (though these are notoriously close-mouthed about where they may be collecting), and by a review of the archaeological literature. In some cases surveys of areas have already been made, or lists of known sites have been compiled by interested persons who foresaw the usefulness of such information as urbanization threatened. (Perhaps the earliest of such surveys is that of the naturalist Rafinesque, who carefully noted all the then known sites, county by county, in Kentucky in 1824.) Finally, excavation reports in the literature provide site locations; few sites of any size have been completely dug, and parts of the larger sites still await examination.

Excavation

Before a site can be dug it should be tested, even before being laid out in grid plan. The nonprofessional archaeologist should not attempt the excavation of a site for which he does not have the experience, manpower, or resources. Sites come in all sizes, from a tiny two-foot by four-foot patch under a rock overhang occasionally used as shelter by hunters on the trail and yielding a few spearheads and stone knives to groups of mounds, like that at Cahokia, Illinois, where the huge Monks Mound has an automobile road running to the top, and to cities like Teotihuacan, which, in its heyday, had an estimated population of 200,000. The temple mounds of the Southeast and the Mississippi Valley, the communities of the Southwest with their ruins of adobe settlements, and even the large village sites in flat fields in the Midwest are projects for large crews working 40-hour weeks and utilizing heavy equipment. Modern practice, for instance, calls for the stripping away of the topsoil from a settlement site in order to uncover the patterns of buildings and palisades outlined by the visible molds of the posts that supported the structures. To do this work by hand would take years; a bulldozer can lay bare a two-acre village site in a couple of days. Professionals do not tackle digs like these without elaborate planning, adequate funds, and a competent staff. But there is still, despite megalopolitan sprawl, enough work of manageable size to be done to keep the nonprofessional busy as long as he can bend his knees.

Excavation is where archaeology begins. It has to be planned, laid out and done within the plan, yet with a keen sensitivity to what turns up that may change the plan. The excavator has to be scrupulous about what actually turns up and report his findings honestly; even professionals have been known to misread, explain away, overlook, downgrade, or even suppress evidence that contradicts pet notions. Excavation, therefore, is not simply digging and recording; it is also a process of forming tentative conclusions about what is turning up which continuing excavation confirms, modifies, or refutes. The amateur digger may content himself with digging carefully and recording meticulously, but somebody should be in charge who has an inkling of when the site existed in time and what its character was, in order to know what direction the study and analysis and, later, the report will take.

Study and Analysis

Since a site is a locale of human activity in an environment from which the occupants had to obtain food and materials for their subsistence, one of the first objectives of the postexcavation study is to deduce from the tools and other evidence found (such as bone, mollusc shells, nut hulls, and the like), the means of livelihood of the occupants: were they mainly fishermen and collectors of shellfish who hunted occasionally, or were they hunters and gatherers of wild vegetal foods who occasionally visited the shores of a stream when game was scarce and plant foods ran short? Hunting tools such as spearheads and knives, fishing tools such as net sinkers and bone gorges, and vegetal processing tools such as manos (handstones) and metates (nether or table stones used in the hand grinding of seeds) not only attest to the practice of these food-getting activities but their ratios to each other establish their relative importance in the site economy. All recoveries must be identified as to function and type (for instance, the types of spearheads, which changed shape through time, can locate a site in time), quantified, tabulated as to materials of manufacture or as to species if they are organic, and plotted as to distribution. These data will usually give rise to questions for which the answers have to be researched.

But the more interesting sites shape their own problems. For the past twenty years my colleagues and I have been digging shell middens on the banks of the lower Hudson River. These middens are simply garbage heaps consisting of oyster shell, with some hard clam and ribbed mussel thrown in, discarded by aboriginal campers for whom oysters were only one item on the menu. One problem for us was this: although the lower Hudson is a tidal estuary and therefore has salty water, it is not salty enough now for oyster breeding and has not been salty enough to support oyster beds for any length of time since about 1000 B.C.

The search for the answer to the disappearance of oysters and other marine shellfish from the lower Hudson led us, surprisingly, to the fact that sea level had been about 400 feet lower some 20,000 years ago. This drop had been caused by the withdrawal of water from the world ocean and its fixing as ice in the Wisconsin glacier, which was, at that time, spread over all of Canada and into the present United States as far south as New York City. About 19,000 B.P.*, the Wisconsin began to melt and its melt waters, returning to the sea, began to raise its level. Sea level had reached close to its present level 2000 B.P. and reached the present level 1000 B.P.

For the 18,000 years of rise the rate of rise was not steady, however; there were periods when it rose so fast that one man in his lifetime would be

---

*The abbreviation "B.P." used throughout this book means "years before the present."

aware of it. There were also periods of slow rise or no rise at all. When the rise was rapid, faster than the rate of accumulation of silt in the riverbed, the lower Hudson was a deep body of water and much of its volume was salty sea water. During such periods oysters found a suitable habitat here. But when the rise was slower than the rate of silting, the estuary became shallow and, since the input of fresh water was nearly constant, the salinity dropped. Geologists have shown that the last of the Wisconsin glacier ice had disappeared by about 7000 B.P. and the rate of rise of sea level began to slow. By about 3000 B.P., when oysters stopped growing in the lower Hudson, the rate of rise was, perhaps, no more than 3 inches per century. By 2000 B.P. it was down to about 1 inch per century.

This was only one of the lines of research, of off-site archaeology, that our shell midden digging led us into. It was eye-opening; our heaps of eroding, nondescript oyster valves (hundreds of such middens have been carted away in the past to surface roads) were clues to great recent geologic events. Even as we were digging our first middens, the archaeologist Wesley Hurt was digging shell middens in Brazil and discovering that the location of the middens was directly related to sea level rise. But, to repeat a caution that will be reiterated again and again: each site is different. Whereas our middens consisted of small, dome-shaped dumps left behind by small groups of aboriginal campers, the shell heaps of California were lived on and the dead were buried in them. The immense shell heaps of the Tennessee River, composed of river mussel shells, were thirty feet deep and so extensive that small settlements were built on them. At Crystal River, Florida, a temple mound (a mound on the top of which was erected a wooden ceremonial structure or temple) was built of oyster, whelk, and coquina valves and is even now about forty feet high despite settling and erosion.

Shell middens are to be found from the Aleutian Islands to Tierra del Fuego and from Maine to Argentina, and they are all monuments to the edibility of shellfish and the human habit of eating them. Beyond that they represent problems to be studied and solved. Such problems may be posed by one site and solved by discoveries at another, so that subjects for study should not be thought of as those that are solved by the recoveries from a single site. After the report has been written and published the excavator may find that a site dug by somebody else holds the answers.

Report

Many excavators find report writing worse than a visit to the dentist. But straightforward reports are not all that painful to write, once the format is understood. In Chapter 13 the reader will find two reports reprinted, one on a simple rockshelter in which the structure of a report shows through, with a little glossing, and another on a more complex site, in which a great deal of material and its interpretation are skillfully handled, but with the structure still recognizable. Whatever the excavator's antipathy to writing, he has already incurred the obligation of reconstructing and construing a site by reason of having taken it apart. Since the more exactly a site has been dug the more absolutely it has been destroyed, the report must return it to useful and meaningful existence; how meaningful and useful depends on how astute the study of it has been. Usually report writing is no more difficult than filling out an income tax form; when the writer has made an interesting discovery either on site or during study, it can be a rare exercise in self-expression.

Publication

Regional and state societies issue periodic journals devoted almost exclusively to site reports, many of which are by citizen archaeologists. These journals do not discriminate as to author, only as to the competence of the manuscript. (As the editor of a state society and a regional journal I do not misstate the situation.) Editors make every effort to find space for all publishable material, even to the extent of overspending their budgets. A second medium for the dissemination of reports is the program of papers of the annual meetings of archaeological societies, for those who can bring themselves to present a paper before an attentive audience. And a third opportunity is offered by monthly chapter meetings.

That he lives in a state or area not covered by a publication, and the opportunity to publish or present a report is scant, does not relieve the excavator of the obligation of writing one. If no other disposition can be found, then the report should be placed in the same drawer, box, or file cabinet in which he keeps the site collection, there to remain until the executor of the will settles the excavator's estate. As extra insurance against loss of the report, it is a good idea to submit a copy to the local historical society. The report is the most important artifact in that site collection, and should all the other artifacts and site materials disappear, the site still exists as archaeology.

THE LOCAL SEQUENCE

These are the five steps in doing archaeology, but they leave unanswered the question of what archaeology does. It provides the record of prehistory and prehistoric anthropology; this has already been said. But what is the product in actual terms? What does it look like, in black and white?

The first product of archaeological investigation is the local sequence, a column of dates and the named cultures to which they apply, ideally from the beginning of human habitation of a locality until the time of the disappearance of aboriginal peoples after contact with white Europeans or Americans. This is a chronological outline that is fleshed out by expanding the descriptions of the component cultures and their relations to each other. There is no definition of culture that satisfies all students because the word can be used in so many different ways. Generally speaking, it means all human activity whether the activity results in or uses material objects or not. Archaeologists recover only material remains but they make inferences from these remains about nonmaterial practices and traits that are equally the content of culture.

By spin-off from the above meaning, the cultures which comprise the local sequence—i.e., the succession of peoples who inhabited a locality over thousands of years—are population units (call them bands or tribes, if you like) distinguishable by characteristic or diagnostic traits. In prehistoric archaeology these traits are, of course, material, manufactured artifacts.

An example of a familiar culturally diagnostic artifact is the Kentucky, more accurately, the Pennsylvania rifle. It began to be made in Lancaster County, Pennsylvania, in the 1730s and by 1750 it was the favorite weapon of the frontiersman and westering pioneer, traveling with guide and wagon train all the way to Oregon. Percussion cartridge rifles like the Henry began to replace it by 1840 and its day was done culturally, although it survives for mantelpiece decoration and as a collector's item. Archaeologists of the year 5000, all records possibly being lost in a nuclear holocaust in the meantime, might very well designate the 100 years of the Kentucky rifle's cultural importance as the Kentucky Rifle Period and the sites at which it is found components of the Kentucky Rifle Culture. But the reader can think of innumerable cultural time markers like this: high button shoes, washboards, Atwater-Kent radios, Coca-Cola bottles, aluminum beer cans, etc.

Because most sites in America are at what were desirable locations—near water, shelter, and food sources—they continued to be resorted to for generation after generation. During these decades, centuries, and even millennia, cultural changes occurred, either through evolution or because different cultures came, stayed awhile, and then vanished. Each cultural change marked by a new diagnostic trait is considered a new culture, and sites where several cultures are found are multicomponent sites. A multicomponent site is a local sequence, or a section of one, in being. When an excavator digs, therefore, he is working on the vertical line of time, the local sequence, the order of events, the chronological history of prehistory.

A culture has no set geographic boundaries. Its locale is defined by the area throughout which its diagnostic artifacts are found; this area may be no bigger than a township, or as big as a state, or it may be a region the size of several states. The size of the area is determined by the correlation of many local sequences. Doing archaeology is searching out local sequences and then finding sequence match-ups in order to make inferences about cultural evolution and advancement, the movements of people, the directions of those movements and the reasons for them.

From about 14,000 B.P. to the appearance of pottery—about 4500 B.P. in Florida, about 3000 B.P. in New York—the principal diagnostic artifact, because Amerinds during that lengthy period lived wholly or partly by hunting, is the stone projectile point or weapon point. The uninformed may call these arrowheads but they were spear, javelin, or dart points, for the most part. The bow and arrow did not come into use in America until quite late, about 2000 B.P. in the Southwest, it is believed, and probably not before A.D. 1000 east of the Mississippi. These projectile points were made in an extraordinary range of types, but it has been proved archaeologically by Joffre Coe of the University of North Carolina that each cultural group made only one type at a time, not several as had formerly been believed. It is this principle, that one projectile point type corresponds to one cultural unit, which has made it possible to develop local sequences. Each new type discovered on a site means a component of a different culture.

On the pages which follow appear a series of local sequences from sites that span the continental United States based on projectile points. What must be understood is that a local sequence is valid only for the locality or area where it has been found. To repeat an earlier caution, each investigator must establish for his locale of operations what that sequence is; it can be stated categorically that the succession of cultures in one locality is never exactly that of any other locality, partly because of the incidental nature of sites and partly because populations were, especially from 14,000 B.P. to pottery times, often intensely local. By "incidental" is meant that there is a high probability that bands which occupied a site simply left nothing diagnostic behind, or lived in the vicinity but did not, for some reason, use a particular site; that culture will be absent at a site where it might be expected to occur. On the other hand, bands which did live in one area for a long time often evolved their own peculiar modification of the projectile point or other diagnostic artifact which differed slightly, perhaps, but recognizably from the main type.

The Carolina Piedmont

The principle that local sequences can be determined through changes in projectile point type was given a firm footing by Joffre Coe's excavation of four sites—Hardaway, Doerschuk, Gaston, and Lowder's Ferry—in the Carolina piedmont region. These sites are on riverbanks that were subject to periodic flooding. When the streams overflowed their banks at these sites they left a silt deposit over the living floors of occupation, separating them from the occupational debris of the people who later returned to the site to camp. This alternation of artifact-bearing layers and sterile silt layers provided positive stratification and the exact sequence of occupations. Because each stratum or layer marked a limited period of time between one flood and the next, it contained the material culture of one group of campers. *Each group, Coe found, made its own characteristic style of projectile point.*

When Coe matched up the sequences of the four sites he arrived at the composite in the accompanying illustration.

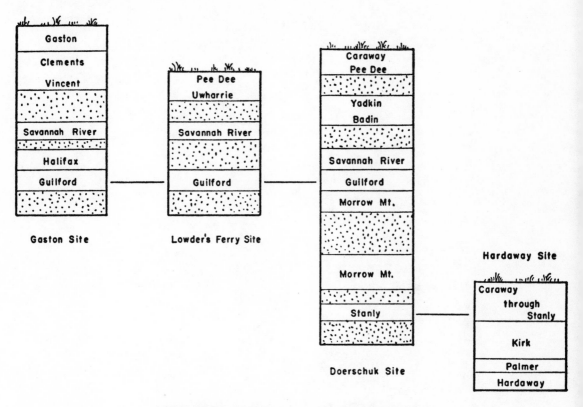

LOCAL SEQUENCE MATCHUP OF COE'S FOUR SITES

The names, of course, are those assigned by Coe and they are meaningless as they stand. They take on meaning, however, when each of them becomes a cultural group distinguished by a diagnostic projectile point type, as in the illustration of the projectile point traditions of the Carolina piedmont. Most readers have seen a movie or a TV program in which the grizzled old scout picks up an arrow from the scene of a massacre, inspects its tip, and says laconically, "Mescalero," the Mescaleros being a branch of the Apache. Coe does, in this

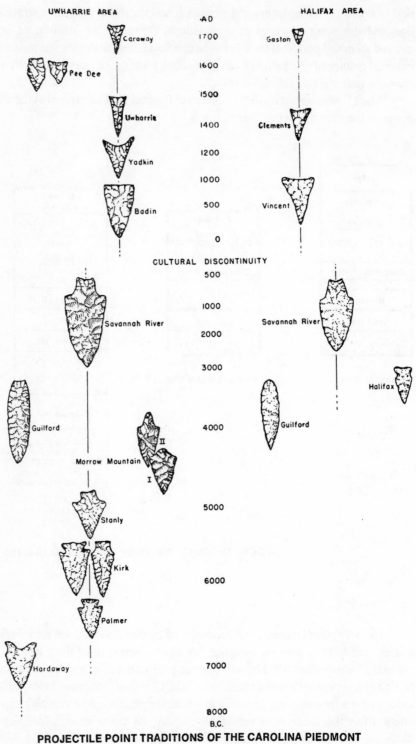

UWHARRIE AREA   HALIFAX AREA

A.D.

1700   Caraway   Gaston

1600   Pee Dee

1500

1400   Uwharrie   Clements

1200   Yadkin

1000

500   Badin   Vincent

0

CULTURAL DISCONTINUITY

500

1000   Savannah River   Savannah River

2000

3000   Halifax

Guilford   Guilford

4000   Morrow Mountain II / I

5000   Stanly

6000   Kirk / Palmer

7000   Hardaway

8000
B.C.

PROJECTILE POINT TRADITIONS OF THE CAROLINA PIEDMONT

diagram, exactly what the scout was doing; he is identifying people or tribes by their distinguishing material culture or artifacts. There is considerably more to each group's material culture than projectile points, but here projectile points are so important that the point type and the cultural (or tribal) designation are one and the same.

Saint Albans

One of Coe's students who assisted him in his work was Bettye Broyles, who later became state archaeologist for West Virginia. In the mid-1960s a site more clearly and deeply stratified than any of Coe's was discovered near Saint Albans, West Virginia, and she has been digging this site off and on, as funds are available, ever since. The top six feet of the site had been stripped off before excavation began and the bottom nineteen feet, as determined by core drilling, remains undug, being below water level and requiring a well-financed project. In the eighteen feet of digging Broyles has found forty zones of occupation, which she has summed up in the sequence of comparison with the older pair of Coe's four sites, shown on p. 31, based on a series of eight C-14 dates obtained from campfire charcoal (the C-14 method of dating is explained in Chapter 8).

It is clear from this comparison that the Kirk people spread from a center east of the Appalachian Mountains northward and westward to the western slopes. (Other West Virginia sites have produced Savannah River points.) Nor did they stop at the Ohio River; Kirk points are found in northern Ohio, Pennsylvania, and New York. The LeCroy people, however, seem to have come more directly northward out of Tennessee and Alabama, where this type of point is frequent. As a matter of fact it is found across the whole southern United States; and a site with a point type very like it, called Pinto, after the Pinto Basin, was found in desert southern California. The LeCroy type point has been found as far north as Michigan, while others in the Saint Albans sequence—Kessells and MacCorkles—have been found by the author in southern New York.

The Modoc Rockshelter

But when one goes further west, into the Mississippi Valley, the sequence looks different. In the early 1950s archaeologist Melvin Fowler dug a site in Randolph County, Illinois, on the eastern edge of the Mississippi Valley about fifty miles south of Saint Louis, Missouri. Called the Modoc Rockshelter, after a nearby village, the site yielded material down to twenty-seven feet below the surface. Shown on p. 33 is the sequence of points, with accompanying artifacts, from the bottom six feet of the deposits, for which the C-14 dates show a period

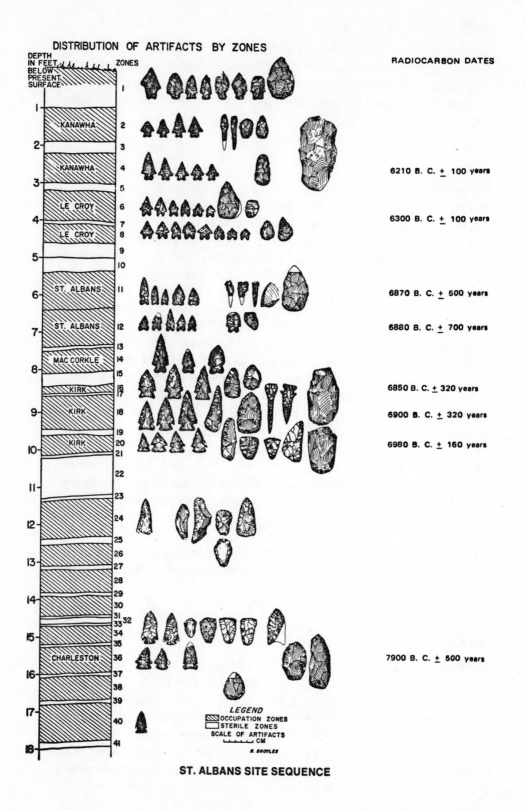

DISTRIBUTION OF ARTIFACTS BY ZONES

RADIOCARBON DATES

DEPTH IN FEET BELOW PRESENT SURFACE

ZONES

KANAWHA

KANAWHA

6210 B. C. ± 100 years

LE CROY

6300 B. C. ± 100 years

LE CROY

ST. ALBANS

6870 B. C. ± 500 years

ST. ALBANS

6880 B. C. ± 700 years

MAC CORKLE

KIRK

6850 B. C. ± 320 years

KIRK

6900 B. C. ± 320 years

KIRK

6980 B. C. ± 160 years

CHARLESTON

7900 B. C. ± 500 years

LEGEND
OCCUPATION ZONES
STERILE ZONES
SCALE OF ARTIFACTS
CM
B. BROYLES

ST. ALBANS SITE SEQUENCE

DOERSCHUK–HARDAWAY   ST. ALBANS

STANLY

6000

KANAWHA

LE CROY

ST. ALBANS B

ST. ALBANS A

KIRK
STEMMED

MAC CORKLE

7000

KIRK
CORNER
NOTCHED

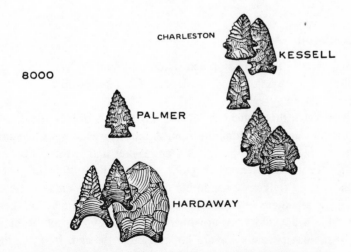

CHARLESTON

KESSELL

8000

PALMER

HARDAWAY

COMPARISON OF SEQUENCES, ST. ALBANS AND PIEDMONT

of use from about 10,000 B.P. to 8000 B.P. The sequence bears little resemblance to the Saint Albans or Carolina sequences. Fowler relates it to material from sites in the Middle South and to Graham Cave and the Hidden Valley Shelter in Missouri. The latter two sites take us across the Mississippi and point us toward the prairies, where the bison-hunting way of life was quite different from the ways of woodland dwellers.

Mummy Cave

In 1962 archaeologists Waldo R. Wedel, Wilfrid M. Husted, and John H. Moss reported on the excavation of a particularly fruitful site, called Mummy Cave, near Cody, Wyoming, about fifteen miles east of Yellowstone Park. The authors of the report wrote:

"Mummy Cave, with its long sequence of discontinuous but undisturbed culture strata dated by radiocarbon, its changing projectile point forms through 9000 years and its relative abundance of perishable materials from the 2400 B.C. and A.D. 720 levels, is of exceptional importance in the correlation, sequential ordering and dating of many single-component sites in the Northwestern Plains and in the adjacent valleys toward the Great Basin." (The Great Basin is the vast semidesert area, comprising Utah, Nevada, and parts of other states, lying between the Rocky Mountains and the coastal ranges.)

In plane form, or outline, the side-notched points that begin to appear in stratum 16 (see p. 34), about 5800 B.C. or 7800 B.P., resemble forms at the bottom of the Modoc Rockshelter; and it seems very possible that these, called Archaic, may have moved across country to the west, to replace the previous lanceolate forms. This change will be explained in the next chapter.

Coastal California

The final sequence in this hop-skip across the continent is a rather skimpy one from California, covering the coastal area from mid-California to lower California.

The fact is that the sequences, local or areal, have been worked out with the detail of the Carolina piedmont, Saint Albans, or Mummy Cave sites for very few areas in the United States. My colleagues and I, for instance, have been digging for twenty years along one twenty-mile section of the lower Hudson, and we are only now beginning to see how the twenty or more sites we have dug fit together. The sequences shown are not refined to a century-by-century time scale and they are open-ended. They do not begin at the beginning of prehistory and some are not carried to the end. It is true they do not summarize all the cultural traits discovered to have been present in the

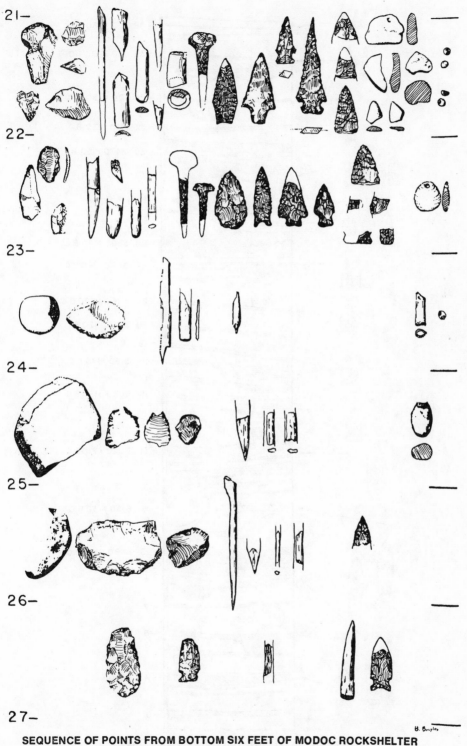

21–
22–
23–
24–
25–
26–
27–

SEQUENCE OF POINTS FROM BOTTOM SIX FEET OF MODOC ROCKSHELTER

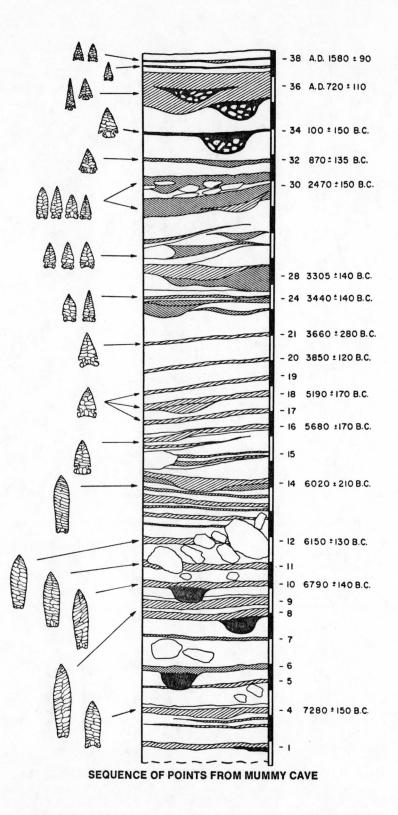

- 38 A.D. 1580 ± 90
- 36 A.D. 720 ± 110
- 34 100 ± 150 B.C.
- 32 870 ± 135 B.C.
- 30 2470 ± 150 B.C.
- 28 3305 ± 140 B.C.
- 24 3440 ± 140 B.C.
- 21 3660 ± 280 B.C.
- 20 3850 ± 120 B.C.
- 19
- 18 5190 ± 170 B.C.
- 17
- 16 5680 ± 170 B.C.
- 15
- 14 6020 ± 210 B.C.
- 12 6150 ± 130 B.C.
- 11
- 10 6790 ± 140 B.C.
- 9
- 8
- 7
- 6
- 5
- 4 7280 ± 150 B.C.
- 1

SEQUENCE OF POINTS FROM MUMMY CAVE

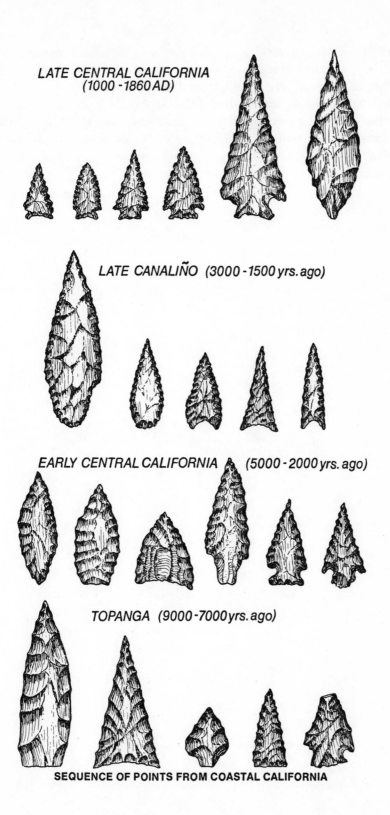

LATE CENTRAL CALIFORNIA
(1000 - 1860 AD)

LATE CANALIÑO (3000 - 1500 yrs. ago)

EARLY CENTRAL CALIFORNIA (5000 - 2000 yrs. ago)

TOPANGA (9000 - 7000 yrs. ago)

SEQUENCE OF POINTS FROM COASTAL CALIFORNIA

area by other investigators but this fact does not contradict the generalization that complete and final sequences do not exist for any locale or area, and it is the lure of archaeological investigation that they do not. Almost any dig can be undertaken with the anticipation of finding something new.

But if there are no completed local sequences, there is still, as a guide for the excavator, the outline, the summary of the main periods of American prehistory to guide him. This generalized sequence will occupy the next chapter.

chapter 3

Prehistoric Man in the Western Hemisphere

AS A SPECIES of animal, man is not native to America. His entrance into the Western Hemisphere was very late in his two-million-year career that began in East Africa with the australopithecines, little ape-men (about the size of modern pygmies) who made the first stone tools. Squalls of controversy have troubled the climate of archaeology for almost a century over the time of that entrance: was it before the last ice sheet spread over Canada and the northern United States, that is, before about 26,000 B.P.; or was it after that ice sheet, called Wisconsin III, had melted sufficiently in places to allow travel southward into warmer, greener, iceless territory, which would not have been until 15,000 B.P. at the earliest?

At issue is much more than a matter of a few thousand years of antiquity. If the entrance was made before the onset of the Wisconsin III ice sheet, then the migrants must have come with a very primitive set of tools, called a chopper-flake industry, not much in advance of that invented by the australopithecines 2 million years before. If so, then all the advances in technology found in America, up to and including the Mexican, Meso-American,

37

and Peruvian civilizations, must have evolved out of those chopper-flake roots within 20,000 years, a remarkable achievement.

Why the people of Eastern Asia, particularly the pre-Mongoloid population of Northeast Asia, whence came the first migrants into America, never improved on the chopper-flake tool kit through 2 million years of evolution will always remain a puzzle. We must assume that it was because choppers and flakes served the purpose of getting a living well enough. In Africa, Europe, and in that part of Asia west of a midline in India, skill in making tools of stone advanced slowly but steadily as man evolved; and about 40,000 B.P., when modern man, *Homo sapiens sapiens,* appeared in the archaeological record, the quality of the work was the ultimate that could be achieved with stone as a material. But none of this know-how seems ever to have been diffused to Eastern Asia until invading Caucasoid peoples possibly from present Iran or Russia brought it into Siberia, perhaps by 25,000 B.P. If man had reached America and was south of Wisconsin III before that time, he had to have been a chopper-flake maker of the native East Asian pre-Mongoloid stock.

But if the first migrants did not find their way into America and to territory south of the ice until Wisconsin III had melted back enough to permit travel southward through it, then they would not have been the chopper-flake pre-Mongoloids but the Caucasoid hunters from the Near East, with their very advanced, even sophisticated, stone and bone technology. The achievement of American aborigines would hardly be lessened, however, if this later migration proved to have been the first. That would mean that their descendants had grown in numbers and skill to erect the civilizations of South America and Meso-America only 14,000 years later.

FINDINGS IN AYACUCHO VALLEY:
A BREAKTHROUGH IN AMERICAN PREHISTORY

The controversy now seems to have been settled. Richard S. MacNeish, one of the foremost American archaeologists (he proved archaeologically that maize is a strictly American plant and agricultural product in origin), reported in the *Scientific American* of April 1971 on excavations in Ayacucho Valley, Peru, by a team of specialists which he headed. In a cave called Pikimachay or Flea Cave in the Andes above Ayacucho Valley (which is, incidentally, in the Inca area of influence) the MacNeish team found, at the lowest level, a crude stone chopper-flake industry with two animal bones, probably from a now-extinct ground sloth. The same industry occurred in the level above this, also with bones of an extinct sloth. These bones gave a C-14 test age of 19,600 years. The age of the older lowest level, formed under different geologic conditions, was estimated at 22,000 years. The chopper-flake industry continued to be found upward through several feet of cave deposits until about 14,700 B.P., when either a new kind of technology entered the Valley from elsewhere or the chopper-flake industry took a rather sudden evolutionary leap forward.

After two years' work on twelve sites, the MacNeish team established a local sequence for Ayacucho Valley from 22,000 B.P. to the present day, making it the oldest continuously occupied locality in the Western Hemisphere known to archaeology. The sequence is a breakthrough in American prehistory; the chopper-flake people were, indeed, the earliest positively dated settlers in the Western Hemisphere and, if they were in Ayacucho Valley in the Peruvian Andes (the Valley averages 6500 feet above sea level and Flea Cave is 9000 feet above sea level) by 22,000 B.P., then their entrance into America must have been on the order of 30,000 B.P. In the first place, these settlers did not travel at a steady pace from the Bering land bridge area, where they crossed into America, directly to Ayacucho Valley, since they could not have had it as a destination; they would have reached it only by slowly extending their living range until they arrived there. And in the second place, the Wisconsin III ice sheet prevented any kind of movement south from 26,000 B.P., possibly 28,000 B.P., to 15,000 B.P. at the earliest, long after the Ayacuchans had huddled in Flea Cave over their first sloth dinner. MacNeish thinks the first settlers may have come 40,000 B.P. or in Wisconsin II time, or even 80,000 B.P., Wisconsin I time

THE WISCONSIN III ICE SHEET

The Wisconsin III ice sheet and the climates associated with its formation and retreat were of such profound and direct importance to the initial settlement and subsequent habitation of the Americas that they merit a fuller, if concise, treatment. The Wisconsin glacier was the last of the four major glaciations that have occurred during the past million years of geologic time. (It has lately come to be believed that glaciations may have been recurrent back to perhaps 3.5 million years ago, but traces of these are hard to come by since each ice sheet, crunching across the landscape, erases most of the evidence of its predecessors.) The four "classic" glaciations, about which all geologists agree, are known, in America, in the order of their occurrence, as the Nebraskan, Kansan, Illinoisian, and Wisconsin. Each of these is set off from its predecessor and successor by an interglacial period of about 100,000 years in length, during which the climate was warmer, often much warmer, than today's.

Even as the Pleistocene or Ice Age consisted of glaciations followed by ice-free interglacials, so each ice period had its internal periods of ice advance followed by periods of partial melting and retreat. During the Wisconsin glaciation there were three advances, numbered I, II, and III, separated by major retreats during which continental glacial ice almost vanished. And each of these advances included fluctuations of advance and minor retreat, or retreat and minor re-advance, responses to short-term reversals in climate.

The American glaciers are named for the states in which have been found the terminal moraines, the piled-up ridges of gravel and clay marking the limits of their farthest advance. The Wisconsin might, more accurately, have been called the Long Island glacier because its farthest advance south was to Long Island, but its designation by the name of a midwestern state places it in better perspective in the series. It was the shortest-lived and the least extensive of the four classic glaciers. The onset of Wisconsin I has been estimated by some authorities at 60,000 B.P., by others as much as 120,000 B.P. A compromise of about 80,000 B.P. is now generally accepted, by archaeologists at least. Wisconsin I and the following interstadial (i.e., retreat period) lasted from 80,000 to about 60,000 B.P.; Wisconsin II from 60,000 to, perhaps, 45,000 B.P., when an interstadial set in, until the beginning of Wisconsin III. This must have occurred prior to 26,000 B.P. because by that time Wisconsin III seems to have been standing at climax position along the Long Island-Wisconsin front. At any one of the three Wisconsin climaxes, and for several thousand years both before and after those climaxes, that is, while the ice sheet was advancing or retreating, men could have walked dry-shod from Asia to North America. The two continents were one land mass joined together by a territory now called Beringia.

BERINGIA: LINK BETWEEN CONTINENTS

For many decades after the phenomenon of glaciation had been fully accepted by geologists the effect of the withdrawal of so much water from the world ocean was almost completely overlooked. The world ocean is, of course, the only reservoir from which could have been drawn all the water locked up as ice in continental glaciers. While it was known that the withdrawal of water from the sea during glaciation had united the British Isles to the Continent, little attention was paid to similar exposures of sea bottom elsewhere in the world. During the past decade the amount of lowering of sea level during the climax of the Wisconsin has been calculated and investigated on a worldwide basis; the values for the lowering of sea level vary from about 400 to 450 feet. Such a drop, it has been discovered, had spectacular effects on the shape of continents. It bared the continental shelves, the "shoulders" of the upthrust blocks of rock that comprise the continents, so that, for instance, the shoreline of the eastern United States was an average of about 100 miles east of its present location. The archipelago trailing eastward from Southeast Asia almost made a land bridge to Australia. For American prehistory the most significant result was the emergence of Beringia, a vast expanse of Bering Sea and Arctic Ocean bottom bigger than Texas, 1000 miles across from north to south and linking Asia and North America together into one continental mass.

This great province of land was low-lying and flat, so that a rise or fall in sea level of, say, 25 feet had dramatic effect on the area of Beringia, but an isthmus or land bridge continued to connect Siberia and Alaska so long as sea level remained approximately 200 feet below present level.

Despite the fact that most of Beringia lay north of the Arctic Circle, it was not glaciated. It lay behind a range of mountains the tops of which are now the Aleutian Islands, and the moisture-laden winds off the Pacific dropped their precipitation on the seaward slopes, little of it reaching the interior of Beringia. But, no snow, no glacier. The land did, nevertheless, receive enough moisture, probably from fog as much as from precipitation, to support a ground vegetation that was, in turn, sufficient to support herds of mammoths and caribou, musk-oxen, and other game animals. Wherever there was such a supply of meat, man the hunter was sure to find it sooner or later. The Caucasoid hunters who invaded Siberia from the west were well enough equipped to make a living in Beringia, and there is excavated evidence that they did, at a site called Onion Portage on the Kobuk River just north of the Arctic Circle.

But this interior Beringia, this Arctic prairie land, was solidly walled off to the south by the pan-Canadian ice sheet. Some geologists think that, after 18,000 B.P., probably no sooner than 15,000 B.P., melting back of the ice sheet had opened a corridor between Alaska and the unglaciated south along the base of the Rocky Mountains. It was here that the mountain glaciers from the Rockies and the continental glacier centered in the east had joined up and where they parted when melting set in. But there is no archaeological evidence that this corridor, if it existed by 15,000 B.P., was used then. Much more probable is that interior Canada remained untraversed until shortly after 11,000 B.P.

The last southward thrust of Wisconsin III ice into the present United States, an advance called the Valders, has been securely dated at Two Creeks, Wisconsin, at about 11,700 B.P. The ice partially invaded the Great Lakes basin and lobed into Wisconsin but otherwise kept just north of the Canadian border. The Valders was in full retreat by about 10,700 B.P., and so rapid was the retreat that at any time thereafter the way was open from Alaska. But it was also open *to* Alaska, and travel into the areas opening to floral, animal, and human life was more likely to have been from the south to the north. By 10,000 B.P. the Wisconsin glacier had dwindled to the degree that geologists have designated that date as the end of the Pleistocene or Ice Age that had begun 1 million or 2 or 3 million years before. It also marks the beginning of the Holocene, the geologic era that is now upon us.

THE COASTAL MIGRATION ROUTE OF EARLY PEOPLE

Those bands, either of chopper-flake people or big game hunters, who crossed the then imaginary line between the Old World and the New into Beringia proper, had no exit southward, then, from, roughly, 28,000 B.P. to, it seems likely, 11,000 B.P. But there was another path, and not much more, that was probably open much longer and reopened sooner. The continental shelf along the Pacific edge of the continent is not so wide as on the Atlantic side but it was there and probably passable until the mountain glaciers from the coastal ranges flowed down the valleys and over it. During a melt period, since the coastal ice front ran along the shore and was at sea level, the ice front withdrew from the shore first. This shoreline pathway afforded one absolute necessity for a primitive people living off the land: a rich food source in the tidal area, where a living could be had for the searching and the picking up. Travelers along this path would have needed no specialized tools; a chopper-flake kit would have been adequate.

The discovery of 22,000-year-old chopper-flake people in Ayacucho Valley lends credence to a shoreline route into the New World. The valley opens on the Pacific side of the Andes and could not have been entered from any direction other than the coast. It must be added that the migration, more accurately the extension of range, of these shore dwellers eventually reached the southernmost tip of South America along this Pacific littoral pathway at the early date of 11,000 B.P. (while the Valders ice lobe still loomed along the Canadian border).

It should not be thought that these early Ayacuchans (MacNeish has named their culture Paccaicasa) were great hunters because animal bones were found in the lower fill at Flea Cave. These were the bones of the slow-moving, though dangerous, sloth, which did not require the specialized hunting tools and techniques employed by the hunters of mammoths and extinct bison. The Paccaicasans may have used wooden shafts with sharpened ends for spears or they may have used nothing that deadly. It is just as likely that they were adept at chasing carnivorous animals away from their prey, or perhaps they skulked in the vicinity until the killer had eaten his fill and then snatched the remains away from other scavengers. There is nothing in the Paccaicasan remains in Flea Cave to indicate that these cavemen were anything but jackallike scroungers. They are, therefore, stratum 1, the bottom and beginning for an American material culture sequence.

THE CHOPPER-FLAKE INDUSTRY HORIZON, 40,000 (?) to 16,000 B.P.

A chopper is a pebble or block of stone from which a few chips have been removed to make an axlike edge for hacking, digging, dismembering, and similar tasks. The chips removed, or chips struck off especially for the purpose, serve as knives and scrapers, since the edges of freshly struck stone of suitably hard material are cutting keen. The pebble tool or chopper-flake stage of toolmaking may be defined as one in which no more tool forms were created than were necessary to the function.

MacNeish reports that the cultural material in that 22,000-year-old cave deposit consisted of "four crude tools fashioned from volcanic tuff and a few flakes that had been struck from tools," further defining the tools as "reminiscent of chopping tools found in Asia." The trail of these tools picks up at Cape Krusenstern on the Alaskan shore of the Bering Sea on the Arctic Circle and can be followed all the way to the Atacama Desert in Chile. The evidence is strong that the trail passed through the Great Basin between the Rockies and the coastal ranges. This probably means that the travelers along the Pacific shoreline wandered up the Columbia River and the Snake and thence southward, breaking eastward out of the Rockies in Arizona. Deeply buried hearths at Lewisville, Texas with a chopper and flake association have been dated at 38,000 B.P. A chopper-flake industry using silicified wood and dating to about 18,000 B.P. has been found in Venezuela. East of the Rockies the best authenticated chopper-flake industry is that found by Don Dragoo of the Carnegie Institute at Wells Creek, Tennessee. Through southern Alabama there was a stone industry called the Lively Complex, using choppers and flakes but including several other tools formed from pebbles, several degrees in advance of the crude tools of Flea Cave but not yet including stone projectile points.

Conservative archaeologists have for years refused to accept the existence of a chopper-flake horizon and even now, with the Ayacucho sequence documented by a renowned archaeologist, the director of the Peabody Foundation at Harvard University, backed up by a team of experts, there will be demurring and counterattack. But that battle is over. Flea Cave is not simply an isolated site. It is the beginning evidence of an uninterrupted human occupation of a locality which charts the orderly progression of an evolving technology and living patterns from hunting through hunting-gathering to plant cultivation to village farming. From now on, the battle will break down into a series of skirmishes not over the chopper-flake, pebble tool horizon but over the assignment to that horizon of a specific site.

And indeed it is not easy to prove a chopper-flake or pebble site to the satisfaction of the skeptic without something datable, but datable materials, which must be organic—bone, wood, antler, shell—do not ordinarily survive for 20,000 years. The industry itself is not sufficient evidence because choppers were made and the struck flakes utilized for knives until the Stone Age ceased to be, which was as late as 1900 in the remoter fastnesses of South America.

What the author believes to be a chopper-flake site came to his attention a few years ago during a survey of a locality called Prickly Pear Hill in Croton-on-Hudson, New York. It was a cache of quartzite in a boat-shaped hole about ten feet long and 40 inches deep in the center; obviously the hole was left by a toppled tree. We took about half a ton of quartzite industrial material and debris out of the hole and from within a radius of about four feet around it. There wasn't another chip, pebble, or sign of quartzite on the sixty acres of that hillside, and it was irrefutable that the quartzite had been collected somewhere else and brought here for working. There were the anvil stones used to strike off flakes and spalls by knocking one stone against another (this is chopper-flake technique) and large and small splits, flakes, spalls, and splinters by the thousand. Yes, there were several choppers and utilized flakes, but no projectile points or other formal tools or tool shapes of later industries. A great deal of stone pounding had gone on at this site; it was from every evidence a workshop, and choppers and flakes had been abundantly produced there—and that is the difficulty. The absence of formal diagnostic tools by which the workmen could have been identified might mean only that these had been made and carried away. For the technology of a chopper-flake industry was pretty much the first step in more advanced industries. Chopper-flake makers stopped there; advanced industries didn't.

Prickly Pear Hill, about 40 miles north of Long Island, was within the glaciated area, but Wisconsin III had melted well north of there by 16,000 B.P. and there was a warm spell about 15,000 B.P. that might have drawn chopper-flake people this far north. At least my colleagues and I count the Prickly Pear Hill site at the beginning of our local sequence. On this premise I would say that it is possible for any excavator at or below the latitude of southern New York to come upon a chopper-flake industry and establish this horizon in his area of interest.

FLAKE AND CORE SPECIALIZATION HORIZON, 16,000-14,000 B.P.

Advance in stonework technology can take place in either or both of two lines of development: emphasis on the creation of more and more specialized tools by further shaping and refining of the flake, which is then called a flake, or uniface, industry; or emphasis on refining and creating tools out of the core or parent material, which is then called a core, or biface, industry.

At Flea Cave, in levels dated between 16,000 and 14,000 B.P., MacNeish found an industry in which flakes had been shaped into saw-edged knives, tools with sharp, perforator tips, flakes with points that might have been projectile heads or plunging knives, and specialized scrapers. The choppers were still there, now more formalized, but the industry was unifacial; that is, the underside of the flake, the surface that had been separated from the core, had not been worked or retouched at all.

At other sites in Peru and in Venezuela, however, the evidence is that at about this time, a bifacial core tool industry was evolving. When chipping is continued all over the parent core, to thin it down, there is created what is called a biface, since both sides are worked. These bifaces, by the very nature of the chipping process, which consists of striking off flakes from the edge, are ovoid or lanceolate; that is, the outside edges are convex curves converging at one end into a point but, in most cases, ending in a blunt "base" at the other end. In higher levels of lithic tool development these bifaces are called "blanks" or "preforms," since they are intended to be refined and shaped later into such tools as projectile points and bifacial knives. Industries regularly producing bifaces are almost always core industries. From about 14,000 years ago until about 3000 years ago, stoneworking in America (except for the Arctic) was overwhelmingly in the core-biface tradition, though this by no means precluded the utilization of flakes as casual tools, a heritage from chopper-flake beginnings.

The flake tradition evolved, however, the utmost in sophisticated stone technology. One development, called Musteroid, was the splitting off of heavy, thick, controlled spalls which were then retouched into tools; but this was never a strong and unmixed tradition in America and usually appears as an element in biface traditions. The second development was the struck, unifacial blade, sometimes called the lamellar blade, occasionally called the strip blade. After shaping the core into a rough polyhedron and preparing a striking area at the top, to allow for a proper striking angle, the flintsmith, by a deft blow, drove off a uniface "blade," a flake with parallel sides, like the blade of a table knife. This was not only a sharp-edged knife of itself; it was a small, easily worked blank, suitable for further shaping into other kinds of tools. This uniface blade-making technique made its appearance simultaneously with modern man in Europe about 40,000 years ago, and swordlike blades up to a foot long have been found in the blade-making period called the Upper Paleolithic. But most uniface blades are three inches long or less; those of about one inch or shorter are called microlithic blades.

There appears to have been a tradition of uniface blade-making in Mexico and northern South America as early as 15,000 to 13,000 B.P., but blade-making was not influential in lithic technology in the area of the forty-eight states until about 3000 B.P. At the previously mentioned Onion Portage site on the Kobuk River, the earliest settlers were uniface blade makers. This tradition may be 15,000 years old in Alaska and undoubtedly represents an eastward extension of those Caucasoid Upper Paleolithic hunters who invaded Siberia from Eastern Europe, or at least of their stoneworking tradition. Uniface blade-making seems to have worked its way down the Pacific coast by about 8000 B.P. and perhaps into the present state of Oregon, but it was not strong enough to displace the indigenous biface tradition; instead the two traditions were fused.

Uniface blade-working does not appear strongly within the contiguous states of the United States until about 3000 B.P., in the mound-building

Poverty Point culture of the lower Mississippi. It had apparently arrived here from Central America or Mexico. It traveled up the Mississippi and Ohio, where it becomes diagnostic of the Hopewell culture of 100 B.C. to A.D. 500. But through the spread of the unifacial blade technique the manufacture of projectile points remained determinedly bifacial.

Unless the excavator knows he is dealing with a site of the Poverty Point culture or a Poverty Point descendant, or a Hopewell site, he had best regard any uniface blades he finds as incidental. A certain number of these appear to have been produced unintentionally during the chipping process by the right combination of striking angle and manual delivery of the stroke.

The flake and core specializations of the period 16,000 to 14,000 B.P. require the same stringent proofs and adequacy of data as a chopper-flake industry. They cannot be isolated by typology, that is, by types of tools and workmanship, from later industries; validation can come only by geological methods and by the dating of associated C-14 testable materials.

The core and flake specialization horizon is short where it is found in South America, and weak in the United States. I am not aware of any sites at all in the United States comparable to the flake specialization level at Flea Cave. But there does appear to be a biface horizon, represented by a site on Manitoulin Island in Lake Huron, by a collection of tools from Pennsylvania called the DeTurk industry, and by a widespread provenience of bifaces, once called "hand axes," in Blacks Fork Valley, Wyoming, and adjacent regions. The Manitoulin Island site alone has a date; it is 9130 years old, but this is a "stop-date forward," a date on a peat deposit lying over artifacts, so that it gives only an age the artifacts cannot be younger than. The age of the artifacts must be pre-Valders (Manitoulin Island was under Valders ice) and thus older than 11,700 years.

These biface sites have, of course, been shrugged off or ignored because, to repeat, bifaces can be interpreted as preforms or quarry blanks, roughed out for transport elsewhere for later finishing. Nevertheless, the site surveyor and the excavator would be wise to keep an eye peeled for occurrences of a biface industry preceding and underlying the manufacture of bifacial projectile points.

PALEO-HUNTER LANCEOLATE BIFACIAL PROJECTILE POINT HORIZON, 14,000 to 10,000 B.P.

There has to have been an overlap between the horizon of specialization of cores into bifaces and the bifacial lanceolate projectile points, when the lanceolate or ovoid bifaces were used as spearpoints though we don't recognize them as such. The biface, dressed down to slimmer proportions for efficiency in penetration, is clearly a tool developed specifically for the hunting of thick-skinned big game—mammoth, bison, camel, horse. Shafts with fire-hardened self-points or tips of bone or antler were no threat to huge beasts like the mammoth or now-extinct bison, armored by hide-covered layers of fat. The lanceolate point, as will be apparent on inspection, is bullet-shaped.

The best known of the big game hunter bifacial lanceolate points is the Clovis fluted type, really a family of types of pure lanceolates. The "flute" is a groove or channel running from the base up the length of the point for varying distances toward the tip. It is formed by striking off one or more flakes from the base, to create a channel in which to lay the halves of the split end of the shaft into which the point was inserted. No weapon points made anywhere else in the world have, as a type, this feature. Points of the Clovis fluted family have been found in all 49 continental states of the United States and in lower Canada; it is the most widespread point type in America. The earliest date for a Clovis is about 11,800 B.P. at the Lehner Ranch site in Arizona, the latest about 10,000 B.P. at the Debert site in Nova Scotia.

But the Clovis is only one among many of the types of lanceolates or modified lanceolates (note the lanceolates at Mummy Cave) used by big game hunters beginning, it is generally believed, about 14,000 B.P. Continuing study of Paleo-hunter sites has turned up an almost endless variety of lanceolates, and modifications of lanceolates recognized by experts in taxonomy as types, bearing such names as Angostura, Long, Milnesand, San Jon, Hell Gap, Cascade, El Jobo, Ayampitin, Allen, Browns Valley, Plainview, Firstview, Agate Basin, Eden, and the much-publicized Folsom, a fluted lanceolate, and the first point to be found in proved association with extinct big game. The shapes vary from the slender Cascade point of Oregon, pointed at both ends, and the similar Lerma point of Mexico and the Southeast, through the stubby Plainviews and Milnesands to those with slight indentations at the side forming stems, like the Eden and Hell Gap.

Regarded as the oldest, in present knowledge, of the lanceolate big game hunter points is the Sandia, which enjoys more fame than it deserves, inasmuch as it occurs only in a restricted area in New Mexico and its seniority is not proved. It was found stratigraphically below Folsom points in Sandia Cave, near Albuquerque, but the oldest date on Folsom is only about 10,700 B.P. However, the Sandia is probably as old as the Clovis. Its appeal resides in its easy recognizability; it is a lanceolate made assymmetric by a stemming indentation on only one side. Since this is a form used for knives in many cultures, more "Sandia points" have been found than ever existed.

The Sandia is certainly not the prototype lanceolate from which all the others derived. The prototype industry would appear to be the El Jobo of Venezuela, wherein, among the plain lanceolates, a few slightly stemmed points are intermingled. This was an industry of big game hunters and is dated, not too certainly, at about 11,000 B.P., not early enough to have

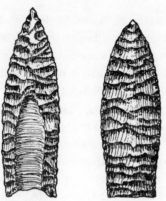

Clovis   Firstview   Folsom

Cascade   Lerma   Sandia I

Sandia II   Sandia fluted   El Jobo

TYPES OF LANCEOLATES

fathered the North American lanceolate. But it was preceded in Venezuela by a stage called Las Lagunas, the diagnostic characteristic of which is "a bifacially worked blade which could have been used as a hand-axe or knife or else have been hafted on a thrusting spear." Dates for bone associated with these Venezuela bifaces suggest they are about 14,000 years old, which is just about right for the time of transition from bifaces to recognizable bifacial points. As the evidence now demonstrates, the lanceolate tradition of big game hunter projectile points developed in South America and quickly moved into North America, probably along the exposed continental shelf of the Gulf of Mexico. But there is also a possible independent center of development of lanceolates in the Pacific Northwest in the Old Cordilleran tradition, the diagnostic artifact for which is the Cascade bipoint. On the other hand, more points of the Clovis family have been found in Alabama than in all the rest of the country combined, and what does that mean? The answers may still lie underground, or in the existing data studied from a different point of view.

THE HERD HUNTERS' WAY OF LIFE

That the Pleistocene era ended officially 10,000 years ago has already been mentioned. Though there was one short return of glaciation, called the Cochrane, about 8000 B.P., the severity of which is disputed, the melt-back from the Valders was the ultimate. But it was not the disappearance of continental glaciation alone that caused the termination of the one- (or two- or three-) million-year-long Pleistocene to be placed at 10,000 years B.P. Geologic ages are set apart from one another not only by major geologic events and conditions, but by the faunal assemblages, the collection of animals that coexisted during particular periods. Ten thousand years ago what happened was that the Pleistocene megafauna, the large beasts, became extinct. These included several subspecies of mammoth, the mastodon, the American horse, the camel, giant bison (*Bison antiquus, Bison occidentalis, Bison taylori*), giant sloths, giant armadillos, giant rodents (the capybara), the giant dire wolf, the saber-tooth cat, the giant jaguar or American lion, and the short-faced bear. Some of these species had disappeared some few thousands of years before 10,000 B.P.; some lingered a millennium or two afterwards. But 10,000 B.P. was clearly the end of an era. The heyday of big game hunting, for which the lanceolate point had been invented, was thus between the "invention" of that tool around 14,000 B.P. and the disappearance of big game around 10,000 B.P.

The rewards that caused men to strive until they had found a means to kill big game are obvious: the huge larder of food they obtained when they toppled a mammoth or bison, and not only food but hides, bone, and horn. An adult Columbian mammoth stood twelve to fourteen feet tall at the shoulder and weighed about five tons, of which some two tons would be usable meat. The kill of such a mountain of meat was excavated at a site near Naco, Arizona, close to the Mexican border, in 1952. Although the skeleton was found in an ancient streambed, the mammoth had not been mired down but had been killed in the open, as a single, free quarry. Eight Clovis points were found in him, all in the target area in the neck at the Atlas vertebra. This was the mammoth's Achilles heel, the one spot where he could be struck and killed by a thrown spear. One of the Clovis points had split the Atlas vertebra; that was the fatal blow.

Probably more typical were the kills of big game found in a creek bed on the Lehner Ranch not far from Naco. In a stretch of about fifty feet of a long-buried stream channel were found the bones of horse, tapir, bison, and nine individual half-grown mammoths. The bone bed excavated is believed to be only half what had been present before washouts had exposed the deposit to decay. Among the bones were found thirteen Clovis points, a chopper, a biface knife, and several retouched and unretouched flakes. Excavation revealed that the creek bed, with sharp-cut, 8-foot-high banks, was used as a game trap. Either the hunters had lain in ambush until animals came here to drink or the quarries had been driven into the trap and speared to death before they could escape. The fact that all the mammoths were juveniles suggested that they had been selectively cut out of a herd and then harried into the trap.

The nonprojectile point tools were certainly for butchering, and the meat had been cooked on the spot. A hearth was found, along with evidence of other fires, and the most acceptable of several C-14 dates for the charcoal was 11,850 B.P., the oldest date for Clovis anywhere.

Very probably, mammoths had to be killed singly. Although there are sites in Europe where mammoths seem to have been killed by stampeding them over bluffs, with at least a dozen mammoth kill sites having been excavated, there are no such sites in America. Bison, however, are something else. They were killed by stampedes in historic times and they were killed by the stampedes of Paleo-hunters. Between 1958 and 1960 parties from the University of Colorado Museum under archaeologist Joe Ben Wheat dug up the remains of one such stampede at a site in Cheyenne County, Colorado. He found the bones of 190 *Bison occidentalis* (considerably larger than the Plains buffalo, *Bison bison*) in an arroyo, long ago silted over, into which they had been driven to their mass death within a matter of minutes on a day that a C-14 test placed at 10,150 B.P.

The three instances just related make a single point: all these kills were of herd animals, and to be a hunter of herd animals was to lead a very special kind of life. Herd animals do not stay put. They not only move day by day, they travel season by season, from summer grass in the north of their range to winter hay in the south. To be a herd hunter was to live at the pace and rhythm of the herds, and in a food-getting routine as different from that of the Archaic hunter-gatherer to be treated in the next section as a day laborer is from a salesman on commission. The Archaic hunter-gatherer stayed within the bounds of his territory; to the herd hunter, his territory was wherever he found the herds.

Wheat has calculated the yield from the *Bison occidentalis* herd at the Chubbock-Olsen site; from 140 animals "heavy" butchered and 30 "light" butchered (i.e., only the delicacies were taken), about 75,000 pounds, or 37 tons, of meat were taken. Half of this was enough to feed about 200 people for perhaps 3 weeks, or as long as it would have been possible to remain in the vicinity of this abattoir, with the stench and rottenness of the meat. It is assumed that while half the amount was eaten fresh, more or less, the other half was dried or made into pemmican. Considering the size of the butchering and preserving job, a crew of 200 does not seem too large. One can imagine a gathering of all the bands within a radius of 50 miles, called in by smoke signal.

This was a life so different from that of the deer-hunting, root-grubbing, fishing, nut-gathering round of existence of dwellers outside game herd areas, that one might think that big game hunters would have been wiped out if the herds were suddenly to have perished. But neither eventuality occurred. Despite the fact that archaeologists cut off the Paleo-hunter period at 10,000 B.P., the herd hunters went right on herd-hunting, with their lanceolate points, if not the mammoth and *Bison antiquus,* then *Bison occidentalis* and *Bison athabascae.* This hunting occurred during the period from 10,000 to about 8,000 B.P., called the Plano. Thereafter there was *Bison bison* to hunt, and the Plains tribes never stopped hunting them until there were no more herds, and that was about A.D. 1880. The buffalo-hunting Sioux and Blackfeet and Assiniboines were nothing more nor less than the mammoth hunters of Naco and Lehner on horseback 11,000 years later.

The Clovis people were *the* Paleo-herd hunters. It was herd-hunting that spread them everywhere throughout what is called the Paleo-East, all the territory from the Rockies to the Atlantic Ocean. Points of the Clovis family have been found from Nova Scotia to Florida and all areas between; beyond a doubt they lie under the waters off the Atlantic coast, for mammoth bones and teeth have been dredged up from offshore where the bottom was dry land during the Wisconsin glaciation. From the High Plains, across Ohio and almost to Pennsylvania, the land lies flat, without a block or hindrance to the passage of herds of mammoth and, on evidence excavated with Clovis points, caribou. At this time, it will be remembered, a glacial ice front lay across North America at the Canada-United States border, and south of it, at least as far as the Ohio River, was an Arctic and sub-Arctic environment, the roaming grounds of caribou and musk-ox. Because the whole succession of environmental zones was moved south by the presence of the glacier, the prairies extended across the Mississippi into Alabama and Georgia, to end in Florida. Probably bison and mammoth were hunted in the Southeast but, despite the fact that more fluted points have been found in Alabama than in the entire West, no site has survived, nor have the bones of the game taken.

Even the hill country of Kentucky and Tennessee has yielded Clovis big game hunter points. But, then, mammoths and bison both inhabited the lush valleys and bottomlands. In Daniel Boone's time the bones of both were numerous around Great Salt Lick, and mammoth vertebrae were used as stools. They are said to have fit the human buttocks very comfortably.

It is no wonder that the Clovis point is a favorite and keenly sought find. It is rare, but not so rare that one cannot hope to find one almost any place; one has even been found at a site on a 3400-foot-high mountaintop in West Virginia, and fluted points have even turned up in the San Joaquin Valley in California. The Clovis point has an easily distinguishable appearance and a built-in guarantee of antiquity. Besides which, no more fascinating Stone Age people ever lived than the Clovis herd hunters.

12,000 B.P. TO CERAMIC POTTERY: THE ARCHAIC NOTCHED AND STEMMED POINT HORIZON

"Archaic" is a confusing term, and archaeologists still use it in a double, often contradictory sense. When the term first came into use, it denoted the period following the Paleo-hunter horizon and the subsistence pattern or way of life that became widespread in America following the disappearance of the Pleistocene fauna and the climatic and vegetational changes that swept over North America, in particular, after the melting of the glacier. Now it is known that the Archaic subsistence pattern is as old as the Paleo-hunter and older, since it was the way of life of the chopper-flake people; the major difference is that the Archaic horizon people made a different kind of projectile point.

The Archaic subsistence pattern is found in areas not suitable for herd animals, that is, in woodlands, rough country, and dry regions. Instead of the free-wandering nomadism of the herd hunter, it was a pattern of scheduled or seasonally adjusted movement, within a restricted territory, gathering nuts and acorns in the fall, frequenting the banks of streams in the spring during fish runs, and hunting deer and lesser animals wherever they were to be found. The subsistence pattern is called hunting-gathering or foraging, and never in their wildest dreams could Archaic hunter-gatherers have imagined taking thirty-seven tons of meat in a single 15-minute game drive. Their major meat animal was the deer, a nonherd animal, and their most formidable the solitary bear. Their characteristic surviving tools are projectile points, woodworking tools such as axes, adzes, and celts, grinding stones for reducing seeds and nuts to meal, and fishing gear—net sinkers, fishhooks, and gorges. They lived from meal to meal, not from mass kill to mass kill, like the herd hunters.

The earliest dates attributed to Archaic sequences cluster about 11,000 B.P.; these are the bottom level dates at Modoc Rockshelter and at another site, Danger Cave, Utah, not far from Great Salt Lake. Though the Danger Cave sequence is called the Desert culture, it is typical of Archaic foraging, adapted to a land too dry to support herd animals or a heavy animal population of any kind. But here were found some of the first cordage, twining, woven basketry, and textiles in the world. A sequence much like Danger Cave was found at Ventana Cave, Arizona; and at this same general time level in Arizona there lived a people, called the Cochise culture, who made no stone projectile points at all and whose most recurrent implement is the grinding stone.

Modoc Rockshelter provides an example of a forest-dwelling Archaic culture, as do the Saint Albans site, Coe's Carolina sites, Russell Cave and the Stanfield-Worley Rockshelter in Alabama, Graham Cave in Missouri, Sheep Rock Shelter in Pennsylvania, Fort Rock Cave in Oregon; the list is endless. There are thousands of Archaic sites both in caves and rockshelters and in the open. The herd hunters were not cave dwellers; artifacts of the hunter-gatherers can be found at every kind of site that provided any two of the three essentials of subsistence, food, water, and shelter.

Archaic sites began to proliferate about 10,000 B.P., at the end of the Pleistocene, because that change of climate brought about an enormous expansion of suitable Archaic habitat. When Wisconsin III stood at its point of farthest advance on Long Island, between that front and the latitude of Carolina was a zone, called a biotic province, of animal and plant life like Canada's today. Not unnaturally, it is known to science as the Canadian biotic province. It consisted of a tundra subzone directly along the ice front, blending into a subzone of taiga—shrubs and bush. These two subzones were natural feeding grounds for cold-tolerant herd animals, and these brought the Paleo-hunters into that province. The next southerly subzone consisted of the low-growing evergreens; after them came the mixed spruce and pine forests, then the pine stands. The latter three subzones had a very limited animal feeding capacity and were probably visited very infrequently. But not far south of the Virginia-Carolina border, and extending westward to the Mississippi, the forest stand of deciduous fruit- and nut-bearing trees began, and here was the home of the hunter-gatherer. While the prairies did extend into Alabama, Georgia, and Florida, as previously noted, the forests of oak, hickory, walnut, beech, maple, etc. occupied the higher ground of hills and mountains, the piedmont, and probably the exposed continental shelf. The Paleo-hunters kept to the prairies and the Archaic hunter-gatherers to the woodlands without, apparently, interfering with each other or influencing each other discernibly.

But as soon as Wisconsin III began its final retreat, the Canadian biotic province retreated with it, and Carolina flora and fauna took over the vacated territory. By 10,000 B.P. mixed oak and pine forests had reached the latitude of New York, and with them came the Virginia deer, its hunters, and the gatherers of acorns. We can be sure of this because projectile points of Coe's piedmont and Broyles' Saint Albans sequences have been found on Staten Island with the remains of campfires dated from 7500 to 9500 C-14 years ago. This trend is marked from New York to Ohio by Kirk points of the piedmont sequence and west of Ohio by side-notched points like those found in the bottom of Modoc Rockshelter. During the 3000-4000 years after the end of the Pleistocene, the forest environment that was homeland to the Archaic hunter-gatherers was being created in the north, mile after mile, year after year, by the climate.

The second major consequence of the melting of the Wisconsin was a relatively rapid rise in sea level. Generation by generation, the sea encroached on the habitable lands of the coastal shelf, pushing the inhabitants of the coast up the stream valleys, which led in most instances to major rivers—the Mississippi, Hudson, Delaware, and Susquehanna, almost directly north. Our investigations of oyster shell midden sites in the lower Hudson Valley show the influx of coastal dwellers to have settled here between 6000 and 5000 B.P. By that time the coastal dwellers had become crowded for living space by the rising waters and had to thrust themselves into territory already occupied, though probably only thinly. There is, however, little evidence of conflict between peoples throughout the Archaic.

By about 6000 B.P. the entire eastern United States (except northern Maine) was woodland eminently suitable for hunter-gatherers, and of no use to herd hunters. Herd-hunting had become regional, restricted to the prairies and the High Plains. The Archaic way of life crossed the Mississippi to the edge of the prairies and even invaded them. Because it meant living off the land in an adaptation to whatever the land afforded, it could establish itself anywhere, even where nature no longer treated the land benignly.

Certainly, the post-Pleistocene change of climate did not treat the West benignly. The patterns of precipitation changed disastrously, and the formerly well-watered Great Basin between the Rockies and the coastal ranges began to dry up. Pleistocene Lake Bonneville, as large as Lake Ontario, shrank to the present Great Salt Lake. The very large Lake Lahontan evaporated away to the present Paradise Lake in Nevada; Lake Mojave is now a playa in the Mojave Desert. The entire Southwest from Texas to Arizona, where mammoth herds had found good pasturage during Clovis times, withered away to desert or semidesert. But man survived with his hunter-gatherer techniques and in the process taught himself such basic crafts as basketry, cordage, and the making of fiber textiles. It may be said, with not too many reservations, that despite steadily worsening conditions no area in the West was without its population, though some locales might have been visited only once in a generation.

As noted before, the Archaic pattern in the Great Basin and Southwest is known as the Desert culture. The whole sequence has been preserved at Danger Cave, Utah, beginning about 11,000 B.P. and following through to a level that is pretty much the culture of surviving Paiute Indians. It is the culture that underlies the agricultural Mogollon, Hohokam, and Anasazi, the latter being ancestral to the Basketmaker-Pueblo sequence.

On the Pacific side of the coastal ranges the Archaic living pattern ended only with the advent of Europeans. The California-Northwest coastal tribes never acquired pottery or agriculture. The available food resources, especially along the fertile rain belt of the Northwest Coast, were so abundant and unfailing that agriculture would have been a waste of effort much better spent in other food-producing pursuits, and pottery filled no specific need for which the crafts of woodworking and basket weaving did not sufficiently provide.

The prairies and the Plains have already been sufficiently discussed; they never had an Archaic. As long as the buffalo grazed there by the millions, what was the need for it? Herd-hunting is a static, dead-end way of life, anachronistic, unprogressive. As long as the herds provided both food and hides for tepees, there was neither compulsion nor incentive to change or improve. To people always packing or unpacking, fragile pottery was a nuisance; the settled life of the farmer was repugnant to the very soul of the herd hunter. Left to themselves, with a plenitude of buffalo, the Plains Indians would have gone on being herd hunters for another 1000 years.

By contrast, the Archaic was a period of constant, even rapid progress toward the fuller, more stable, more complex living pattern we call civilization, even though no people within the limits of the United States ever attained it. The exploitation of hundreds of different micro-environments, each with its own ecosystem of food resources, evoked as many food-hunting strategies and stimulated invention in tools and toolmaking. The grinding of stone into axes, adzes, and celts with cutting edges, and into shapes like bannerstones, plummets, gouges, pipes, and pots (all these will be explained in Chapter 8) was an Archaic, not a herd hunter trait; the herd hunters went on using choppers and "teshoas," flakes broken off the outside of pebbles, until the white man traded them iron axes. By 4500 B.P. and very probably much earlier (ground-bit, hafted stone axes date from at least 7000 B.P.), Archaic peoples were living in permanently placed, pole-framed houses in settlements, though certainly not all year round. The first mounds, the only structures surviving from prehistory (except the Pueblo complexes of the Southwest), were built by an apparently late Archaic group, the Poverty Point culture.

Nor did the Archaic people advance in material culture alone. Though the earliest discovered ceremonial burial, at a site near Renier, Wisconsin, a cremation with red ocher sprinkled over the bone ash, included Plano herd hunter points, it could not have been a herd hunter burial. It also contained an Archaic side-notched point; soon after, there developed an Archaic ceremonial burial complex in this general vicinity, but there is no record anywhere in North America of such burial practices by herd hunters. The Wisconsin culture with which ceremonial burial, even to the point of interment in cemeteries, is associated is called the Old Copper because it made use of the abundant native copper, much of it obtainable from the surface in the Lake Michigan area, in the manufacture of artifacts. These were hammered out of the 99 percent pure copper, either cold or slightly heated. The artifacts are quite distinctive in shape and were, in a few cases, ornamental—bracelets and rings. The metal is not regarded as having been metallurgically treated; the copper was worked simply as a stone with special, nonchipping qualities. Stone tools, nicely finished, were made by the Old Copper smiths as part of the complex. The Old Copper culture, dated as early as 7400 B.P., influenced Archaic developments in the north central and northeastern United States, from Minnesota to Maine, and adjacent areas in lower Canada for the next 5500 years, spreading both its burial practices and native copper throughout the territory. It was within this Old Copper sphere of influence that the spectacular Hopewell focus developed, beginning about 2000 B.P., in which are found the same elements of ceremonial burial, shamanism, and the use of native copper.

To summarize, the Archaic gives an impression in the beginning of the restriction of the hunter-gatherer pattern of subsistence to a relatively small territory broken up into regions—the Southeast, the Great Basin, the Northwest—while the herd hunters roamed the length and breadth of the land. But the end of the Ice Age contracted herd hunter habitat while it expanded hunter-gatherer habitat, and certain hunter-gatherer groups, like the Kirk and LeCroy people, took immediate advantage of the opportunity to extend their range. That is why Kirk and LeCroy points are horizon styles, that is, styles widely distributed within a limited era. After the settling down of migrant groups, localized adjustments in tools were made and point types became differentiated into local varieties. But this process was complicated by new arrivals from the south in the thinly populated northern regions.

The Great Basin situation was quite different, however. It was not expansive at all. As the age of aridity intensified, the hunter-gatherers had to cover more territory to make a living, but there was no inducement to migrate. Conditions were bad everywhere. New strategies and discoveries were probably diffused by contacts between bands so that the entire population of the

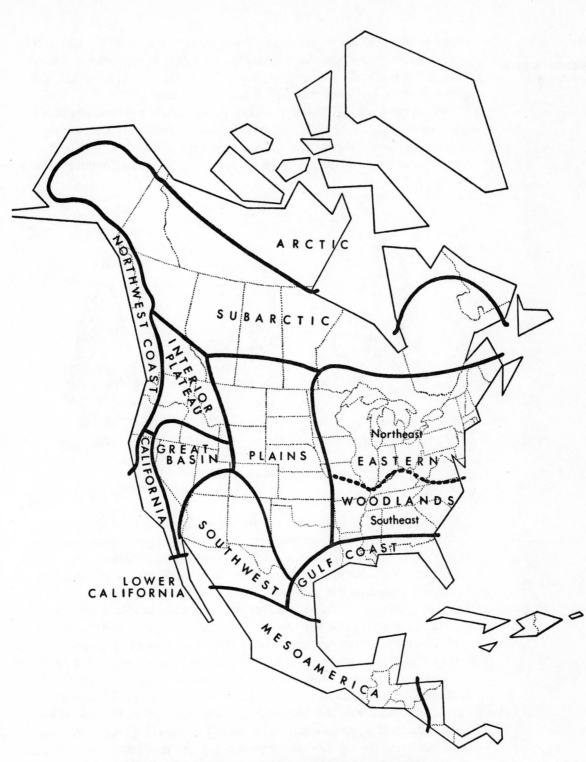

ARCHAEOLOGICAL CULTURE AREAS OF NORTH AMERICA

region participated in the generalized Desert culture, with only trivial, though archaeologically important, local variations. Along the Pacific coast, certainly from San Francisco northward, conditions never really worsened and the settled residents had every reason to be content with their lot.

Thus the Archaic is both time period and way of life, a generic way of life made up of hundreds of variations, broadly alike regionally, specifically alike only locally. What the excavator is looking for is the local and the specific. For most of the Archaic this means projectile points. As the heading of this section

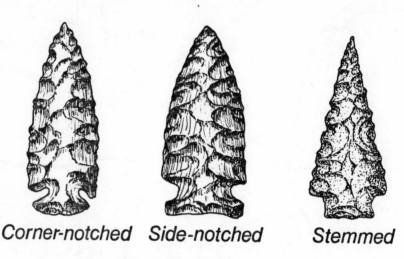

Corner-notched   *Side-notched*   *Stemmed*

ARCHAIC PROJECTILE POINTS

indicates, these differ markedly from the big game hunter lanceolates in that they have notched or stemmed treatments of the base to provide what is known as, in tool terminology, a shank. Usually called a haft in archaeology, the shank is that part of the tool which connects the handle to the blade or acting part. Why notching and stemming is peculiar to Archaic points will probably never be known. It cannot have to do with killing effectiveness, since the lanceolates were used on the biggest game with entire satisfaction to those who depended on them. Nor is there an advantage in manufacture. The notched points and some of the stemmed types go through a blade or preform stage in manufacture which is in form a lanceolate or triangular point. If the process stopped there, the blank would be a proper projectile point, haftable to the shaft exactly as lanceolate and triangular points are hafted. Notching and stemming narrow the blade to the width of the shaft, which probably makes the attachment of the point to the shaft more secure, but that additional security does not appear, at least to the modern investigator, to have been of any great importance. Eventually, in the last few hundred years of prehistory, unhafted triangular points achieved a wide popularity, apparently as arrow points; notching and stemming do not seem to have provided any special advantage in their case.

There are exceptions to the universality of notching and stemming during Archaic time. The reader will have noticed unhafted triangular points in the brief California sequence pictured in the last chapter. These probably represent evolutions from earlier lanceolates. The same kind of evolution seems to account for a tradition of unhafted triangulars found in the Archaic of the lower Hudson Valley. The Paleo-hunters in this vicinity, when the Carolinian biotic province spread over it, did not give up and move out; they adapted to the new environment successfully, and among the changes were the shape and size of projectile points, from unhafted lanceolate to smaller, unhafted triangulars. It is a quite plausible transition and it will have to serve until a better explanation is offered.

Those who, by reason of the sites they dig, specialize in the Archaic will find it an absorbing and inexhaustible subject.

THE POTTERY AND AGRICULTURAL HORIZON
FROM THE END OF THE ARCHAIC TO EUROPEAN CONTACT

No dates are given for this horizon because none would be valid for all areas and for both pottery and agriculture. For the archaeologist working in the United States the Archaic is considered to have ended with the addition of ceramic pottery to the material culture. But that one trait did not transform the way of life in any important respect; only agriculture could do that, and did.

The first ceramic pottery known within the United States was found in Florida and dates from about 4500 B.P. Ceramic pottery developed a little later in the Middle Atlantic states, and the earliest pottery in the Northeast, from the Ohio River to upper New York, dates at about 3000 B.P. Curiously enough, pottery did not appear in the Southwest, despite the proximity to early pottery-making cultures in Mexico, until about 2000 B.P. Branches of the Archaic Cochise culture became the Mogollon, the Hohokam, and the Anasazi in archaeological classification when they began to make pottery. Although in the Mogollon territory corn, and possibly squash and gourds, had been cultivated since about 5000 B.P., this could hardly be called agriculture. The corn ear at that time was a little thumb-size nubbin and could not have been much of a dietary staple.

In the Northeast—New Jersey, eastern Pennsylvania, New York, and New England—the ceramic period was preceded by a short period from about 3600 to 3000 B.P. when cooking vessels were made of steatite, or soapstone. In the extreme Southeast—South Carolina, Georgia, and Florida—steatite pot-making was adopted by people already making pottery, possibly because steatite was better than the ceramics of the time which were strengthened with grass and other vegetal fibers. In the Southwest there seems to have been no preparation for pottery. Storage receptacles of dried, not fired, clay were made but apparently had nothing to do with the introduction of ceramics, which were Mexican in origin.

Plant cultivation—to the degree that it had a significant effect on the economy and encouraged an increase in population and settlement living and therefore may be called agriculture—dates from about 3000 B.P. in the Southwest, when beans began to be cultivated, along with pumpkin or squash, gourds, and an improved variety of corn. But this may not be the earliest agriculture in the United States. The great mounds and earth works of the Poverty Point culture of Louisiana (representing one million cubic yards of earth-moving) could hardly have been erected by bands of hunter-gatherers who could not remain in one spot longer than a few weeks as they followed their food-collecting rounds. In his summary of Poverty Point, Clarence H. Webb, leading authority on the culture, says, "Agriculture or horticulture is not proved, but it is implied by the riverine settlement pattern; by the usual association of agriculture with large, year-round villages and ceremonial centers . . . and by the occurrence . . . of artifacts . . . which are associated with agriculture in Mesoamerica." All this Poverty Point had, and steatite and sandstone vessels, but no ceramic pottery, until perhaps the very end. Webb places the culture in time between 3500 and 3000 B.P.

At that time the Ohio River did not enter the Mississippi at Cairo, Illinois, but in Louisiana. Poverty Point influences traveled up both streams, it now appears, to instigate separate centers of the exuberant mound-building Hopewell culture in Illinois and Ohio. But agriculture seems not to have reached either center until about 2000 B.P. The precedent Adena culture in Ohio, which was latterly contemporary with Hopewell, cultivated sunflowers, but this was certainly not true agriculture.

It was the Hopewell people, religion, or cultural emissaries—nobody is quite sure what Hopewell was—who seem to have spread the agricultural doctrine into the Southeast as far as Florida, whence it worked its way northward into the Middle Atlantic states. But, though Hopewellian artifacts and even a Hopewellian mound or two have been found in upper New York, corn-beans-squash agriculture did not reach Iroquois country until about A.D. 900. Very probably, it took centuries to develop strains of these crops adapted to the shorter northern growing season. But the pre-Iroquoians had been making pottery for 2000 years before the proto-Iroquoian Owasco people made a success of agriculture.

The appearance of pottery, then, ends the Archaic as a formal archaeological period and initiates the Woodland period, except in the Southwest, where no general name has been given to the pottery period. Agriculture ended the Archaic way of life, and brought along with it permanent villages, palisaded or otherwise fortified for defense as the consciousness of territoriality intensified; greater political complexity, both within the village community and between communities, leaguing together in socioreligious-ethnic statism; great public works, principally mounds for religious purposes, like the flat-topped mounds surmounted by temples; burial mounds for honored interment; enigmatic mounds like the animal effigy mounds; and the earthworks, usually in geometric patterns, of undivined usage but in some cases, as at Poverty Point, probably village layout plans. The later in time the community, the more complicated a problem in excavation it usually becomes because less and less does the material culture reflect the whole social-economic-religious organization, and the single site reflect the whole culture. The archaeologist is only one of a half-dozen or more specialists whose skills and knowledge must be applied to the investigation of advanced societies. Project archaeology by coordinated teams, like those MacNeish took to Ayacucho Valley, alone is capable of performing the task.

THE CONTACT PERIOD, A.D. 1500 TO A.D. 1800

The contact period is as scalloped in outline as the end of the Archaic; it is a kind of brief twilight or dawn, depending on the point of view, before the setting of the sun for American aborigines, or the rising of the sun of European-Colonial occupation of the United States. For the archaeologist it is the period during which items of the white man's manufacture—beads, kaolin pipes, iron knives, hatchets, gun flints and guns, liquor, brass and iron kettles, buttons, etc.—appear as trade goods on Indian sites. As early as 1500 French, English, Spanish, and Portuguese fishing fleets began visiting the Grand Banks off Newfoundland for the cod season. Landfalls appear to have been made there and along the New England coast, probably for food paid for in European goods. In 1513 Ponce de Leon discovered Florida and initiated the incursion into the present southern United States by Spanish adventurers, the most widely traveled of whom was Hernando De Soto, who traversed the South between Florida and Arkansas between 1539 and 1541, discovering the Mississippi in 1541. The contact period on the Middle Atlantic seaboard began earlier, in 1526, with an abortive Spanish attempt to found a colony somewhere between the James River and Cape Fear. This and unsuccessful English attempts to gain a foothold before 1600 along the Atlantic coast of the present United States, did not breach aboriginal culture, but they did presage the end.

In 1534 Jacques Cartier initiated the French fur trade, which was to influence powerfully the history of North America north of Mexico for the next 200 years, by sailing up the Saint Lawrence River. European items were introduced into Indian culture in enormous quantities during those 200 years by both

French and English traders, with the result that more and more tribes became dependent on them. This is the real contact period, the time when Indians were abandoning their aboriginal crafts and developing a hybrid, dependent culture. They never adopted the ways of the white man or aspired to learn his technology. All they wanted were the artifacts of his material culture with which to pursue their own lifeways. It can be said that the Indian never acculturated, was never absorbed into white civilization. In that sense the contact period never ended.

THE HISTORIC PERIOD, A.D. 1600 TO A.D. 1900

Historical archaeology is becoming an increasingly practiced specialty of American archaeology because the awareness that our non-Indian past is disappearing along with our Indian past is making funds available for digging. Historical archaeology does not really fall within the purview of this book. It has its own literature, its own classic on how to do it, Ivor Noel Hume's *Historical Archaeology* (American prehistoric archaeology can offer no equal to it), and its own structure of organizations, conferences, and publications. Prehistoric and historical archaeologists both follow the same methods, standards, and principles in their digging; it is what they dig that makes all the difference—or nearly all of it. The prehistoric archaeologist has nothing to do with written records, since there are none for his sites; he digs the only record there ever was. But the first task of the historical archaeologist is to compile a dossier on the site under investigation from land records, diaries, letters, wills, and contemporary literature, tradition, and gossip; he is as much a delver among archives as an earth mover.

Historical archaeology has its periods, too. The Colonial period—on which millions of Rockefeller dollars have been spent in the excavation and restoration of Colonial Williamsburg, Virginia, the Dutch patroon estates at Phillipse Manor at Tarrytown, and Van Cortlandt Manor at Croton on the lower Hudson—comprises the nearly 200 years between the first settlements and the end of the Revolutionary War; it is confined to the original thirteen colonies of the Atlantic seaboard. West of the Appalachians the earliest period is the frontier period, which begins with the migrations of land-seekers into Tennessee and Kentucky in the 1750s, moves westward with time, and ends on a precise day, December 29, 1890, when the massacre of Sioux Indians at the "battle" of Wounded Knee Creek in the Dakota Badlands snuffed out the Indians' last illusion of autonomy.

The Federal period following the Revolution, when communities and cities west of the Appalachians were founded, and the Civil War period both have left behind physical evidences that belong properly to archaeology as they fade from memory, are buried, or are being destroyed. We cannot resurrect and restore our own past in its entirety or there would be no place for the present, but historical archaeology can help revive enough of it to keep our sense of continuity with it alive.

And so we have run out of time within which the archaeologist works.

SUMMARY

Despite the sketchiness of this outline of prehistory, it should provide a background for the reader and a chronological scale by which to measure the sequences he uncovers. It is impossible to reduce the outline for all its sketchiness, to a table that will do justice to its intricacy and multifariousness, but the following is a summary for a quick reference.

Chronology of Archaeological Periods

Date	Cultural Events	Site Locations
30,000 B.P.	Chopper-flake, pebble tool industries	Ayacucho
14,000 B.P.	Flake specialization industry Biface blade specialization industry	Ayacucho Venezuela
13,000 B.P.	Bifacial projectile points first appear	New Mexico (Sandia Cave)
12,000 B.P.	Clovis herd hunters first appear	Arizona (Lehner Ranch)
11,000 B.P.	Early Archaic of the Southeast first appears Midwest Archaic first appears Desert culture first appears	Carolina piedmont Illinois (Modoc Shelter) Great Basin (Danger Cave)
10,000 B.P.	Pleistocene animals become extinct and Plano bison-hunting tradition begins	High Plains, Colorado, Montana, Wyoming
4,500 B.P.	Pottery first appears in Southeast First corn appears in present United States	Florida Arizona (Bat Cave)
3,500 B.P.	First agriculture inferred	Louisiana (Poverty Point)
3,000 B.P.	Pottery appears in Northeast and initiates Woodland period Agriculture converts Cochise Archaic into Mogollon, Hohokam, Anasazi	Ohio, Pennsylvania, New York New Mexico, Arizona, Colorado

| 2,000 B.P. | Agriculture appears in Hopewell culture and spreads to Southeast | Ohio, Illinois |
| 1,000 B.P. | Agriculture reaches Northeast | New York |

It must be emphasized that everything the excavator finds belongs somewhere in the foregoing and it is up to him to discover or deduce where. This can be done and, to repeat, it *must* be done as a local sequence. How it works out can be shown from our work in the lower Hudson. In 20 years of excavation we have accumulated a great deal of material and although we don't know where it all belongs, we do have this much:

Local Sequence in the Lower Hudson

14,000 B.P.: The Prickly Pear Hill chopper-flake cache; no date; inferred from the type of material found.

11,000 B.P.: One blade section of a Clovis fluted point, found in a collection but known to have been found on the surface at a local site.

10,000 B.P.: Several lanceolate points, points verging from lanceolate to triangular and believed to be transitional from herd hunter lanceolates to triangles used after 10,000 B.P. by descendants of herd hunters adapting to the Carolinian biotic province. Hypothetical as yet. From a site called Piping Rock.

9000 to 6000 B.P.: A Kirk point and two Taylor points (related to Dalton points of Coe's sequence)* from an early shell midden site called Dogan Point; C-14 dated *older than* 5100 years by an unknown factor. A Kessell and a LeCroy point, like those found in Broyles' Saint Albans sequence, at Piping Rock. MacCorkle points, as at Saint Albans, at Piping Rock. A shell midden site called Twombly Landing, and an inland site called Hanotak Rockshelter.

More than 5100 B.P.: Shells lying on top of certain points, which had been left behind before the shell was deposited on them, have been C-14 dated at three places at the Dogan Point site. The points were a side-notched variety like those in the lowest level at Modoc Rockshelter and two types called Vosburg and Otter Creek. The latter two are strictly New York-New England styles and apparently mark a period of regionalism, after the traditions of the Carolina Archaic had died out.

4750 B.P.: A C-14 date at Twombly Landing sets this as the date when those people who were pushed upriver by sea-level rise reached this area. They

---

*Both the Taylor points found here and the Hardaway points found by Coe in the Carolina piedmont are probably varieties of the Dalton, a supertype.

made rather crude, small, stemmed points quite unlike the notched and triangular points that preceded them in the lower Hudson. This tradition, which is called the Taconic, remained about 1000 years.

3600 B.P.: Two varieties of points of what is called the Broad spear tradition, the Perkiomen and Susquehanna, occur by ones and twos regularly on the riverbank sites. They are dated at slightly over 3600 B.P. in nearby Pennsylvania and are associated with steatite vessels.

3000 B.P.: A point style called the Fishtail occurs at riverbank sites in about the same numbers as Broad spears. The fishtail is associated on Long Island with the earliest pottery type in the Northeast, called Vinette I, and has a C-14 date of 3000 B.P.

1500 B.P.: An assemblage consisting of a steatite platform pipe, a gorget fragment (this is an ornament worn at the breast on a string suspended from the neck), a native copper awl, points called Jack's Reef, and a pottery type called Wickham Corded was found at Piping Rock. This is the very characteristic association of a culture of upstate New York called Kipps Island, dated about 500 A.D. It is probably distantly related to the Hopewell culture of Ohio, which died out about A.D. 500.

Susquehanna

Fishtail

Perkiomen

POINTS FOUND IN THE LOWER HUDSON

1000 B.P.: Quite common in the lower Hudson is a type of usually large triangular point called Levanna. Such a point, from Prickly Pear Hill (not associated with the chopper-flake industry) was C-14 dated at A.D. 970.

Contact times: We have dug in the barnyard of the Rockefeller-restored Van Cortlandt Manor where Indians had camped for 5000 years or more, but it yielded, not surprisingly, contact material, including 50 or more sections of Dutch kaolin clay pipestems broken in lengths about 1 inch long for beads, some gun flints, and a George III penny.

This detailed tabulation, to which further references will be added, has been set down to give some idea of how local sequences are arrived at and how they actually do synchronize with the main periods in American prehistory.

c h a p t e r   4

Finding and Recognizing Sites

THE FIRST STEP that must be taken in doing archaeology is to locate a site. The two indispensable elements in archaeology are the digger and the place to dig; the two must meet and interact. But much more is required of the archaeologist then merely wanting to meet and interact. The author was thirty-five years old before he found his first site, on the banks of the Ohio River, which are really almost one continuous site from Pittsburgh to Cairo. And then he had to do it all over again when he moved to Ossining, New York, on the banks of the Hudson, which is not, at this point, a river at all, but an arm of the sea and an environment totally alien to a midwesterner. The simplest way to meet a site and see artifacts in their native habitat—and it is recommended as the first attempt to make—is to join the local chapter of the state archaeological society. Local chapters are usually engaged in digs, and their members know where the sites in the vicinity are to be found.

But when the author came to Westchester County, populous though it is with citizens of the educated upper middle class, there was no chapter of the New York State Archaeological Association within sixty miles. This experience leads him to suspect that at least 75 percent of the readers of this book may find themselves in the same frustrated isolation, condemned to bland library research. Until archaeological societies and sites are listed in the telephone book, site location is going to be the blank wall that stops the aspiring archaeologist from becoming a sweating one.

But the fact is that there are explorable sites within a short automobile trip of nearly every resident of the contiguous United States, Alaska, Canada, Mexico, and Central and South America; and they are to be found for the looking.

Looking for sites is—when conducted according to plan—survey, and the methods of survey are determined by survey objectives: to find a site, just any site, to make a beginning; or to find a certain kind of site, or a site of a given period; or to discover the total archaeological resources of an area. But before your attention is turned to these matters, buy a U.S. Geological Survey map of the quadrangle in which you intend to work.

THE U.S. GEOLOGICAL SURVEY MAPS

The United States has been surveyed in its entirety and divided into quadrangles of various sizes, depending more or less on how thickly populated is the area within the quadrangle. The largest scale maps of these quadrangles belong to the 7.5-minute series, so named because the maps cover 7.5 minutes of longitude (east-west) and 7.5 minutes of latitude (south-north). Maps in the 15-minute series cover 4 times as much territory, being 15 minutes on a side, so that, printed the same size as maps in the 7.5-minute series, they are smaller in scale; i.e., everything is closer together on the maps. The 30-minute series is still smaller in scale, and certain areas of the mountainous and desert West have been mapped in 60-minute (1-degree) quadrangles. These U.S. Geological Survey maps are topographic, showing elevations (for the 7.5- and 15-minute series) on 10-foot contours, and they accurately locate all natural features. In addition, they include "cultural" or man-made features (buildings, mines, dams, roads, railroads, trails, etc.) as of the time of the survey. The maps may be purchased from map dealers such as Hammond and Hagstrom and sometimes from book stores and dealers in engineering supplies; they may also be had in some states from certain state agencies, such as state geologic surveys and departments of public works, but the surest source is the publisher, the U.S. Geological Survey of the U.S. Department of the Interior. The price should be less than $1.00 per quadrangle.

SITE NOTATION

The quad map's principal use is in survey, but its first use is for site notation. The finder dots in the exact locus of the site discovered as another datum

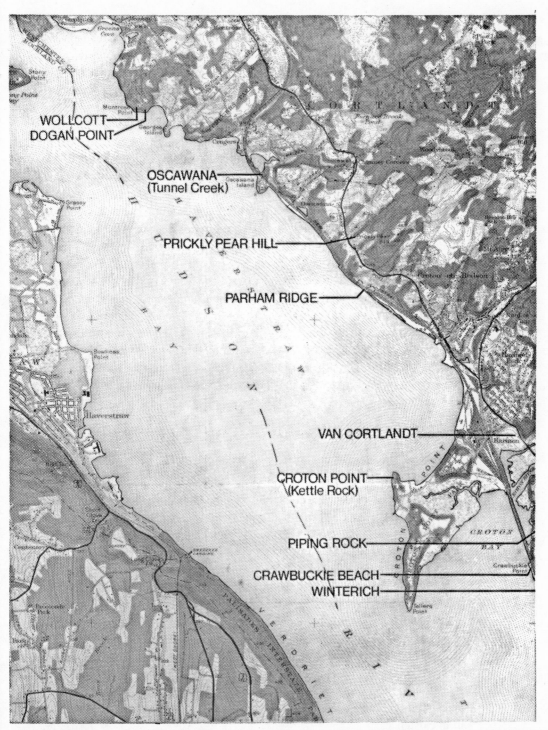

WOLLCOTT
DOGAN POINT

OSCAWANA
(Tunnel Creek)

PRICKLY PEAR HILL

PARHAM RIDGE

VAN CORTLANDT

CROTON POINT
(Kettle Rock)

PIPING ROCK

CRAWBUCKIE BEACH
WINTERICH

SITES EXCAVATED BY AUTHOR MARKED ON U.S. GEOLOGICAL SURVEY HAVERSTRAW QUADRANGLE MAP

on the map. In some states, such as New York, sites are given their designation by quadrangle in a state register of sites kept by the state archaeologist; for instance, Hav-2-1 would mean the first site in the northeast quarter of the Haverstraw quadrangle. The final digit stands for the site, and the first digit stands for the quarter. The northwest quarter is 1, the northeast 2, the southwest 3, and the southeast 4. This system differs from the method of site designation used by federal agencies such as the River Basin Survey. The latter consists of a number which is the position of the state on the alphabetical list of states (using the old 48-state list), followed by a two- or three-letter abbreviation of the county of occurrence, followed by a serial number. Thus this same site in Westchester County, New York would receive the designation 30 We-1. The reader, poring over the literature, may encounter such designations and they should not puzzle him; there is nothing esoteric about them. It was formerly the practice to include in the designation a symbol for the kind of site—i.e., shell midden, mound, village, etc.—but this practice has been abandoned. The trend is unfortunately not toward the New York model of location and designation by U.S. Geological Survey quadrangle, and the second system described above is generally used.

Nothing compels the finder to submit his survey information to the state archaeologist, but he should. Most states maintain a site register, with site locations kept confidential if the finder so requests. The finder should think of a site as public property and of himself as the custodian of its archaeology, not the owner.

SOURCES OF INFORMATION ON SITE LOCATIONS

With his U.S. Geological Survey quad map pinned to the wall awaiting its first site dot, the reader, anxious to get into the field, had best look for that first site by reportorial techniques; i.e., he should seek out and question the likeliest source of information. One of the best, the local historical society or museum, should be near at hand. There is probably no community in the United States as much as fifty years old in which a group of residents have not formed an organization for the preservation of the history and antiquities of the vicinity. Materials and records are usually gathered together in a room, building, or repository that serves as a museum. Among the accumulated materials will be donations of collections of "arrowheads" and other Amerind equipment, cleaned out of attics or turned over by the executors of estates who don't know what else to do with them. In most instances some clue can be provided as to where the collection came from, and the eager searcher has his site, or several sites, if they are still in existence.

This is an especially enlightening way to find a site because it gives the searcher a look at actual discoveries; he can see the kind of stones used in tools and the kinds of tools and utensils used (these collections rarely contain anything but artifacts) and form impressions that will give him the feel of the site he is about to dip into. Further, by comparing this real material with what references he can muster, he will be at least partially informed on where, in the area sequence, he is beginning his work. There is no better way to begin archaeology than to study site collections already in being because, among other lessons, it will show how exasperating it is to deal with materials unscientifically and unsystematically "picked up."

Pot hunters are diggers, and the aspiring archaeologist who can win the confidence of one to the degree that he will reveal the location of his digging has special talent as a salesman. But the effort is worth making. Since pot hunters are looters by instinct, they are extremely careless and unmethodical in their grabbing and running and often abandon a site half-dug, leaving valuable information behind. A pot hunter may be worth cultivating for just such information. The student can frequently put together the pot hunter's material with what he digs properly himself and arrive at a reasonably accurate interpretation. Just don't be undiplomatic enough to call him a pot hunter. He thinks of himself as a relic collector. One thing can be relied on: pot hunters know where the sites are. However, if they will not be helpful, some sleuthing is called for. They are usually digging on private or public land without permission.

The beginner, if he lives within travel distance of a college or university, may do well to present himself at its anthropology department and offer his services. If the department is doing any local archaeology, he may be accepted as a member of a digging party. Or, if he can convince the person in charge of his sincerity, some information may be shared with him. But, by and large, anthropology departments with courses in field methods in archaeology as a part of their curriculum will themselves be looking for sites. There are others, however, which have lists of sites longer than they will ever be able to get at.

EXPLORING FOR A SITE

If other means fail, the beginner may take to his car and go looking in a likely stretch of countryside along a permanent stream, making inquiry of the owners of the land through which it runs. Property owners are naturally suspicious of snoopers but it is surprising how often they will, when civilly and candidly approached, become interested in the possibility of having prehistory uncovered in their own back lots. One of the commonest acknowledgments in archaeological reports is of gratitude to a landowner not only for permission to dig but for even more substantial help and hospitality.

The Field Survey

A field survey is a walking tour. It may have the objective either of finding just any site or a special site, and it may be an absorbing and complete project in itself, consisting of the discovery and inventory of every visible outcrop and evidence of aboriginal occupation in a given area. The formal field survey is highly recommended as a beginner's first archaeological activity, to precede plunging into a dig relatively dewy-eyed. The investigation afoot, undertaken with reference to a selected natural, geologic feature, say a stream valley and its watershed as determined from the U.S. Geological Survey quad or quads, affords incomparable familiarity with the environment with which Amerinds lived so intimately. The land, its features and natural productiveness, gave shape to the life of the Amerinds—their food-getting, shelter, travel, and defense. Every site consists of the natural environment as well as the camp or village; the Amerinds chose their campsites for the accessibility of water, food-yielding plants, game habitat, seasonal shelter, and needed materials. Civilization is organized to nullify the natural environment; Amerinds had to live with it as they found it, since they had no power to change or control it, and technology sufficient only to gain a living from it and defend themselves against it.

In a survey the archaeologist does with his feet what he does with his mind's eye when he scans a U.S. Geological Survey topographical map, trying to imagine where Amerind camps and settlements would have been. A survey is walking a main watercourse valley and checking out the fields that border it, the bottoms, the unexpected niches and coves that are sheltered from the prevailing winds, the bluffs, the rock faces on which petroglyphs may be engraved, and the outcrops of flint, quartzite, or steatite that were quarries or mines for tool material. It means trudging up side streams peering at eroding banks and their debris for tell-tale chips and for the buried stratum of black "Indian dirt"* that reveals the surface once lived on and now covered by the humus accumulation of 2000-3000 years. It often leads to old ponds, lakes, and swamps where all kinds of local wildlife congregate even today, as the archaeologist looks for nearby, well-drained knolls where camping would have been most comfortable. He keeps an eye peeled for artificial-looking mounds and for big old oaks, beeches, and other nut trees, survivors of ancient groves. He climbs the hills looking for caves in limestone country, and rockshelters and high hidden valleys suitable for wintering in. With permission from the owners, he surface hunts the plowed and planted fields, and examines the banks of all excavations, including road cuts.

---

*"Indian dirt" is a former living surface stained by organic matter, grease, charcoal, and other such dark pigments of human usage. It is a culture-bearing zone. The blackness differs from humus by being greasy-looking.

Surface hunting is simply walking over a site and picking up whatever has been exposed by weathering. To hunt an archaeologically productive field on a sunny March day after a rain when the surface is bare or newly plowed is one of the pleasantest avocations.

To pick up an artifact or other evidence of occupation by Amerinds lying in plain sight is a good deed; it saves the piece from breakage, from being possessed by the uncaring, or from being covered over and lost again. But to pick it up is also a responsible act; the item should not be merely pocketed and then stored in an empty coffee jar. What turns surface hunting and pot-hunting into archaeology is record-keeping. The "arrowhead" picked out of a ditch should (1) receive an acquisition number, which is inked on it, (2) be catalogued in a simple serial number register, and (3) be recorded as to provenience, that is, place of discovery.

Step 3 can be done on a property survey map, but it can be accomplished as easily on a sheet of graph paper on which a few landmarks on or near the site—trees, rocks, banks, fences, streams, etc.—have been marked in the proper approximate relationship to each other. The locations of finds are then jotted in by acquisition number on this sketch, to which is appended such descriptive notes as are appropriate. Something like the diagram on the following page will result.

A student can take this record and, together with the artifacts, make a great deal of it, certainly enough to tell him where to dig. The knoll is, clearly, a "hot spot," or concentration of evidence suggesting a camp; but it also may be only a living area within a village which happened to be higher than the surrounding area and more subject to erosion and leveling by plowing. The scattering of finds over the whole field is suggestive of wider occupation of the field than merely on the knoll. When a surface hunter does this kind of notation, he is doing archaeology; if he expands it with information on the kind of soil, environmental resources, and the history of the site after it became white man's property, he has readied the site for digging by himself or by any competent excavator.

Sites found by surface hunting should be entered in their proper location on the appropriate U.S. Geological Survey quadrangle map.

If no more than a tin medal or scroll were awarded to a resident in each quadrangle for such a survey, the remaining archaeological resources of the entire United States and a good part of Canada could be known within five years, and attention could be directed toward their preservation. Theoretically, the survey should produce evidence, throughout 90 percent of the United States, of prehistory up to 30,000 years ago. It may be assumed *a priori* that every stream valley in America south of the last phase of the Wisconsin glacier must have been explored, traversed, or camped in, and every lake and food-producing locale must have been known to wandering aborigines from

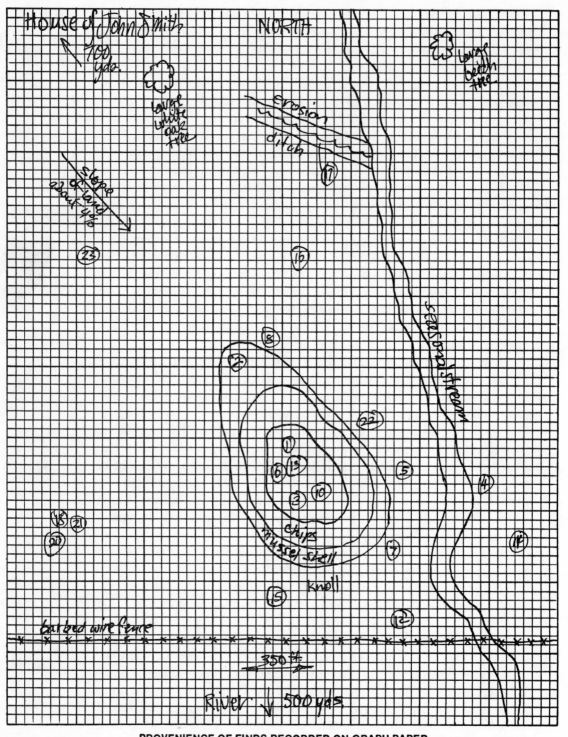

PROVENIENCE OF FINDS RECORDED ON GRAPH PAPER

the beginning. That they left physical clues of that beginning, out of the slim stock of possessions of their transient way of life, clues that could withstand ages of weathering and which are not buried forever out of sight, is another matter. But who is to say in what quadrangle all these conditions will be met?

The Special Site

The beginner will hardly be looking for a special site, that occurrence of material that fills in a blank in an archaeological program, a village site of a given period, a component yielding a wanted type of pottery or assemblage of traits, or an environment especially preservative of organic remains. But the process of locating such a site consists of a canvass of the sources listed above, an examination of all known collections and relevant reports, and direct inquiry. Curiously enough, the most sought-after kind of special site, and the rarest, is the latest—the villages and camps occupied just before and during Amerind-white contact. All of these were literally on the surface and so were quickly scattered or pre-empted by white men for their farms and other enterprises.

But when all these measures fail, the searcher for the special site has no alternative but to hitch on his pack, take his U.S. Geological Survey map in hand, and strike out on a field survey.

EQUIPMENT FOR THE SURVEY

Field survey combines many kinds of pleasures—hiking, picnicking, overnight camping, birdwatching, specimen collecting, camera tripping, and breathing fresh air—but how the surveyor will equip himself for these is a matter for individual choice. One is best prepared to survey when one's burdens are light. The following lists what is needed for archaeological survey only:

- A clipboard for writing on, to which is attached: (1) the U.S.G.S. quad map of the area (the discovered site should be immediately dotted in on the map and given a serial number and a name, from a place name in the vicinity, if possible), and (2) several sheets of graph paper on which to make sketches, like that given in the section on surface hunting.

- A short axe for cutting blazes on trees to mark the site (sites can easily be lost under some circumstances).

- A keel or engineer's crayon, for the same purpose as the above when there are no trees to blaze.

- A short shovel or trenching tool. (It is important to know whether a site has depth and/or is stratified. A test hole will usually need to be sunk.)

- A digging trowel, in case something is uncovered that requires delicate excavation.

- Collecting bags of cloth or heavy plastic (the recoveries from each site should be kept in its own tagged bag).

- A notebook and ball point pens for observations and site summaries.

- Several survey forms, one to be filled out for each site (see the example).

- Binoculars, to scan the faces of cliffs and steep hillsides for rockshelters (they save legwork).

- A camera. (Pictures of wooded or open field sites don't usually show much; but mounds, petroglyphs, caves, rockshelters, and such prominent configurations make good subjects and should be photographed.)

- A 50-foot steel tape (not an absolute necessity but helpful in measuring a site for scale drawings).

- A companion. (Two pairs of eyes and their differing angles of vision are better than one, a corroborating witness is comforting, and there are sometimes tasks that require two pairs of hands. Besides which, a surveyor can turn an ankle or be bitten by a snake.)

FORMS FOR RECORDING NEW SITES

Reproduced on pp. 78-79 is a form used in recording new sites discovered by survey and other means. It is used by the West Virginia Geologic and Economic Survey, Section of Archaeology, and is oriented toward prehistoric sites. Many variations of this memorandum form are in use, and the surveyor may even devise his own. However, the Imaginary Site Outline included in this chapter may furnish guidance to the beginning surveyor. (The information in parentheses following "e.g." is of the author's own invention.) Its purpose is to show how concretely a discovered site should be located and described in the memorandum the surveyor files on it.

To sum up, the field survey is exploration afoot in a given, limited area to discover sites by surface hunting or by test-pitting (see Chapter 5). But what is a site?

SITES PLAIN AND FANCY

A site is an area, plot or tract of land, locus or place where is found evidence of former human habitation or other activity, the limits of which are set by the evidence. That is, the site is where the evidence occurs. As self-evident as this definition may appear to be, it should not go unheeded. Archaic campsites may

Imaginary Site Outline

Site Serial No. 1 (in the order of the surveyor's visitation)

Site Name: (as given by original finder whether this finder or a previous one)
Lat. & Long. _____   USGS Quad. _____
County Georg̲e̲   Township Washingto̲n̲   Owner of Record John Doe

How Discovered (survey, inquiry, information given, previous excavation)

Accessibility (e.g., on foot only; no major obstacles)

Location (e.g., on right bank of Bloody Run 1000 ft. plus or minus 100 ft. south of
    Bloody Run bridge on Rte. 123, 2 miles east of village of Smithtown)

Identification: (e.g., live black oak 3 ft. diameter near center of site; downed tree
    across eastern end; blackberry patch on perimeter)

Description and Extent: (e.g., half-pie-shaped flat lying 100 ft. along present stream
    course which is entrenched about 6 ft. deep. Flat averages 50 ft. wide, between
    present stream and old meander scar. Hillside rises steeply behind scar, giving
    shelter from northwest; exposures of bed rock on opposite bank with land
    gently rising and in pasture; owner's barn, distance 1000 yds., is visible in that
    direction. Ground cover under oak is leaf mold, with some poison ivy; beyond
    tree shadow are low bushes, blackberry canes, shrubs. Cattle sheltering on site
    have left droppings. Hillside to northwest was lumbered over in the 30s; now in
    poor stand of second growth hardwoods—oak, hickory, beech.)

Collection: (e.g., broken Kirk-like side-notched point eroded from creek bank; flint
    chips in creek; 2 chips and 1 black flint core in bare spot at tree base. Pebble
    hammerstone on surface though no pebbles in creek bed. Broad-stemmed point
    [Savannah River type?] in leaf mold near blackberry patch. Chips also found
    on opposite bank.)

Test: (e.g., two 2 X 2 ft. holes, 10 in. deep. Chips to 8 in. Clay begins at 9 in.)

Evaluation: (e.g., very promising undisturbed Archaic site. Probably occupied
    before meander channel was abandoned and stream took present course
    through site. Black oak is apparently in center of occupied area; will cause dig-
    ging problems. Some stratigraphy possible, depending on stream flooding.)

Status and Availability: (e.g., Owner will permit excavation but wants half of ar-
    tifacts. State plans to reroute Rte. 123 as 4-lane highway over site within 5 yrs.
    Because it is sheltered from prevailing wind, could be dug in early spring or
    late fall. Relatively safe from prowlers and claim jumpers.)

Past History: (e.g., owner has 1 ground ax, 2 Kirk-like points. No other known
    collections.)

Site Sketch: (tied into USGS map)

WEST VIRGINIA GEOLOGICAL SURVEY
SECTION OF ARCHEOLOGY

SITE SURVEY RECORD

*1. Site No. 46-Bo-1   2. Site Name Horse Creek Petroglyphs

3. County Boone   4. District Scott   5. Elev. 610

6. Quadrangle (7.5 min.) Julian   (15 min.) Madison

7. Location On face of cliff on the end of a point, on the north
bank of Horse Creek, ¼ mile from its mouth. Railway cuts
through this point back of the site.

8. Owner Jacob Price   9. Address Julian, W. Va.

10. Tenant None   11. Address
                    Present owner's
12. Previous Owner father   13. Address deceased

14. Attitude toward excavation Favorable towards vicinity of site.
                    Incised lines and designs on smooth areas
15. Site Description: along 80 feet of the face of the cliff.

16. Type of site Petroglyphs

17. Dimensions: N-S o   E-W 80 ft.   18. Depth -

19. Vegetation None on site   20. Soil none

21. Surrounding soil Alluvium   22. Cultivation None

23. Erosion None   24. Nearest site 46-BO-66 ½ mile SE

25. Possibility of destruction None foreseen

26. Nearest water Horse Creek, 25 ft. S.

27. Nearest buildings, roads Dirt road & house 500 ft. NW, RR 100 ft. N.

28. Features None noted except petroglyph designs.

29. Burials None known

30. Informants Site well known locally more than 150 years
                    31. Address

32. Private collections None known
                    Olafson, "Rock carvings in Boone Coounty,
33. Published references West Virginia Archeologist, No. 2.

34. WVGS Acc. Nos.   35. WVGS Photo Nos.

36. Recorder Sigfus Olafson, 1960. Revised   37. Date 6/5/1971

WVGS Form #1
WEST VIRGINIA SITE-RECORDING FORM (FRONT)

38. Site No. (Name) 46-Bo-1, Horse Creek Petroglyphs

39. Co-ordinates locating site on Julian Quadrangle (7.5-15 min)

    a. 7.45 inches from (~~north~~, south)

    b. 1.87 inches from (~~east~~, west)

40. Map of site and surroundings, taken from quadrangle:

*41. Visited by WVGS _____ *42. Date _____

*43. Culture _____

44. Excavations _____ 45. By whom _____

46. When _____ 47. Address _____

48. Remarks:

*49. Recommendations:

*Items thus indicated will be filled in by WVGS representative.

WEST VIRGINIA SITE-RECORDING FORM (BACK)

cover no more than 10 square feet, or, as at Saint Albans, a single horizon or definable stratum obviously contemporaneously occupied may run for a mile. Village sites may be a quarter of an acre or ten acres in extent. One can be embarrassed to give a site a number, excavate it, and then, on exploring the area further, discover half a dozen loci in the vicinity, all separate sites in one sense yet all related to each other because the locale had been a traditional camping grounds for several thousand years. A site is defined by its extent and by its function.

By function, sites fall mostly into the broad categories of habitation, food-producing, industrial, and ceremonial, with certain minor categories, such as trails and fords of lesser importance, observable but often not excavatable. But this is not to say that several activities might not have been carried on in the same vicinity, in which case the correlation of the activities constitutes the site. But, since the purpose of archaeology is to explain the evidence, it is best to attempt to derive function from the evidence. The following breakdown is not necessarily exhaustive but should be helpful:

Types of Sites

Habitation

    Villages, nonagricultural.

    Villages, agricultural, open.

    Villages, agricultural, fortified.

    Camps, central.

    Camp sets, single-fire camps.

Food-producing

    Shell heaps, often associated with camps or villages.

    Kill sites, such as the Olsen-Chubbock, the Naco, and the Lehner Ranch sites.

    Game pounds, artificial or natural culs-de-sac into which game was driven.

    Fish weirs, pounds, or traps. A noted example is the Boylston St. (Boston, Mass.) fish weir dated at about 3850 C-14 years ago.

    Fishing stations, usually distinguishable only by the presence of numbers of net-sinkers.

    Gathering places, usually oak or nut tree groves or stands of wild rice or other harvestable vegetal food, yielding mostly nutting stones and hand grinding stones. One of the strangest gathering sites was reported in a recent survey of the Flathead River in Montana. It was a grove of ponderosa pines from which the bark had been partially stripped. Indians ate the cambium layer under the bark in times of scarcity. They also fed bark, particularly cottonwood bark, to their horses during the winter.

Industrial

Quarries and mines, where flints, quartzites, rhyolites, and other such rocks used in tool-making were wrenched or dug from outcrops and roughly worked and where steatite (soapstone) for vessels was mined. In the western Great Lakes native copper was mined from the numerous deposits there, mainly on Isle Royale in Lake Michigan. In the Midwest catlinite, fire clay, and pipe clay were mined in several places.

Chipping stations or floors. Probably most stone artifacts used in America were made of river pebbles and other stones picked up on the surface. The chipping floors where there occur concentrations of the debris, the "debitage" or waste, from reducing these pieces to rough or finished artifacts will be found in or around camps or on the banks of bodies of water with gravel beaches.

Caches. Blanks, roughs, or preforms—that is, specimens of the working stage intermediate between block or core and the finished artifact— were often stored away in caches for "seasoning." The caches were usually in damp ground, the dampness preserving the chipping quality of the flints. Other caches contained finished artifacts, actual hoards of treasured possessions hidden away for safekeeping. Some caches may even have been ceremonial offerings.

Bedrock metates and mortars. Very often the best stone available for use as a nether or table stone in seed grinding was an exposure of bedrock. Such sites are listed as industrial because they were food-processing loci, whether the stone served as a metate (little table), used with a mano (hand stone), or as a mortar, used with a pestle of stone or wood.

Specialized processing sites. The surveyor or excavator will occasionally come upon sites where the assemblage of artifacts suggests a specialized processing or manufacturing activity. A variety of cutting and scraping tools and "hot stones" indicates a locus of hide working. (Hot stones are pebbles heated and placed on the outside of the hide to scorch off undesirable epidermis.) A collection of adzes, choppers, and heavy scrapers suggests the locus of manufacture of a dugout or bark canoe. The drying of foods—flesh, fish, vegetal—for winter keeping can be recognized by large, usually stone-filled hearths over which the food was cured on racks. The author knows of no reported locus of ceramics manufacture in most of the United States, but in the late cultures of the Southwest kilns are sometimes found, surrounded by thick layers of the sherds of broken pots.

Ceremonial

Cemeteries and burials. Deliberate burial (no matter how bare the grave or bereft the remains of evidence of ritual) may be regarded as ceremonial because interment is a ceremony, an act or pattern of acts performed in response to a belief not related to the necessities of living. Strictly speaking, cemeteries and burials should be counted as sites only when they are isolated from other activities, such as habitation.

Constructed mounds. The principal kinds of constructed mounds (in contrast with accumulated midden mounds) are temple mounds, burial mounds, effigy mounds, and ritual mounds. There is no need to justify any of these as ceremonial sites; their contents or form are defining enough: (1) The pyramidal temple mounds are so called from the "temples" or houses of ritual erected on their flat tops. They are found in the Mississippi Valley and the Southeast. (2) Burial mounds are sometimes—as among the Adena, who inhabited the Kentucky-Ohio region 3500-3000 years ago—accretional; that is, they consist of a series of burials over an extended period of time, with each new burial placed on top of the earthen heap of the earlier ones and covered over with its own little mound. (3) Other burial mounds are above-ground tombs covered monumentally with heaps of earth. (4) Effigy mounds are earthen constructions of zoomorphic shape— animals, birds and, as in the case of the Great Serpent Mound of Adams County, Ohio, reptiles. They are usually devoid of content, being artifacts in themselves and should not, as a rule, be destroyed by digging. (5) Ritual mounds are usually piles of stones where ceremonies that left little evidence of their nature took place. At the Perch Lake stone mounds of northern New York State the ceremony involved the use of fire. But on the high points of bluffs overlooking the Ohio River the stone mounds, heaped up of cobbles carried from the valley 200 to 300 feet below, are wholly enigmatic. A mostly eastern phenomenon, found from Canada to Kentucky, stone heaps or mounds have been reported from most states but without plausible explanation of their use or significance.

Earthworks. These are embankments laid out in geometric forms (circles, squares, hexagons, etc.), are apparently related to the Hopewell culture, and are considered to have enclosed "sacred precincts," areas where ceremonies and sacred mysteries were conducted. Like effigy mounds they are without archaeological content and should not be dug. They are apparently related to the "sacred circle" circular embankments of shell sometimes up to 300 feet in circumference, found along the seacoast and on the sea islands of Georgia and the Carolinas. Sacred circle shell embankments are believed to derive from the Caribbean coast of South America. These ceremonial embankments should not be confused with the banks of irrigation ditches of the Southwest or the ditch-and-embankments surrounding a village palisade.

Arrangements. Outlines, usually of circles, formed by gathered stones laid out on the surface of the ground, are to be found all over the buffalo habitat of the West. Many of these are undoubtedly "tepee rings," the stones used to weight down the skirts of tepees. But others are also arrangements used in ritual; some may even be astronomical devices or models for seasonal rites. Stone arrangements have also been reported that may be effigies or symbols.

Petroglyphs and Pictographs. Petroglyphs are figures incised, pecked, or scored into the surface of stone; pictographs are painted figures. Unfortunately, much of this rupestrian art in America is to be found not in caves but on the faces of rock exposed to weathering. It scarcely qualifies as art in the narrow sense. The figures are sometimes realistic, more usually schematic or symbolic, and may have had meaning in hunting magic, dream fulfillment, shamanistic medicine, or as clan insignia. Obviously, such sites are not dug but are recorded in various ways—by photography, drawing, and mold-taking.

Ritual Caves. Found throughout the West from Lincoln, Nebraska to San Bernardino County, California, but most numerously in caves in the Grand Canyon, have been some 200 animal figurines made from split twigs, usually willow, apparently representing deer or bighorn sheep. These are usually found in caches in caves that show no other signs of occupation; no cultural material that might identify the makers has ever been found in association with these little effigies, but the C-14 dates of the wood place their construction earlier than 4000 B.P. The caves must have been used for some rite, probably of hunting magic. Caves in California are also known to have been used in female puberty rites. Caves seemingly empty of cultural material should always be examined thoroughly for evidence of ritual use.

TELL-TALE SIGNS OF SITES

The kind of site that the surveyor will be looking for most intently, the kind that is most rewarding to dig and the most difficult to find, is the buried habitation site. If it is buried too deeply, of course, it will not be found unless the surveyor detects the evidence in a streambank, road cut, or erosion trench. But when it is visible, what is this evidence? How do you know a site when you see it?

Shell

The most certain and easily detectable evidence that a site is in the vicinity are the valves of marine or freshwater shellfish. Unless the surveyor knows he is near a modern dump, cannery, or shucking station, when he comes upon a heap, scattering, or even a fragment of shell he is treading on a site of some kind. Shell is the most durable of the organic garbage Amerinds left behind because, being calcium carbonate, it resists dissolution in high acid soils. It is, for the same reason, an excellent preservative of organic materials enclosed within a heap of it. Some shells, such as those of oysters, suffer from weathering more than others, such as those of hard clams; but, once humus has formed over a heap, decay slows down. Oyster shell heaps 6000 years old have been found in relatively whole condition, except for the weathered outside. It must be remembered, however, that shell middens are simply accumulations of discarded shell and are only features of a site, not the site itself. Only where the midden is stratified, that is, where there have been successive deposits of shell alternating with soil layers, will there be found within a shell midden fuller assemblages of cultural materials. This occurs because, in some cases, when a heap has weathered down and become by intermingling with humus a usable soil surface, later campers may have used that surface for camping. The living area will be found, usually, near the periphery of a heap. Amerinds apparently did not mind the stench.

Archaeological shell heaps are by no means to be found only where there is salt water. Deposits of freshwater mussels have been found in such unlikely places as Montana, and the river mussel deposits along the Tennessee River, now lying behind Tennessee Valley Authority dams, were 30 feet thick. The Hopewellians of Ohio and the later Mississippian peoples must have gathered millions of river mussels, to estimate from the number of pearls (of no precious gem value) found in their graves. It is not exaggerating to say that to find a shell on the bank (not the beach) of any body of water is to find a site.

How to Recognize Worked Stones and Pebbles

But what if there is no shell? What, then, are the marks? Stone. Stone artifacts, rejects flawed in manufacture, stone chips, stone blocks or cores from which the chips were struck, fire-cracked stone, hammerstones, grinding stones, stone net sinkers, boiling stones (used in basket cooking before pottery was invented), stone potsherds, and manuports, that is, stones carried to a site and never used or used for a purpose that left no signs of wear. Stone, though damagable, is imperishable and throughout the occupancy of the Amerinds, were it 90,000 or 30,000 B.P., they made tools of stone; all these tools, or their fragments, are still in the earth, except for what has been removed—a tremendous quantity but still only a minor fraction of what must have been made and used by people who made and used them daily. Add to this the prodigious amount of debris of manufacture and it would seem that there must be a chip, core, or artifact of stone for every square inch of American territory, though not deposited so uniformly.

What kinds of stone should you look for? Keep your eyes open for the shine or glitter of chipped flint, quartz, jasper, or chalcedony, or the pebbles that are out of place geologically, water-rolled stones in a field without stone, or full of country (local) rocks like gneiss or sandstone. The best stones for chipping are blocks and chunks of cryptocrystalline rocks (the crystal structure is microscopic)—the flints, cherts, jaspers, chalcedonies, agates, quartzites, and obsidians. These were preferred when they were available, but all dense, hard rocks could be successfully shaped by the skilled knapper; and the truth is that there is hardly a stone, including slate, shale, and siltstone, that Amerinds did not reduce to form by flaking. The beginner will simply have to learn by experience to recognize the duller stones—basalts, andesites, rhyolites, argillites, sandstones, arkoses, hornstones, greenstones, and crystalline limestones—though it is very likely that for quite a while he will identify half of them as flint. Except for stones with a lens or platy structure, like slate and shale, the above stones chip very much alike.

Unless he knows something about the methods of chipping stone and the few simple characteristics of worked stone, the beginner may find himself puzzled to distinguish between chipped stone, fire-broken stone, and naturally broken or weather-split rock. The three methods of working stone are (1) direct percussion, (2) indirect percussion, and (3) pressure flaking. Direct per-

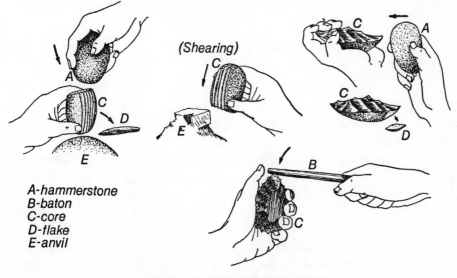

(Shearing)

A-hammerstone
B-baton
C-core
D-flake
E-anvil

METHODS OF DIRECT PERCUSSION

cussion is the direct striking of the stone to be shaped by another hard object (not necessarily a stone). In indirect percussion the point of a blunt-pointed punch of antler or hard wood is placed precisely at the spot from which the flake is to be removed, and the butt end is struck with a stone. Indirect percussion can be used anywhere direct percussion can be used, but its unique usefulness is in tight corners, for notching.

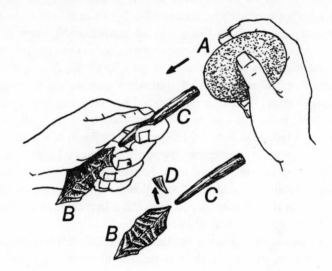

A-hammerstone
B-core
C-flaking tool
D-flake

INDIRECT PERCUSSION

In order to have any control of the flake he is taking off, the stone knapper—whether he is using direct or indirect percussion—must have an edge or projection to hit. This is called the striking platform; quarried stone has the angles and planes that afford striking spots. These may not be in the right place, however, and the knapper will trim one end of the block to give him the striking platform and angles he needs to strike off accurately.

Pebbles (the clastic classification of stones up to six inches in diameter) are something else. Their water-rolled smoothness presents no built-in striking platform and they must therefore be split. In the lithic debris in a site the excavator will happen now and again upon a piece that he will swear is a petrified patella or kneecap. It is the crown or boss knocked off a pebble to achieve a striking platform. But quite large cobbles (the stone size above pebbles) can be split by the knapper who has the touch. The cobble is laid on a log (a knee will do, in fact) with 60 percent or more of its length unsupported. A single, sharp blow at about midpoint will shear the stone in two.

The author once found half of an egg-shaped cobble of quartzite about eight inches long that had been split the hard way—lengthwise. The knapper had whacked each end about half a dozen times before he found the break point, after which the cobble had split cleanly.

The opening up or exposing of this one striking platform is only the start of the work. Striking along the edge of the platform, the knapper drives off flakes—in the case of pebbles to trim off the cortex or weathered "rind", but in any case to give himself some longitudinal edges to work on. In order to thin down the core he must strike off flakes from the side, across the core. This is the precise part of the work, for, if a flake struck from the edge does not run at least half-way across the core and a hump is left in the middle after all edge-striking surfaces have been used up, the piece is ruined. To hit that hump will break the piece in two. Large cores may be used to strike off large spalls or flakes, and these spalls or flakes then become secondary cores; but this will seldom give good results if the original core was a pebble. The spall will probably come off with sharp edges all around and thus afford no side-striking surfaces.

Thin flakes can be further worked by what is called pressure flaking. This is done by pressing a pointed tool (a nail works passably well but the Amerinds used antler, bone, or wood, which are much better) against the surface of the stone and twisting; the tiny flake detached comes off, curiously enough, from the underside, the face opposite that where the pressure is applied. Very fine "retouch" and finishing can be done by pressure flaking. Australian aborigines have been observed pressure flaking with their teeth; Amerinds could certainly have done the same.

Pressure flaking was also used in the production of prismatic blades, which can be and have been at various times produced by direct and indirect percussion. In Mexico the production of prismatic blades from fine, glass-pure obsidian was almost a factory process. The blades were "punched" off the core, resting on the ground, by the worker leaning his body weight on a long stick with a breast rest that looked like a crutch.

Another method of working thin stone utilized what is called a baton or soft hammer, usually a length of hard wood the thickness of a broom handle or a little thicker. It gives better control of thinning, because it drives off broad, flat, thin flakes. How much the soft hammer was used by Amerinds is disputable; it is most effective with good grade materials and is disappointing with poor material. Probably the soft hammer was a technique most flintsmiths knew about and used when appropriate.

The above steps were not taken as a matter of course by Amerind stone-

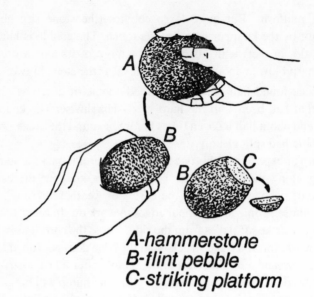

A-hammerstone
B-flint pebble
C-striking platform

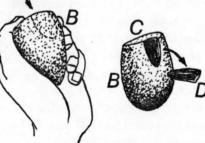

A-hammerstone
B-flint pebble
C-striking platform
D-flake

TOP: MAKING A STRIKING
PLATFORM, AND *BOTTOM:*
DRIVING OFF A FLAKE

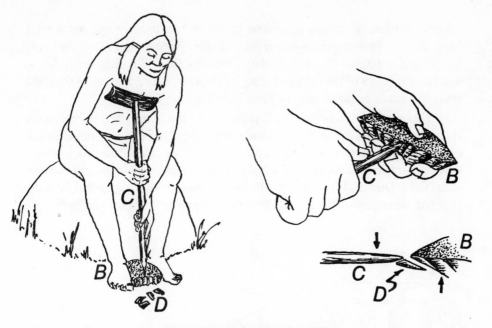

METHODS OF PRESSURE FLAKING

Left: Worker punches blades (D) off the core (B) by leaning his body on long stick with breast rest (C). *Right:* Worker presses pointed tool (C) against surface of stone (B) and twists. Flake (D) is detached from underside of stone.

smiths. Direct percussion by hammerstone and by baton, indirect percussion, and pressure flaking are all regarded as separate and sufficient techniques; and each could be used exclusively to effect the final shape of chipped artifacts. For instance, though direct percussion is thought of as a technique for roughing out, it is by no means confined to that, and some edge retouching once thought to have been done by pressure flaking is now conceded to have been possible by the right control of the right size and weight of hammerstone. Its only real limitation is in routing out narrow grooves and notches that no hammerstone can get at; broad or shallow notches are certainly not beyond accomplishment by this method. A survey of Amerind stone artifacts suggests that all three methods have been known for at least 10,000 years (how else than by indirect percussion or pressure flaking could serrated edges have been made?), but that the principal reliance was on direct percussion, with indirect percussion and pressure flaking as auxiliary and finishing techniques. There is a very widespread tradition in stemmed projectile points in which not only was no technique but direct percussion ever used, even for edge retouching, but which never went through a real blank or blade preform stage, the shape being chipped out of the parent block or pebble whole and entire, at one sitting.

There is a 50-foot shelf of literature on lithic technology, and the reader who is tempted to learn the trade is advised to familiarize himself with it. He is advised, further, to wear goggles and gloves and to use a stone, not a steel hammer to strike with; steel hammers slip on stone just enough to spoil the blow. Learning how to chip flint is a matter of practice in conditioning the reflexes, and close scrutiny of the material being worked on, in order to select the right striking place. Practically anybody can learn pressure flaking.

This may seem an overlong preliminary to the following few statements about the industrial debris of flakes and cores to be found on a site, but it is necessary to understand how that debris came about. The reader will now know why the first thing to look for in a flake is the vestige of striking platform at one end of the flake. Directly beneath it he will find a fatness or swelling, called the bulb of percussion because it is the result of the hammer strike. That platform-and-

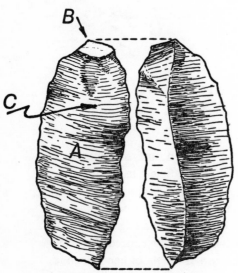

HOW TO RECOGNIZE A MAN-MADE FLAKE

A-inner or bulbar face
B-striking platform
C-bulb of percussion

bulb combination is proof positive that the chips are the product of human effort; under some geologic circumstances nature can produce chips, but these could never have been present at a site. Plows can't make chips, nor booted heels nor steel-shod hoofs, nor picks and shovels. The only agent that could have directed the bulb-making blow is the flintsmith; the platform-and-bulb combination is as certainly indicative of human technology as a skyscraper.

Flakes may be of various shapes. The natural disposition of the cryptocrystalline series and most dense rocks is to break conchoidally, or like a Venus clam shell; that is, the flake tends to be round or squamate, scab-shaped. But this all depends on the topography, as it were, of the block below where the blow is struck, which may have excrescences and bulges in it. The shape also depends on the strength, the follow-through, and the angle of the strike. The right coincidence of these can produce the flake or strip blades mentioned in Chapter 3, with parallel edges like a table knife; or thick, tabular spalls to be used as secondary cores.

A flake or spall that runs the length of the core will thin out to a razor edge on the end opposite the striking platform, and that end will be rounded or sharp. But if the flake does not run the length of the core but breaks off short, it terminates in what is called a "hinge fracture," which is blunt and square across. This happens more often in the making of flake blades than in routine chipping.

About 90 percent of flakes, chips, and spalls are subsumed in the foregoing explanation; the other 10 percent will be atypical in that they show no striking platform or bulb of percussion. These are called "resolved" flakes and there are experts who say they were struck by lucky accident with a baton. "Lucky" is not here a carelessly tossed-off synonym for adventitious. The platform and bulb of percussion very often constitute a nuisance; this thickening seems to have been very difficult to reduce further by chipping and probably always remained an unsatisfactory and awkward factor, although it could be minimized by using a baton instead of a hammerstone.

Before we leave the subject of chipped stone some additional advice should be given to the beginner. At least 50 percent of the chips, flakes, and spalls, large enough to have been held with the fingers, that are found randomly on a habitation site will show edge wear; they were actual, though amorphous, tools. The student, before consigning these flakes to his chip bag, should look for the polish or edge irregularities caused by cutting and scraping, and for minute retouch. About half the remaining 50 percent were probably tools also, but show no wear damage. Fred Kinsey of Franklin and Marshall College, conducting some empirical tests with flakes as knives, butchered a raccoon with a flint flake about one square inch in size without any discernible damage to the edges. But that was, of course, flesh, fat, hide, and ligaments; not wood, antler, or bone. Altogether, Amerinds must have used several times more casual, informal flake tools than classic tool types in their day's work.

Every pebble found where pebbles would not naturally be present should be assumed to be site evidence. If pebbles are out of their proper geologic environment, then they had to be transported—manuported—out of it by man. Visual examination will show some of these to be artifactual: pebble hammerstones will have a pattern of pecking at one or both ends or even on the side, where they were used to strike with; pebble anvil stones will have such a pattern on a flat face; nutting stones will have cuplike depressions in them for holding nuts to be cracked; pebble manos will have a flat face, caused by attrition from being moved back and forth across the metate surface in grinding seeds, which movement may also cause scratches or striations on the face; pebble net-sinkers will have shallow notches to hold the ties; bola stones, used in the tool employed by Argentinian cowboys, will have similar notches.

Unworked and Fire-split Stones

But the pebbles showing no wear or alteration must still have had a use or an intended use. Some were undoubtedly carried to the site as tool stuff but never worked; others were weights, ballast, props, whetstones or abrading stones, or boiling stones. Before the adoption of stone and ceramic heat-resistant pots, stews and soups were made by putting water and ingredients in caulked water-tight baskets and dropping hot stones into the liquid. Many stones were heat-broken in the process, but some would not have been; these can sometimes be identified by their fire-reddened color. Large pebbles and cobbles were used to outline hearths, though most campfires during the Archaic were laid on the ground surface or in very shallow scoop-outs. The hot-stone roasting method used considerable quantities of pebbles and cobbles: a fire was built in a pit, usually elongate, and allowed to burn down to a bed of coals; a layer of stones was then spread over the coals and the food to be roasted was placed on the stones.

Since fires were in daily use and cookery usually required heated stones, as hearth stones, boiling stones, or pot props, fire-broken rock is common on habitation sites and most rocks broken into ragged-faced chunks will have been fire-split. Plows almost never break rocks and even less often break them into sections as fire does. Although heating will cause spalling or scaling off from the outside, in typical fire breakage the stone literally falls apart, sometimes actually exploding, from the center into fractional sections of halves, thirds, or quarters. Those who have understood the section on chipping will never confuse fire-cracked rock with chipped cores; the striking platforms and flake scars of the latter make them as identifiable as a whittled stick.

Industrial debris, innocuous-looking pebbles, shapeless cracked rock—this is what will usually confront the surveyor when he discovers a site. But his eye may also spot artifacts. The shape and workmanship of most of these will be obvious evidence of human manufacture. There are so many kinds of these that they will not be described here; they will be treated in chapter 9, "Guidance in Classifying Artifacts."

Bone, Antler, and Ceramics

Bone, antler, and tools of these materials do occur on sites, but these are quite perishable and do not last for long when exposed. Ceramic potsherds are second only to stone as the tell-tale litter to be found on the surface at sites. But most Indian ceramics, unlike high-heat, kiln-fired white man's pottery, will disintegrate on surface exposure; besides which, pottery has been made by Amerinds only for an average of about 3000 years throughout the United States. Ceramics, bone, and antler are most likely to persist subsurface.

SITES AS GEOLOGIC STRUCTURES

It is almost too obvious that all sites are structures, natural or artificial. They are not often thus described; yet to think of them that way gives the excavator a very exact sense of what he will be doing, demolishing that structure. While it is something of an infringement on the forthcoming chapters on excavation to touch on this theme, the surveyor cannot begin too soon an assessment of a discovered site with an engineer's eye. It is how the site grew or was put together that will determine his work.

Mounds, earthworks, ditches, still standing houses like those of the pueblos of the Southwest, being of human construction, will not concern us here. Man recognizes his own works. The following deals with geologic structures.

Accretional Structures

Riverbank Sites. For some curious reason the importance of sites on the banks of rivers which periodically overflow was not recognized at all until about 1960, when word of Coe's excavation at the riverbank sites in the Carolina piedmont began to circulate. Yet these are the only sites in America that can provide anything like fine stratigraphic sequences; the alternation of habitation zones and layers of flood silt builds up a simple and reliable geologic-chronological site structure. It is the perfect site type, since it is accretional through time and, even when the outlines of the silt and habitational members or strata are not discernible, measurements of depth have high reliability as measurements of time. American archaeology has taken a giant step forward since riverbank sites have begun to be actively sought for excavation. The 38-foot-deep Saint Albans site, already mentioned, and the 12-foot-deep Onion Portage site on the Kobuk River just north of the Arctic Circle in Alaska, found by the late J. L. Giddings and excavated by Douglas Anderson, have clarified the position of the Archaic in the south and the north. An important riverbank site about 18 feet deep is being dug in Illinois by Stuart Struever, and Fred Kinsey and Herbert Kraft have dug 6- and 8-foot-deep sites on the upper Delaware River. The results of one such dig will be found in the sample report by Kraft in Chapter 13. Surveyors should constantly be on the lookout for riverbank sites, which deserve first digging priority.

Caves and Rockshelters. Since these are protected from surface erosion, they are accretional, though not as clearly stratified as riverbank sites. Some are, as a matter of fact, streambank sites into which water has flooded from time to time; and many of the caves of the Great Basin region, in the vicinity of extinct Pleistocene lakes, have gravel deposits among their strata because of the fluctuation of the level of the lakes during the Wisconsin III period of glacial advances and retreats.

The three agents that build up deposits in caves and shelters, aside from the water deposits cited above, are eolian (wind-blown) soil, rockfalls and the detritus from disintegration of overhead and walls, and input by man. The net amount of accumulation due to man may be a considerable element even though he may have tracked out soil as well as brought material in. The structure of cave and shelter deposits is therefore quite complex as compared with riverbank sites, where there is only one accretional agent. At Modoc Rockshelter the stratum below 21.5 feet is waterlaid sand and clay, from the time, apparently 11,000 B.P., when the shelter opening was at the level of Barbeau Creek, which runs past it. The fill above that level came from (1) wind-blown soil, (2) soil washed over the cliff above the shelter, and (3) cultural debris, ash lenses (lens-shaped deposits of ash, usually the remains of a fire), and fired areas. This is such a mixture that no strata are observable, though the upper half is of a slightly different shade of yellow-brown than the lower. Modoc, in consequence, could not provide the cultural and time differentiation of a site like Saint Albans.

In Flea Cave about the same depth of deposit built up in approximately twice the length of time. Here rockfalls and cave detritus constituted the main ingredient of the fill, with wind-blown soil next in bulk, followed by cultural debris, animal bones, and a certain amount of industrial debris and materials. The zones at Flea Cave are more consolidated than at Modoc and hence more easily distinguishable. Their character as strata was established by a novel method: the measurement of their acidity. Because of Flea Cave's height above sea level, the surrounding territory was very sensitive to climatic change. A stratum within the cave with low acid reading meant the mountainside was grass-covered. When scrub woods grew about the cave, the soil blown into it was acid. These zones provide a broad stratification, over long periods, sufficient to establish the general cultural trend, while the compression and consolidation guarantees that the artifacts will be found within a few inches of where they had been left behind.

The structure of cave fill is upward, then, even though all the geologic members cannot be identified. The only disturbances in cave fill are rockfalls, which depress the surface, and man, who scuffs and shifts the surface about and makes holes and pits in it, all of which activities can alter the level of deposit of cultural items. Caves are second-priority sites in the establishment of local sequences.

Shell Middens. Though shell heaps are man-made, on deposit they become geologic features, instant strata, man-made geology. When they are deposited on humus, they "kill" it (see Living Soils under Static Structure, below) so that it is no longer a living soil and mark the beginning of a new geologic horizon. When a heap ceases to be added to, its surface begins to weather and to collect blown dust and leaves, forming a thin soil layer where plants will begin to grow. This becomes a band or stratum and eventually campers will begin to camp on it again (nobody in his right mind would camp on a heap of sharp-edged shell) and, perhaps, dump more shell on it. Thus shell midden sites become accretional and the horizons of shell have stratigraphic value. Reading the stratigraphy is tricky, however, for the stratigraphy may not be horizontal. A shell heap may stand exposed to the weather long enough to weather on the sides as well as on top; later shellfish gatherers may not deposit their shell directly on top but beside it, and shells at the same horizontal level may be hundreds of years apart in age. The interpretation of this kind of structure must be approached with caution. Artifacts that appear to be within a heap are most likely to be actually from the weathered layer on top of or surrounding it, so that they date later than the shell they appear to lie among. No general rule covers the structure of shell midden sites. Within a 10-foot square it can change three or four times.

Static Structure

Living Soils. Most open field sites are covered by a living soil, a dynamic geologic stratum the opposite of the dead strata found in deep stratigraphic sequences. This living soil is a metabolic system, the body of which is in constant movement by reason of the two forces of depletion and increment. Plants growing in a soil add to its surface annually their increment of foliage, dead stalks, branches, etc. which, in decay, make the humus cover or otherwise add to the bulk. But these same plants deplete the subsurface by taking from it the nutrients on which they feed. The input is from the top; the outtake is from within the soil, depending on the shallowness or the depth of root reach. Thus there is a "flow" of soil from surface to interior, and it is in constant though very slow movement. In addition there is the effect of rain, which beats down the surface and also carries materials in solution lower and lower, the leaching effect. This effect can actually be observed in shell middens where percolating water dissolves the surface of the shell and transports particles of calcium carbonate which precipitate out on other shells or stones encountered.

Other forces operating on or within living soil to alter its structure are surface erosion by wind and water, which act differentially, affecting some spots more than others, and freeze-and-thaw heaving. And this is to say nothing about animal disturbance such as burrowing by rodents and the incredible amount of soil-turning that can be done by earthworms. A factor that is also of importance is soil creep on slopes, the response of soil to the weak but unrelenting pull of gravity, aided and abetted by water which flows downhill both at the surface and subsurface and by the dislodging effect of freeze-and-thaw.

A living soil is the net accumulation in the balance of aggrading and degrading forces listed above. In the Northeast the accumulation is between eight and fifteen inches, the entire deposit since the glacier retreated from the region. But curiously enough, this is also the depth of soil build-up in nonglaciated regions once covered by forests—Alabama, for instance. This depth seems to be a measure of the balance between soil anabolism and catabolism, but only in the temperate zone. In tropical jungles, where deadfalls decay in a matter of weeks and are almost immediately consumed by the riotous vegetation, the soil level is only about 3 to 4 inches, barely enough for root coverage.

Thus a living soil is both static and metabolic, a stasis of counteracting living forces, and at no time can the placement of artifacts within it be regarded as having stratigraphic chronological reliability. Stone sinks through humic and loamy layers until it meets a hard object or barrier layer, usually the subsoil. In consequence, artifacts of all ages may end up at approximately the same depth. That this is what happens has been archaeologically demonstrated by Coe.

Before he dug his famous riverbank sites, Coe had been engaged in establishing a local sequence by digging or examining the collections from some 100 of these open, living soil sites. The then-conventional method was to compare the materials and data from the sites; when assemblages of similar artifacts were found to be recurrent over several sites, they were regarded as a cultural "complex" and the products of a related people. The results of this comparative study were published in *The Archaeology of the Eastern United States*, regarded at the time as authoritative. In this work Coe, the authority on the coastal and piedmont Southeast, set up a sequence of cultural "complexes." One of these was the Badin "complex" of the first pottery-making period of the area. But after his excavation of the genuinely stratified riverbank sites, Coe discovered just what this "complex" was worth. In the assemblage he had ascribed to the Badin complex he had included artifact types, principally projectile points, that were 6000 to 10,000 years old, while the pottery was only 1500 years old. What had caused the assemblages of materials from a group of sites to be replications was not that the same cultural units had occupied them, but the same *sequence* of cultural units. Soil metabolism had mixed the artifacts as thoroughly as with a cocktail shaker.

A living soil is, to summarize, rather like brandy: each year there is added to the basic stock an amount of new brandy equal to the amount that evaporated during the year. It, therefore, has no age. Archaeologists use a device called seriation, which will be explained in Chapter 11, to deal with soil's interior activity, but it is not very satisfactory.

Deflation Structure

Desert Pavement. The surface of vast tracts of the desert West consists of millions of naked stones lying exposed on a hard-packed subsoil, sand, or bedrock. The stones are where they are because the soil in which they were once enclosed was eroded away by wind and hard-driving though infrequent thundershowers. The deflation or removal of soil is believed, on the basis of experiments, to have been as much as thirty inches, most of it in the last century and a half, when the current phase of aridity set in. Natural stones and cultural materials that in the early 1800s lay on a surface thirty inches above where they are now have dropped down and lie intermingled with stones and materials 8000 to 10,000 years old, from the time when a living soil covered the area. Clearly the archaeology of desert pavement is surface hunting, but not for the hobbyist who does not know thoroughly the sequences and the literature of desert cultures. The vertical placement of artifacts has been destroyed but the horizontal placement has not been, and, because it is all there is left, must be handled very carefully.

Though the subject of survey has not been exhausted, enough has been said, it is hoped, to enable the reader to discover sites, to "see" and to evaluate them. To find sites before the bulldozer gets to them is the first step in saving the most significant, the most irreplaceable ones.

chapter 5

Getting Ready for Excavation

ONCE A DESIRABLE-LOOKING site has been located, before a full commitment is made to excavate it, common sense suggests that, if it is of any extent at all, it should be tested and probed. Where are the "hot spots," the concentrations of material that indicate living or other activity areas? The competent supervisor, estimating the man-hours of labor he can get out of his available work force, will want to plan the project for maximum results. Further, is the site worth digging? More than one site will prove, on testing, to be too contaminated, disturbed, or featureless to provide sound data. To waste time on ruined sites when the threat to good sites is imminent violates all rules of economy and conservation.

An instructive instance of this kind of waste is related here because the reader can deduce from it a whole chapter of lessons. The supervisor of the dig was a young university instructor in anthropology-archaeology who had undertaken to teach a required summer field methods course of four weeks' duration to a class of twenty students. The site selected was a 10-acre field which had been surface hunted for decades and had yielded a considerable collection of artifacts. For the last twenty years or so it had been in pasturage for a herd of cattle. The locus of the dig was determined by summoning one of the former surface hunters and asking him where, in the nearly half-million square feet of area, he had made his finds in the 1930s and 1940s.

The outcome of this impetuous and naive approach was, if not inevitable at least highly predictable. Laboring for twenty days, those twenty field hands recovered some rusty nails, fragments of bottle glass and nonprehistoric ceramics, fewer than twenty flint chips and one artifact, a projectile point, found outside the excavation during a lunch break. Moreover, at no time during the excavation was there any indication in the profile of the trenches of a stratigraphy or a soil geology of any usefulness in determining artifact provenience.

Survey—the surface hunting of a generation ago—had established the field as a site; the field itself, sloping gently to a small river, was the credible setting for a site, series of campsites, or possibly a village, but the young supervisor did not know the most important requisite of doing archaeology: there must be some archaeology to do.

HOW TO TEST A POTENTIAL SITE

The first mistake in planning this project was not to have surface hunted the field in March, when the grass was thin and snow melt runoff and rain had cleared the ground for looking. The second mistake, and it is a teaching mistake as well, was not to have given over two of the project's twenty days to a program of surface hunting by the students despite the July stand of grass. Something has already been said about surface hunting for archaeological purposes; in this case a crew of twenty could have sectioned off the field in 50-foot squares and hunted it, one student per square with forty-five minutes devoted to each square. At the end of two days the supervisor would have known where to dig, or whether to dig at all, if the search had been diligent. Diligent search means bending one's spine to the task; the probability of making surface finds decreases in inverse ratio to the square of the distance between the ground and the end of the searcher's nose.

Had this been done, the supervisor would soon have had sections with cloth or paper flags tied to sticks, marking where a chip, fire-cracked stone, or alien pebble had lain. He would then have sent workers with shovels and hand sieves to these markers to dig test holes. Was the find a random piece or was it a surface signal of a subsurface archaeological occupation? A 3-by-3-foot test hole would have been sufficient to expose the subsurface information: the occurrence of cultural evidence, including midden or occupationally discolored earth, and soil structure.

Before he plans a dig or lays it out, an excavator should know the following facts: (1) where the concentrations of occupational evidence are, (2) the depth of the occupation-bearing layer, and (3) the structure or geology of the site. Only then is he ready to stake out his grid plan.

THE GRID PLAN

A grid plan is a simple system of coordinates, the staking out of a site as though it were a very large sheet of graph paper. In America, the squares of the grid or graph are most often five or ten feet on a side; elsewhere, of course, the meter or two-meter square is usually used. It is being assumed here that the excavator is not a surveyor. If he is, he does not need any instruction in laying out and staking such a grid. Others may need an explanation.

The construction of the grid plan begins with a datum point, from which two baselines take off in compass lines of direction. Usually, though not always, it is possible to lay out a site with baselines running north-south and east-west. This is desirable principally because it makes it easier to figure right angles, but the two baselines are any two lines perpendicular to each other.

The datum point is a point fixed or inscribed in a permanent immovable feature—if at all possible, a tree, rock, or solidly implanted stake, at or near a corner of the site. The primary baseline is a line running north-south—from 0° to 180° on a compass—from the datum point, and the secondary baseline runs east-west, through the datum point, that is, from 90° to 270°. An ordinary Boy Scout magnetic pocket compass with locking dial for carrying will suffice for lining up. The excavator does not have to fret over the correction for the difference between magnetic north and true north, but he does have to be wary of the error caused by metal, such as an ax or shovel, within the field of attraction.

A steel 100-foot tape is expensive but, for staking out the baselines, it will repay its cost in accuracy. The tape is stretched from the datum point along the chosen compass direction of the baseline and stakes are driven in every five or ten feet, depending on how the supervisor intends to schedule the dig (which in turn depends on how much manpower he has at his command). The best stake is the two-by-two-inch wooden stake used by surveyors. It has four sides broad enough for lettering on the numbers of the four squares for which it serves as the point of junction. Thus the stake at the line between 2N1E and 2N2E will bear, on the appropriate faces: 1N and 2N, 1E and 2E.

Once the baselines have been staked out, completing the grid is only a matter of staking out parallel lines. As can be seen from the accompanying diagram of a grid plan, it is indefinitely extensible in all directions.

THE SITE PLAN

Since the grid plan is a graph, it transfers to graph paper exactly, but it is not yet a site plan. Trees, boulders and other aboveground features must be

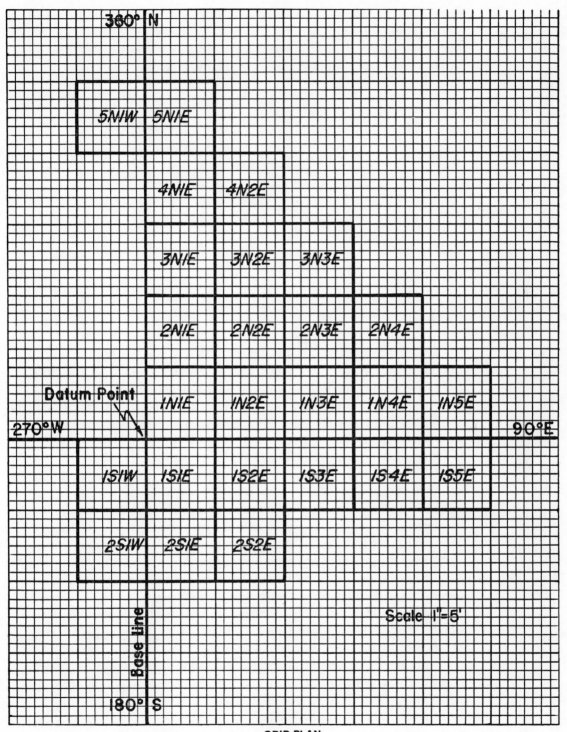

GRID PLAN
(Plan reduced, Scale: ¾″ = 5′)

located, and the topography sketched in. This may as well be done as the grid is being taped off, and it requires nothing more than a ball of cord, a 6-foot folding rule, and a short line level, usually three inches long with a hook on each end to suspend it from the cord when that is stretched out.

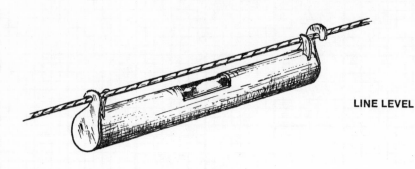

LINE LEVEL

(Those who know how to use a plane table and who can borrow one, or who can use a surveyor's instrument level or a hand sighting level will probably prefer to use one of these instruments for preparing the topo map. We use a hand sighting level, which can be carried in the pocket. The instructions here are for those who are not familiar with the more sophisticated methods and who want to do the job for $3.00; $.75 for cord, $.75 for a line level, and $1.50 for a 6-foot wooden folding rule.)

Let us assume that the datum point is a nail in a tree six feet above the surface of the ground. A line is stretched from the datum point along the prime baseline or along any line of stakes to a point which is level with the datum point, the levelness being determined by the line level. The elevation of the ground at any stake is the height of this datum line minus the distance between it and the ground as measured by rule (see the diagram).

This datum point can be tied into the actual elevation of the site by reference to the U.S. Geological Survey quadrangle sheet.

There will be noted in the diagram the small, abrupt hump or outcrop between stakes 5N and 6N. This elevation should be taken (it can be done very easily), as should the elevations of any humps or hollows within any square, for these may later be discovered to be subsurface features, or surface features related to subsurface discoveries; graves, for instance, may show up as either mounds or sinks, where the earth has slumped.

The site map is made by joining points of equal elevation, so as to show the surface contour as related to the grid plan (see the diagram).

The level datum line is the equivalent of the surveyor's line of sight through his mounted instrument or hand level, and is actually more versatile in that it can be run through foliage that would obstruct a line of sight. But this kind of work should be done, if possible, in the seasons when the foliage is off the trees and bushes and the ground is bare.

The grid plan superimposed on the topo map constitutes the site map, the basic document in excavation. It is a set of reference points on the plane for the location of all finds and data. It is not, however, an *excavation plan*. There is nothing in dogma or logic that says the excavator has to begin at square 1N1E or 1N1W, that is, at a square that adjoins the datum point and to pursue from there a trench relentlessly to the end. If he has test-holed the site and has the objectives of the dig clearly in mind, the choice of a beginning comes naturally. (The author can't remember a site in twenty years of digging where he began at the beginning of a grid plan.)

On most sites the first objective is to discover the sequence of occupation; the first square dug should be, therefore, where the sequence seems to be most

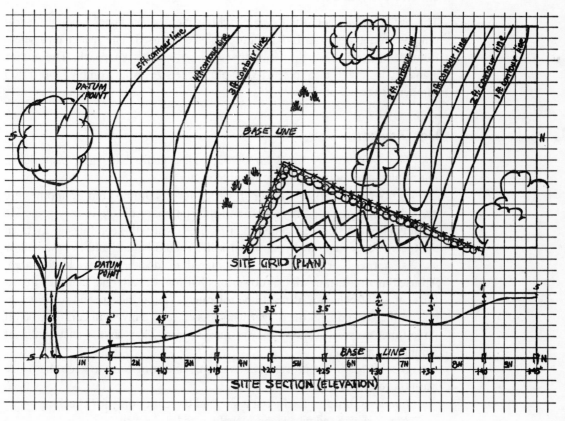

SITE GRID AND ELEVATION

clearly represented, so that its components can be followed with some confidence through the ensuing excavation. But the choice of the initial square should not be made without one pragmatic consideration: where is the back dirt to be piled? To pile it in your own path, on squares you may later want to dig, is not very prudent. This problem will be discussed in Chapter 7.

But there are other projects, such as the excavation of a house plan or settlement pattern, in which the wanted evidence occurs at a single level and the site is not trenched at all but uncovered by stripping. Or it may be that the excavator wants to expose a single feature, such as an isolated shell, stone, or dirt mound, and then excavate it. Archaeology requires the kind of planning that goes into any project, from painting a house to buying a new car, the difference being that doing archaeology has its own set of conditions. Once the planning has been done, so that the work will not turn out to be a dry hole like the 10-acre field site, the excavator is ready to move dirt.

GEAR FOR THE DIG

The individual digger usually carries his gear in a backpack, though everything from book bags to Indian burden baskets is used. The reader may select from the following list the items that will go into his knapsack. The author manages to cram into his 15-year-old large-size Abercrombie and Fitch camper's pack, all of these:

Light Equipment

First Aid Kit. A small kit of band-aids, gauze bandages, bactericide, tourniquet, ammonia ampules, salt tablets, etc.

Spray Can of Insect Repellant. Biting insects of one kind or another are abroad from April till November, and the stationary digger is easy prey. He should spray himself well. Smoking a pipe or cigar will keep bugs away from the face. A spray can of flying insect killer should be on hand in case yellow jackets, hornets, or wasps are encountered or decide to invade the area. Aroused to attack, they all can do serious harm to the allergic, and they are so treacherous of behavior as not to be tolerated. Yellow jackets and some wasps hive in the ground, and the digger who gets close to a hive will certainly be bit three times before he knows they're mad at him. They have a nasty habit of aiming for the head.

Work Gloves. To prevent blisters, cuts, and stings and to keep the hands warm in cool, wet weather.

Compass. Used in laying out a site and thereafter only for checking.

Line Level. Used whenever a level has to be checked.

100- or 50-Foot Tape. Used in laying out a site and thereafter only if something goes wrong, such as stakes being uprooted.

6-Foot Folding Rule. For depth and other short measurements.

Trowels. There is a great deal of amusing snobbishness and mystique about the use of digging trowels. The favorite among professionals—and they often make a snap judgment about a digger's knowingness on nothing more—is the 4- or 5-inch Marshalltown pointing-up trowel. It is a very "in" thing to have this ground down to about three inches. The Marshalltown is a good, but expensive, implement, the shaft or shank of which is forged into the blade and thus will not break at the elbow, as will cheaper trowels the blades of which are welded to the shank. Cutting the blade down to a three-inch stub reduces the chance of breakage, but also the amount of work that can be done at a stroke. The author uses a Goldblatt K.C. trowel, equal in quality to the Marshalltown. In selecting a trowel, remember that the mason-plasterer's pointing trowel was not made for digging and that the garden trowel, with its one-piece blade and shank, and the shank inserted directly in a straight line into the handle, was. The broad-bladed garden trowel is indeed a clumsy instrument, but a narrow version is available, the 6-inch-long blade tapering slightly from about 2 inches wide at the shank to about 1½ inches just behind the blunt point. The steel is heavy-gauge, the slight dishing in the blade gives it rigidity, and there is just enough bend or arc in the end-to-end length to make it easy to handle. Because it can be used for prying, without danger of breaking, it is particularly suitable for shell middens, in which the valves are often so tightly interbedded and cemented with earth that they have to be either pried or chopped. The best trowel the author ever owned had a 10-inch-long blade, about 2 inches wide; it had been ground down from a 10-inch-long mason's trowel used by the brickmason's gang in a steel mill. The blade was of steel as fine and flexible as a Toledo sword, as it should have been. Such trowels cost about $12 each. The important thing is that the trowel used should be suited to the work and to the hand and habits of the user. You can do very well with a 4-inch trowel that sells at $.60 to $.75. It's all in the user's dexterity.

Hoes. There is a school of technicians which prefers a short-handled hoe for the same flat-plane kind of scraping for which the other school uses the trowel. The wooden handle of a garden hoe is cut at 4-6 inches from the shank, and the hoe blade is ground down to a depth of 2-3 inches. Garden shops now carry hoes with this depth of blade, so that all that has to be done is to cut off the handle to a wieldable length. Garden shops also sell a short-handled, two-headed hoe with a narrow solid blade at one end and a three-tined scratching blade at the other. The solid blade is too narrow for efficient scraping but the tined end is very effective in shell, in ground full of fine roots, and for scarifying very hard clay. All of these hoes and trowels have their specific usefulness, and it is puzzling to see teachers of field methods insisting that there is only one "right" tool. It is a good idea to carry both kinds of trowels and both kinds of hoes because, in a single day's digging one can expect to encounter (1) a soft, root-filled humus with shell fragments, workable with the pointing trowel, (2) close-packed whole oyster valves, best worked with the garden trowel, and (3) a clay subsoil which can be scraped with a hoe when moist but which, when dry, is as hard as adobe because of the leached-in calcium carbonate and has to be scarified before scraping. There are other compositions of soil to be dealt with and it is only good craftsmanship to select the proper tool for them.

Root Clippers. These are the ordinary small, one-hand pruning clippers and are indispensable for snipping rootlets which are found even in desert soils.

Short-handled Ax. "The Boy Scout ax" is needed to cut out larger roots and saplings.

Clipboard and Field Book. For field recording we use a standard copyrighted engineer's notebook, 8½ by 11½ inches, with one page graphed and the facing page lined. This is kept on the clipboard, which provides a smooth, hard writing surface. The book and board are stowed in a plastic bag cover, which keeps the book tolerably clean and dry. Pencils, a 6-inch plastic rule, small plastic draftsman's triangles, and a protractor are included in the assemblage.

Aluminum Foil. The accepted method of packaging datable materials such as charcoal, shell, nuts, etc. is in aluminum foil. We cut pieces the size of the field book and keep them pressed either in the field book or between it and the clipboard.

Slate Board. A 6- by 8-inch child's writing slate or square of metal, wood, or chipboard on which is chalked the appropriate information about a feature, profile, etc. and which is placed in a photograph in order to identify what is photographed. It is, in short, a photograph caption board or card.

Chalk. For the above and other marking purposes.

Tweezers. For picking up charcoal crumbs and small items that require careful removal.

Brushes. Paint brushes are needed for the fine removal of dirt about skeletons, the bones of which are seldom in good condition. Whisk brooms are used to clean profiles before photography; tooth brushes are used in the scrubbing of artifacts. On-site cleansing of artifacts is sometimes necessary to make accurate identification; this is especially true of pottery, with its meaningful but shallow surface markings.

Magnifying Glass. Fine or faint marking, striations, discoloring, and other details sometimes have to be studied in the field under magnification. A wide field reading glass, with 2X magnification should be sufficient. Too great magnification and too small a field will often expand the design under examination out of coherence.

Ball of Heavy Twine. Used in laying out the site and for other line establishment.

Styrofoam Pad or Rubberoid Sheet. It is not good for the joints of either old or young to be in contact with damp, cold earth, and digging cannot be done for long from a squat. Sooner or later the digger has to go to one or both knees, or even sit. Rheumatoid arthritis was one of the commonest of afflictions among Indians and they got it from exposure in the very places in which you will be digging.

Knives. A long, thin-bladed knife will often be needed in the "surgery" of freeing bones from the soil matrix. Grapefruit knives are a favorite with some. A fisherman's or Boy Scout knife will do as well.

Nails, Matches, and Sundries. The digger never knows when he is going to need them, for repair work, or any of half a dozen emergencies. It often happens that a pair of pliers or a tube of glue is needed to join two pieces of pottery or a broken projectile point.

Cameras. These are not, strictly speaking, knapsack cargo, but belong in the inventory of essentials. The choice of camera makes and models is a personal matter. Two cameras are needed, one to take pictures to be developed as slides to accompany the reading of reports before audiences, the other to take pictures for prints of record and for journal publication. (Incidentally, prints for publication should be glossy finish.) Polaroid cameras produce only pictures for record and their only advantage is that the digger can snap away, at considerable cost, until he gets what he wants. They are not recommended. What is recommended is that the amateur archaeologist become not only a proficient photographer but learn to develop his own pictures. Most commercial development is unreliable and, in the case of archaeological photographs, usually disappointing. A developer who knows what the picture is supposed to show can usually bring it out in the developing. (Some helpful pointers on photography will be found in Chapter 10.)

Collecting Bags. The recoveries from excavation units are kept together in bags. Paper grocery bags may be used but they are not very reliable when wet. Plastic bags are better and cloth bags are best. They can be purchased or stitched on the sewing machine from old bedsheets.

Radio. A good, small transistor radio will keep you in touch with the weather reports and traffic conditions for the trip home.

Heavy Equipment

Brush Scythe, Machete, Sickle. These are site-clearing tools and need to be on site only once or twice during a season, the tool being related to the vegetation that has to be removed.

Rake. For clearing leaves, etc. from the surface.

Ax, Saw. A small bow saw is very useful to have around, for cutting roots, small trees, stakes, etc. Only large downed trees will require a woodsman's ax, but a single-bit ax is good for driving stakes.

Shovels. There is no avoiding bending over a shovel; excavation means moving dirt again and again. The short-handled round-point shovel is for short pitches and tight places; the long-handled round-point for longer pitches, such as when the excavation reaches a depth of five feet. If a safe place can be found, these ought to be left on the site; they're a nuisance to carry.

Picks and Mattocks. A railroad pick is sometimes necessary for breaking through such hard surfaces as cemented shell layers. Hardpan or dried clay can only be cut through with a mattock. The author uses a short-handled tool about fifteen inches long with a mattock blade on one end of the head and a pointed pick at the other. The excavation of a culture-bearing layer of hard clay by mattock requires a light mattock and a sensitive touch to avoid breaking artifacts.

Sledgehammer. There is only one way to break up the ever present rock fallen from the roofs of rockshelters, unless one of the diggers is an experienced dynamiter, and that is by sledgehammer and bull-point. As much as the sledgehammer is needed somebody who can swing it without danger of heart attack.

Scale Pole. A 1-foot-long wooden or metal pole or lath painted alternately in white and red or black stripes should appear in photographs showing depth, to provide a scale for measurement and perspective. Other kinds of scales may be used, but the painted pole is the simplest.

Bulldozer. Anybody who can command the use of a bulldozer, tractor, or four-wheel-drive vehicle with a bulldozer blade should not hesitate to use it on overburden or to move back dirt. Professional archaeologists, when their objective is to uncover a settlement pattern which is revealed by postmolds in the subsoil, often hire bulldozers with skilled operators to peel off the topsoil overburden. Testing sometimes reveals that the culture layer is buried under a depth of sterile overburden, and the saving in labor and time accomplished by using a bulldozer to remove the overburden should not have to be argued. But a bulldozer can't be used on sites full of stumps or trees of any size, even if it is powerful enough to uproot them, because the uprooting causes too much subsurface disturbance.

Trash Cans. It is only good housekeeping to use a trash can for the inevitable accumulation of debris, with the intention of burying it later in the back dirt or fill. It is an even better practice to stipulate that diggers take their trash home with them.

Pumps. Water can constitute both a problem and a tool. Sites in swamps, below water table depth, or where the excavation has been flooded by heavy rains or rising streams will have to be drained by pumping if work is to continue. Portable gasoline pumps can be rented in most communities; occasionally they can be borrowed. It may in some instances prove desirable to bring water under pressure to a site. Water can be used to reduce hardpan or dried clay in order to get at the inclusions. The reduction can be accomplished by dumping the hardpan into a sieve and hosing it down. This method has been used very successfully at the previously mentioned Saint Albans site, with the pump drawing water from the Kanawha River, on the bank of which the site is located. It is the only way to deal with soil from the Ohio terrace mentioned earlier where the innumerable fire-cracked stones embedded in the clay give the soil below plow zone the appearance and resistance of a cobblestone pavement.

Screens. These range from one-man hand sieves to motor-driven shakers on large projects that are so well staffed they can afford a maintenance mechanic. But since they all perform only one function, sifting dirt, the important thing is the size of the mesh, and this is selected according to what is being looked for on the screen. If you're working a burial site where wampum, tiny embroidery work beads, or trade beads are scattered about, something about the size of the wire cloth found in window screens will have to be used and the earth will have to be washed through. On some digs where the concern is a maximum of dietary and/or ecological information, astonishing amounts of seeds, small bones, and other minutiae have been recovered by flotation and screening with $\frac{1}{16}$-inch mesh. Generally speaking the screen should be of sturdy hardware cloth; $\frac{1}{2}$-inch mesh is standard for most projects with no special screening needs. Mesh of $\frac{1}{4}$-inch can be used in dry, sandy earth without rootlets, but it becomes impermeable almost instantly when filled with wet earth full of hair roots. If there are any of these in the soil at all, the $\frac{1}{2}$-inch apertures very quickly shrink to about $\frac{1}{4}$-inch to $\frac{1}{3}$-inch and small pebbles obstruct them so that there is little likelihood of losing items smaller than $\frac{1}{2}$-inch in diameter. Hand sieves are simple rectangular frames about 15 by 20 inches or so, with light boards 4 to 6 inches wide (too big and/or heavy a sieve will strain the spinal column). We keep three or four hand sieves on hand on our digs, but our system of screening centers on one large central sieve. This is a stationary sieve about 5 feet long by 3 feet wide, on legs that bring it up to about elbow height to save back-bending and set out where the back dirt is being piled. Our diggers scrape the trowelled dirt into a plastic dustpan, a scoop made of a cutaway plastic gallon-size bleach bottle, or even a wooden scoop. The dirt then goes into a plastic bucket, is carried to the screen, and spread on it. If the dirt is light and dry, spreading alone will do the sifting. Soils in mucky or lumpy condition must be pulverized to make sure an insignificant blob of dirt isn't concealing something. Spreading the dirt first, rather than shaking it, provides a hedge against losing very small items before the load is glanced through. We don't much like to have items turn up on the screen, however; they should be

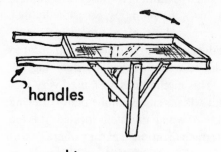

handles

rocking screen

ropes or wires to
trees or scaffolding

swinging screen

hand screen and table with rollers

TYPES OF SCREENS

found *in situ,* that is, in place, during the scraping by trowel. There are several other kinds of sieves and shakers, including one suspended from a tree branch or tripod (borrowed from oldtime plastering practice), but the reader should not be deprived of the pleasure of "inventing" his own ingenious variation of this basic machine.

Canvas Shelter Half. If the project is far from shelter, some sort of overhead protection is advisable in case of sudden rains.

As long as this list has grown it still does not include all the tools, equipment and devices which may at one time or another or under one set of circumstances or another be put to good use. Archaeological equipment is pragmatic; it consists of that apparatus and those appliances that will get the work done within the objectives and standards of archaeology. The handyman type will find more than one opportunity to improvise. But as long as the list is, except for the bulldozer and pump little is called for that can't be found around the normal household or at little expense at the neighboring hardware store or discount house. Nor does all the equipment have to be on the project at the same time, only that necessary for the stage of work in progress. There is nothing listed, nor is there an assemblage necessary at any stage of the work, that can't be carried by the diggers—except the bulldozer and pump. We have trekked to and from a site as far as two miles and a half in a round trip with everything needed.

In the foregoing list of equipment mention has not been made of the most indispensable: the perceiving eye and the inductive-deductive logical mind. Without them no dig will turn out well.

chapter 6

Deciphering
Archaeological Finds

"ARCHAEOLOGISTS TRACE THE evolution of cultural systems by analysis of stratified deposits."

This is a statement so simply put and generally accepted that the man who wrote it (Robert E. Fry of Purdue University) in a review in *Science* magazine dated January 14, 1972 would not immediately recognize it as his. Chapters 2 and 3 outlined the results of its application to American prehistory. Now that we are on the verge of digging, it needs some expansion and clarification as to how it shapes the attitude of the digger.

In their *Explanation in Archaeology* (Columbia University Press) Patty Jo Watson, Steven A. LeBlanc, and Charles Redman explain well the frame of mind in which an archaeologist undertakes excavation. They point out that the excavator has a problem in mind to which the data uncovered at a site may furnish a solution but that he is not surprised if such data do not provide exactly those answers which he has been seeking. The authors enumerate three functions of hypotheses as follows: "to give direction to research, to determine what further data should be collected and to guide the analysis of the data." As an archaeologist works on a site, his conceptual understanding of his work changes "through the interaction of *a priori* plan and hard data," a process the authors call "the ongoing dialogue between the scientist and his material."

Introduced in the foregoing is the procedural relationship between data and hypothesis or theory stated as proposition. But what are data?

LOOKING FOR THINGS IN ASSOCIATION

What is the archaeologically motivated digger looking for as he dissects the corpus of soil in which he expects to find the evidences of a dead culture? Things, certainly, all the kinds of evidence so far described—artifacts, chips, bone, potsherds, etc. But not things alone and by themselves. What he is looking for are things *in association*.

The entire site is, of course, an association of some kind of everything found there, a system of pertinent units the relationships of which are close or remote; it is the digger's business to determine how close or how remote. When he comes upon an artifact, his automatic reaction should be to ask himself, and find the answers to: (1) Exactly where is it, and (2) Why is it there? *Where* it is can be determined by measurement from his reference points, the corners of the square; but that is only half of where it is. The digger must also ask: Where is it in reference to other finds in that square and adjacent squares that are within the same sphere of human use and circulation? If where it is in relation to other artifacts appears to constitute an association, then the digger may have the answer, or the beginning of the answer, as to why it is there.

Often the digger will not perceive any immediately satisfactory answer to *why,* from the circumstances of *where,* because losing an item or casting it aside are not patterned behavioral activities from which persuasive deductions can be drawn; and it may be assumed *a priori* that few items were deliberately placed where they are found, to say nothing of the probability of their displacement after their last possessors laid them down by either unrelated human activity or forces of nature. Nevertheless, everything found got to its last resting place through the action of one or more agents, and the digger must learn to hypothesize the agent and the action. It is the objective of the archaeologist not only to discover local sequences but to be able to describe anthropologically the components of each sequence.

HYPOTHESIZING

Hypothesizing should be distinguished from indulgence in fancy and the pursuance of a bias, although it is possible that imagination might lead to insight and bias to systematic theory. One archaeologist has for years been interpreting every crudely made artifact he finds as "boy's work," and every stray pebble of likely heft as "a boy's throwing rock." That crude artifacts are of juvenile workmanship and not the result of untoward breakage of the material, haste, or leaving a job half done, it is not safe to assume. Nevertheless, since boys and girls probably threw missile stones by hand or sling, they may have had more to do with the distribution of artifacts on a site than most archaeologists credit. Any parent who has raised children to postadolescence knows the juvenile habit of constantly picking things up willy-nilly and laying them down somewhere else. The children of aborigines may have been more disciplined than our children and certainly there were fewer things lying around loose, but the effect of children's activities at a habitation site has never been given the anthropological weight it must have had actually.

Hypothesizing in archaeology is not going to be fully grasped, however, until it is explained by example. The example used here is the set of conclusions we have arrived at from excavation of a series of oyster shell middens on the banks of the lower Hudson.

Through C-14 dating we have discovered that the use of oysters for food and the deposit of the discarded valves in heaps dates back to at least 6000 years ago. The older heaps are on the edge of eroded banks, and have themselves been eroded by pounding waves. Since sea level rose steadily and at times rapidly from 15,000 B.P. to about 1000 B.P., and the lower Hudson is at sea level, as the water level rose it gnawed higher and higher into the banks. How much midden has been wrested from the banks there is no way of knowing, but oysters were probably growing in the lower Hudson at least 10,000 years ago, and Amerinds were gathering them. But when the rate of rise slowed down to a creep, around 3000 B.P., oysters ceased to thrive here because the sea was no longer putting enough salt water into the fjordlike lower Hudson.

Over and over again at the bottom of the older middens, there is found a stratum of shell called the "GO" (for giant oyster) horizon because many of the oyster valves are very large, six to eight inches in length and thirty to forty years old—quite old for this upriver, marginal oyster habitat. (The approximate age of an oyster can be determined by a count of the plates that compose the shell, a new plate being grown each year as trees grow rings.) This GO period ended about 5600 B.P. (which is why it is called a horizon), and for about 500 years the stretch of the Hudson where we are digging seems to have produced no oysters at all. But when they did return, about 5100 B.P., a new people had entered the area. Either the GO horizon people had left the vicinity during the 500-year dearth of oysters, or they had been displaced by the new people who invaded the valley with the return of oysters. We were most anxious to discover the cultural identity of the GO people.

But, dig as we might in GO shell, we could find nothing culturally diagnostic. We found occasional flint chips and scraps of animal bone—deer and elk—but none of the projectile points with which this game had been killed.

Charcoal was scattered through the shell and now and again we would find small stones of the gneissic local rock, shells of the delicate ribbed mussel, barnacles, and the shell of a moon snail, an aquatic variety. A few hammerstones and manos used as hammerstones were the only real artifacts. Who could make anything of such rubbish? But, as this association of material kept recurring, a hypothesis formed. It went like this:

The oyster-gatherers, probably the women and children, must have scooped up the oysters off the bottom at low tide with their hands or some sort of scoop, and whatever came up went into the gathering basket. Thus the random stones, ribbed mussels, barnacles, and mud snails. The gathering basket was carried to the oyster heap of the moment and dumped, its entire contents of oysters, mud, and the rest being spilled on the heap. Then the gatherers sat down to shuck their harvest. There is practically only one way that an Amerind, with no thin steel-bladed knife to prize and cut, could open an oyster; the means would be heat. A flame applied to the shell will cause the oyster to open its valves wide enough to insert a pry or fingers. Thus the scattered charcoal. The shuckers must have used small, flaming sticks, or small fires of twigs (there was nowhere enough charcoal or signs of burning to suggest a hearth) to apply heat to the oyster. But the oyster still had to be cut loose from the shell, and thus the flint flakes. The bone fragments, most of which are splinters with sharp ends, were probably used as forks to spear the slippery oyster meat out of the shell and into the mouth or cooking basket. The hammerstones suggest that some shells may have been pounded to break them open, though there is little evidence of this.

What pleased us considerably was the find, now and then, of an oyster that had never been opened, its two valves together as they had been in life. It had simply been overlooked by the shuckers. This probably would not have happened had any other procedure been followed than dumping the gathering basket on an already existing pile of shell. Our deduction was that the oyster meat was eaten raw on the spot.

If this hypothesis were true, then it was highly likely that we would never find a diagnostic projectile point in a GO heap. And we have never found one. The heaps are not total refuse dumps onto which all the camp garbage and discards were thrown; they are the remains and evidence of only one activity: the opening, followed by the eating, of oysters. The locus of other activities—cooking, the preparation of other foods, hide- and woodworking, sheltered sleeping—was elsewhere. Acting in accordance with the hypothesis, we took our dig to a likely place at some remove from the GO horizon heaps, and found our GO horizon people, the Archaic Vosburg and Otter Creek people mentioned under Local Sequence in the Lower Hudson at the end of Chapter 3 as being, at Dogan Point, older than 5100 years.

There is hardly a statement in the foregoing which is not a hypothesis, and our feeling about the soundness of our hypotheses covers a broad spectrum, from the tentative to near certainty. These hypotheses are what we pursue our digging to test, and at any moment we may uncover something that is confirmatory or incompatible. We think these oyster gatherers camped here for two- to four-week periods in the early spring, after leaving their winter quarters in caves and sheltered places in the wooded hills. The reason is that spring comes to the sea level riberbanks two weeks before it begins to stir in the interior uplands. But the water would still be very cold for collecting oysters. On the other hand, the upriver runs of shad and other anadromous fish begin in March and continue about a month. With game hunted out in the woods and winter-gaunt, the plenitude of fish must have been powerfully attractive to people at the end of their winter store of food, cold water or not. Almost no fish bones have been found in the shell middens, and the shell would preserve them if they had been thrown there, but our hypothesis stipulates that they were not thrown there.

The camp sets are almost tiny, consisting of a single fireplace on the surface of the ground; no pit was dug nor were the hearths stone-encircled. Few tools occur about these hearths and very little stone tool manufacture was done; most of the chips of any size were used as knives and scrapers. There is never any evidence of a shelter, and we have supposed that the dwelling units were wickiups, made of bent saplings and thin poles covered by bark and hides, not large enough for more than a family of perhaps two adults and a child or two.

But the projectile points, manos, and pestles are evidence that oysters and fish were not the only foods exploited; and it is likely that the food quest kept the members of the band scattered far and wide most of the day. The hearth was, to put it simply, the kitchen, to which the members of the band resorted only briefly for their share of the meal, which they ate elsewhere. There may have been a certain amount of sitting about the fire in the chilly evenings, but it seems doubtful. The hearths were not big enough to be warming; they must have been merely cooking fires. Like the oyster heaps, the hearths must have been loci of limited and passing activity. We cannot, therefore, be sure how many people composed the camping band, which was the basic social unit. So we keep digging. We know we are probably overlooking evidence and failing to see associations, but some slight new clue may someday provide insight.

To sum up, excavation is not the digging of square holes according to a grid plan. It is the mind wielding a trowel or shovel in search of the elements of hypothesis.

chapter 7

How to Recognize and Expose Features and Artifacts

THE PLACE TO begin excavating is at that test pit where the evidence has been most promising of quick results. Nothing so fortifies the soul for the days of scarcity, which are inevitable, as a good beginning that inspires confidence in the productivity of a site and stimulates the excavator to his first hypothesis. Of equal interest is the practicality. If the 3-foot by 3-foot test pit has been dug as suggested, the digger already knows where he is stratigraphically. The supervisor should himself enlarge the test pit to a standard 5-foot by 5-foot square. It gives him a good view of the four faces of the pit from which he must choose the direction he wants his trenches to take. This choice will determine his balks.

BALKS

A balk is a wall of earth left standing on the side of a trench to provide an illustration of the stratigraphy or subsurface soil structure. It is, conventionally, 6 inches wide, 3 inches on either side of the boundary line of a square; but the nature of the soil will determine how wide it must be. For projects manned by volunteers working over weekends, or any project where the balk has to stand for some time, the balk should be sturdy enough to sustain weathering; a driving rain can make a shambles of a balk of sand or loamy soil.

Some instructors in field methods prefer to leave balks on all four sides of a ten-foot square, so that, from above, an excavation looks like a waffle. At some excavations each five-foot square is balk-enclosed, a practice that is hard to justify since it leaves too much unexcavated earth and interrupts the continuity of both the excavation and the stratigraphic picture.

It is better to leave long balks the length and breadth of the site with each balk, if possible, not a balk at all but the face of a trench backed by solid, unexcavated earth that may weather but will not collapse. The plan followed by the author is to begin with a single square, as described in the first paragraph in this chapter, with two diggers standing in the square. Then the diggers dig four adjacent squares—one each to the north, east, south, and west. From each one of these adjacent squares, in turn, the diggers dig all of the adjacent squares to the north, east, south, and west, except those squares which have already been dug. (In the accompanying diagram, squares numbered 2 are dug from square number 1, squares numbered 3 are dug from squares numbered 2, etc.) The digging continues in this manner until a couple of dozen squares have been dug or something is encountered that alters the plan.

This may seem cumbersome and slow at the beginning but it soon develops enough squares for the size crew that will turn up regularly on volunteer projects. In the beginning there is plenty of other kinds of work to be done, such as site-clearing. The disciplinarian supervisor with ten diggers at his command would marshall them at the baseline and set them all going at the blast of a whistle, but on volunteer crews the workers don't all show up at the same time.

But there is a good reason for going about digging this way: the digger is always working on a block with one vertical face exposed to view for guidance. If he is digging by natural level, that is, by stratum or by visible change in the soil of either color or texture, the digger knows where he is in relation to these levels by consulting as a chart the soil profile into which he is digging. He is equally oriented if he is digging by arbitrary levels, that is, by 2- or 4- or 6-inch levels. Yes, a digger can begin on flat ground and sink a square down like a welldigger, but he is not as sensitive to levels because he is moving dirt over dirt and sometimes obscuring what he does.

Sometimes this is not a feasible procedure because of trees or boulders in key squares. But surely the supervisor will know how to modify the plan in these circumstances. It will do well enough for sites up to about 4 feet deep. If the site is really deep, like Saint Albans, the plan can be used to take it down by 4-foot decrements; that is, a 40 foot-by-40 foot or 50 foot-by-50 foot section will be cut down by 4 feet before digging any deeper.

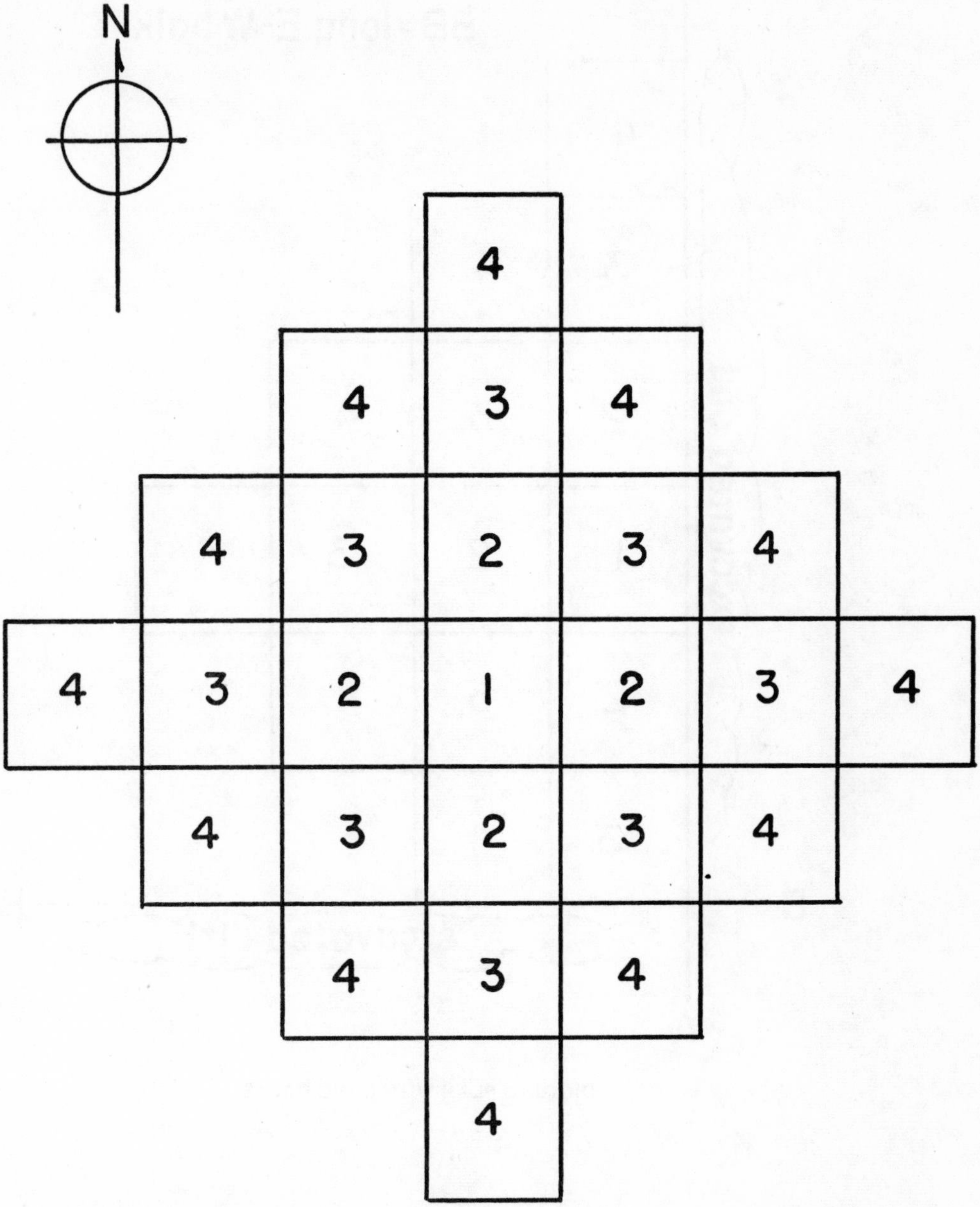

N

			4			
	4	3	4			
	4	3	2	3	4	
4	3	2	1	2	3	4
	4	3	2	3	4	
		4	3	4		
			4			

DIGGING PLAN

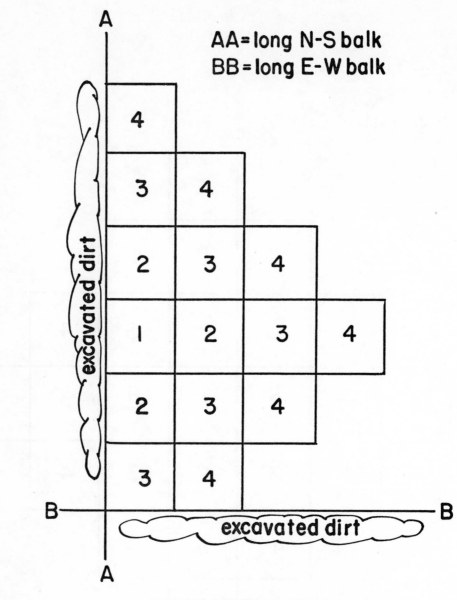

A

**AA = long N-S balk
BB = long E-W balk**

DIGGING PLAN WITH LONG BALKS

This is not to say Saint Albans was dug in this way; it wasn't. Broyles used a step-in method, which resulted in the isolation of a central block which exposed a central block. This method was chosen not only to expose occupational interlarded with sterile water-laid strata and to keep the stratigraphy intact but also to save the crew from being buried under a sudden slump.

This isolation of a central or specimen block which is then very carefully dug by trenching on all four sides is one of the several alternate plans of attack that may appeal to the supervisor. A third is to pursue a series of parallel trenches, leaving a 5-foot or 10-foot strip unexcavated between them. This is a more exploratory, less intensive plan than either of the other two and it has its proper use. The first plan, however, by pursuing trenches in right-angle directions, combines exploration or probing with intensive excavation. If either of the trenches probing the length or breadth of the site strikes a significantly productive area, the supervisor will assign his forces to that area.

The Value of Long Profiles

In the first excavation plan outlined above, the primary balks or walls charting the profile of the subsurface structure are the walls of the primary perpendicular trenches. The faces of these trenches must be kept clear as long as the site is being excavated; because they are in solid earth, not narrow balks, they will survive weathering, and a little work with a trowel will restore the profile for study.

The practice of keeping the long profiles open and legible for the duration of the excavation is, probably, an extreme view, but not peculiar to the author. After all, the profile can be drawn square by square and a continuous record thus kept; theoretically, as soon as it is recorded, it can be covered. But the fact is that the eye does not always see in short segments of profile what may prove to be the significant continuities in longer ones. Our shell middens are an example. A 5-foot or even a 10-foot square shows a tangle of several lines and a jumble of disordered masses. But in one profile 120 feet long is the tolerably clear picture of how the midden developed, camping episode by episode.

The value of long profiles was revealed by Coe's basic excavations in the piedmont Archaic. He relates that he dug a 5-foot test square at the now famous Hardaway site in 1948, and found the depth to be only 28 inches. Since 40 percent of the fill was aboriginally worked or broken stone, the profile looked rather like a cultural gravel pit and made no sense at all. In 1951 he dug another 5-foot square and found it almost solid occupational debris and visually a jumble. But these two squares yielded the incredible number of 1500 artifacts and, loath to give up on such a rich deposit, Coe returned in 1955 and laid out a grid plan. He dug ten 5-foot squares by arbitary 6-inch levels, keeping meticulous records of the profiles but filling the trench behind him as he dug. Again the effort drew a blank. But he felt that there had to be some sort of zonal differentiation; the cultural debris was too compacted for there to have been any vertical movement or natural displacement within the soil. Six weeks after this unproductive test he went back to Hardaway for the fourth time and exposed a 20-foot-long face. And there it was, a profile showing four zones of occupation, faintly but visually discernible. On the effectiveness of the long profile, then, rests the achievements of the excavation that, for the first time, demonstrated the antiquity of the hunting-gathering Archaic subsistence pattern, established the principle that projectile point types were valid diagnostic traits, and described these types. Standard operating procedure would never have—in three trials it had not—disclosed the key to this Archaic cryptogram.

What to Do with the Back Dirt

The standard operating procedure is that used by Coe on his third try: back-fill your trench with the dirt you take out of the squares as you advance. On those sites which must be restored to their original state—and most landowners expect this—it is the most economical solution to the always vexing problem of what to do with the back dirt so that it does not have to be moved over and over. But it is obviously incompatible with the maintenance of the exposed long profile. The author's procedure is to pile the dirt from the primary trenches on top of the long balks, from which it can be shoveled back into the trench, which is what anybody would do. But the dirt from the interior squares becomes increasingly embarrassing if the cultural depth of the site is over about twelve inches. The ridge of dirt along the balks becomes unmanageably high and has to be broadened; replacement then becomes really onerous. After a block of interior squares has been cleaned out, the situation eases. A back dirt pile is begun in the excavated area, and there is no difficulty thereafter. The pile spreads as the earth is cleared and has only to be spread to restore the interior of the site.

This method does not make for pretty slide pictures suitable for showing at conferences but, after all, taking a pretty picture is not the objective of excavation. The picture that satisfies the critic that the work was competently done is a gridiron of well-trimmed balks, with each square looking like an emptied carton. Such work is admirable, but balks are balks in the fullest sense; they are obstructions to movement and, often, to a view of the site's integrality. They do one job only: they are instant references to what happened geologically at that place.

The emphasis on long balks does not mean that other balks are not to be maintained, if they serve the above purpose. If a change in subsurface structure is encountered that is nonconforming or cannot be tied into a long profile, its profile should be preserved in a balk. A balk can be left wherever it does its job. I have often left, moreover, specimen balks where the profile of the subsurface structure was most vividly delineated. Such specimens often stave off strenuous arguments. But they are warts on the nose of pretty pictures.

SCRAPING THE 5-FOOT SQUARE

The piece of work to which each digger, equipped with trowel, pruning clippers, notebook, and collecting bag, is assigned in excavating by grid plan is, of course, the 5-foot square. His task is to scrape it down evenly, being careful to make square corners and perpendicular sides. Some diggers never seem to learn how to achieve square corners and straight-up-and-down sides, because they never learn how to use a trowel. The sides are for surface scraping but the point is for scoring along the sides, and a good digger can dig a plumb, cubic hole, square to the cord line running between stakes, without ever changing his scraping motion over the surface, that is, without ever stopping to "smooth" the sides. Such diggers don't even need a line to dig by. There is nothing that looks so amateurish as a square with sides sloping in toward the bottom. It makes for a shoddy profile and a general air of dishevelment.

The scraping over of a 5-foot square (25 square feet of area) has to take into account the factor of the length of the human arm. The whole area can't be scraped unless the digger does a certain amount of trampling on it and scraping dirt over dirt. If there is no feature which has to be uncovered in plan, over a broader area, it is good procedure to work on half a square. The digger stands or kneels on the floor of the last excavated square, reaches in 2.5 feet and scrapes dirt toward himself, into a scoop. (Some diggers make scoops by cutting away plastic gallon containers of the kind that liquid laundry preparations are bottled in, but others prefer to make their own wooden ones.) The scoopful of dirt is dumped into a plastic two-gallon bucket and conveyed to the standing sieve for screening. No trampling, no stretching, no double-scraping; a single stroke brings the dirt off the surface cleanly being scraped into the container. If something is overlooked in the scraping, the digger knows where it came from, within close limits.

Theoretically, nothing should ever be found on the screen. The objective is to uncover artifacts and evidence *in situ,* that is, reveal them without disturbing them from their age-old resting place, so that they can be photographed, if that is called for, and their location measured from the reference stakes. A light, deft handling of the trowel usually accomplishes this, if the soil is light, grainy rather than lumpy, and neither too wet nor too dry. The digger will discover quickly enough when it is not, when it is viscously wet or cloddy or hard-packed. But even when the soil is at its most workable, the safest course is to screen. Small artifacts can escape the quickest eye and it is better to be slightly chagrined than to miss them.

DIGGING BY THE LEVELS

The phrase "digging by levels" is very nearly a misnomer. It is not the digging that is done by levels; it is the collecting and recording. Digging by arbitrary levels, as has been explained, is scraping down a square by predetermined units of any thickness, from one inch to one foot (four inches is the usual arbitrary layer) but, more to the point, it is the recording and sacking together of everything found in that layer. When natural levels, soil members that there is reason to believe were formed at different times and under different climatic or geophysical conditions, are present, excavation is guided by such levels; and all that occurs within each member is recorded and sacked as of that level. (The collection bag or cannister is within reach at all times, to receive those bits and pieces not requiring recording, as well as those that do.)

Digging by neat levels is not usually as easy as cheerful verbalizing makes it seem. There are two main frustrations: stones and roots. It is the invariable rule that stones be left *in situ,* the digger scrapping around them until they are exposed to the base and the level at which they rest. Large stones can be part of a fireplace or other cultural feature or association and, until it is shown that they are not, they should not be moved. Roots are to be clipped (the digger's second most used tool is a pruning clippers), chopped, or sawed; they should not be pulled out, since they usually run through levels and abrupt removal disturbs the levels.

Pseudostratigraphy of the Soil Profile

The structure of soils has already been treated at some length in Chapter 4, but it may do well to say something here about the pseudostratigraphy of the natural soil profile. The average soil found in the southern part of the temperate zone where deciduous trees once covered the land is called a forest brown earth. Where it has not been plowed or otherwise altered, it consists of four zones: the duff on top consisting of loose, decaying vegetal material; the black humus layer of fully decayed vegetal material, dust, and other particulate matter, labelled the A_1 zone; the A_2 zone, grading from brown at the top to yellowish at the bottom, strongly leached from percolation; and the B zone, of yellowish color often tinged with red if there is iron in the soil. In undisturbed, standing soils, this profile develops very quickly by the chemico-physical action of rainwater through the whole depth and the chemistry of weather. That weathering is an element in the establishment of soil profiles is demonstrated by the fact that there develops in the northern part of the temperate zone a quite different soil profile called a podzol. The profile of a podzol is as follows: raw black humus, called the A_0 zone, the A_2 zone of soil leached white, and a B_2 zone of yellowish red which contains considerable humus.

The digger may find it convenient to dig by the pseudostratigraphy of soil development, but he should not be deluded into thinking he is dealing with actual levels, though the zones may be quite differentially colored and textured; the lower zone may be sandier and contain more pebbles and stones which have gravitated to the lower zones. The fact is that the whole soil, forest brown or podzol, is a single geologic member and all that occurs in it can be understood to have been deposited during its "lifetime" of perhaps 10,000 years.

Some soils that are 3 feet thick and of nearly the same humic black from top to bottom contain wrought nails 100 years old at the same depth as flint chips and artifacts 1000 to 2000 years old. In such soils the "contaminating" agent was not man but nature itself, with its constant moving of soil downhill and mixing of humic soil with humus and humus-in-formation at just the right rate. In one such soil the whole 3-foot column, by index (diagnostic) artifacts that lay on the bottom (steatite potsherds; for chronological position see Chapter 3), dated the bottom black dirt at about 3500 B.P. Within 20 feet of this deep profile the black-brown zone was 12 inches deep and rested on a terrace deposited by the melting local lobe of a glacier, on the surface of which were artifacts 10,000 years old. In short, the 12-inch soil represented 10,000 years of formation; the 3-foot soil represented only a third of that. The reason was that the 3-foot soil was at the head of a draw which had long been a drainway. About 3500 B.P. the draw ceased to be a drainway and a soil began to build up there; particle soil movement (not erosion wash) down from the slopes that drained into the draw added further soil until this formerly low spot had been built up to the level of the adjacent area.

FEATURES

As the digger scrapes the surface by ½-inch or ¼-inch cuts, he must be alert to detect the discolorations or color contrasts that identify features. These may show up at any depth in either the arbitrary or natural level. The kinds of features he may expect to find are hearths, pits, the postmolds of houses or other structures, living floors, and burials. When a feature is discovered, digging by squares and levels ceases and the digger adjusts his procedures to expose the feature and what may be associated with it, as completely as they survive.

Hearths

The stone-enclosed hearth, consisting of a circle of stones usually about a deposit of charcoal, has already been mentioned. Other hearths are simply dark areas of charcoal and other debris on the surface of the ground or in shallow pits, the earth about which is often fire-reddened. A third hearth type is the "barbecue pit," a pit filled with stone laid on top of a bed of glowing embers to roast food or to dry or smoke it for preservation.

Pits

Pits, burials (which are simply pits with a human skeleton in them), and post-molds (holes in the ground from the driving of stakes or of poles for house or other construction) are all recognized by the circular or oval stain in soil of a lighter color. They are invisible or nearly so in dark soil but may, in the case of pits, be detected by the greasy look of the fill. Since the orifice of the pit is at the level of the culture which dug it, it is important to detect the orifice as soon as possible.

Pits were dug by aborigines in almost all cases for storage, and after they became unusable by reason of insect or mold infestation or were no longer needed, they were often used for refuse disposal. Frequently enough, when filled with refuse, they became hearths. Their use, after abandonment for storage, as places to bury the dead is far from unknown. But pits entirely devoid of cultural material or any hint of what they once contained may be expected. At one site about 140 pits were excavated without so much as a scrap of flint to show for the work.

Pits come in many shapes and sizes, and the combination of shape and size is often a culturally diagnostic trait. They may be excavated in either of two ways: by emptying out the contents from the top, or by sectioning. The more laborious of the two methods, sectioning, consists of cutting a wall face in which the pit shows from top to bottom in profile. To show the shape and size in full, the excavation face has to be cut through the diameter of the pit. It is possible that a pit was made by one cultural group and filled by another, that two groups contributed to its filling, or that nature alone did the filling, and the excavator should be aware of these possibilities. The evidence he should be most alert for, however, is vegetal—corn grains or cobs, beans, squash or pumpkin seeds, nuts and acorns, this being the kind of food stored. Since storage pits were often lined with bark or grass, these may be found either in their original state or as carbonized, decayed remains.

Postmolds and Structural Patterns

Postmolds, dark circles in the surface, from an inch in diameter up to, very rarely, eight inches or more, are excavated when they are first encountered in section to prove they are postmolds and not the channels of decayed roots. The stakes and posts driven or set by Amerinds were sharpened at the end, not necessarily for driving but because that was the way the tree was cut. This sharpened point should show in the profile of the postmold. As soon as a postmold is authenticated, the search begins at the level where its orifice was discovered for the next one, and the next. The pattern of postmolds outlines a house, stockade, or other structure, always a major find.

It is becoming standard procedure, since Dr. Don Dragoo of Carnegie Museum first initiated the practice, of stripping off topsoil from the level where postmold orifices surface in order to reveal the postmold alignments. This technique has resulted in a highly desirable increase in the amount of information about settlement patterns. But for those who cannot command the services of a bulldozer and skilled operator, the technique used is flat-shoveling, familiar to anyone who has ever cut sod: a flat shovel or spade is shoved horizontally along the postmold orifice level and the soil overburden is removed. Where the structure is an Iroquois longhouse 120 feet long and 30 feet wide, or a stockade enclosing a village covering 3 or 4 acres (in Pennsylvania a village on the upper Susquehanna River covered 10 acres), this is no light task. Without bulldozers little settlement pattern work would get done.

The practice is, generally, to empty postmolds of their contents after the pattern has been determined and recorded. They will probably not contain artifacts, though occasionally they do, but a portion of the post may still remain for C-14 dating. As soon as the hole is cleaned out, a small marker stake should be placed in the hole; it will help the excavator to detect a structural shape among the plethora of postmolds he may encounter. In house patterns any number of distracting postmolds may be discovered, patterns of annexes and of interior structures such as bunk banks, vestibules, and anterooms. And this is to say nothing of the possibility that a later house was built on the site of an earlier one.

Living Floors

The excavator may be alerted to look for postmolds, or he may be able to determine where the house interior is by the presence of a floor, a surface hard-packed by being trod on, and discolored by grease, charcoal, and other offal. Hearths and pits may be expected to be found within houses, and either of these may have burials beneath them or, in the case of pits, in them.

When he is uncovering a house or a settlement pattern—a community of dwellings—the excavator is dealing with a major association, the best evidence he can ever hope to find of organized social behavior. This is paleoanthropology, the study of ancient man within his own society. Haste to complete an excavation should not be allowed to engender neglect of *all* evidence, physical and relational.

Burials

The burial pit must be excavated larger than the original grave in order to give the excavator space to work around the interred skeleton or skeletons, exposing the bones and "grave goods" or "furniture" *in situ*, drawing and photographing the remains, preserving the bone, and preparing the whole interment *en bloc* if that is the plan. This is a shovel operation, of course. The grave fill may, however, contain materials that were in the pit originally or accidentally included in the fill where the grave was.

Preserving Bones. The first concern in uncovering a burial should be for the condition of the bones. Whether they are in poor condition or not, the bones and other material subject to decay should be painted with a polyvinyl glue (such as Elmer's) thinned to the consistency of skimmed milk. For years several elaborate and not wholly satisfactory measures were taken to safeguard bone and preserve it intact so that it could be handled or at least studied. But, confronted with an unmanageable quantity of bone, the 190 bison skeletons at the Olsen-Chubbock site, Joe Ben Wheat, the excavation director, came up with the glue expedient. It proved to be the perfect treatment. The water kept the bones moist, preventing them from checking, splitting, and drying into dust. The glue formed an integument or skin that held the water in and the parts together. (In the case of very fragile bones several coats were applied, to be safe.) The bone was not discolored by the glue, which could be washed off if and when desired. The treatment works equally well for any organic remains and for pottery. In the case of delicate cordage, leather, or bark, there may be difficulty in applying the solution. It may be sprayed on by atomizer or dripped on by eyedropper.

There is no predicting what may be found at the bottom of a grave or burial pit; findings include ceremonial burials with red ocher and "killed" (deliberately broken to release their "spirits") artifacts, forlorn single individuals without a token of regard, pathetic mother and infant burials apparently performed after the death of both in childbirth, mass burials, a grave on top of or beside another grave, burials of whole or cremated bone bundles, cremation burials where the corpse was burned in place, and ossuaries, where the bones of many long deceased were deposited and burned.

Even the simplest single individual burial is tedious work for the excavator. The dirt matrix must be removed from around all bone and any accompanying material without disturbance or damage. This is done by brush and knife blade. A bulb syringe is helpful in blowing dirt out of places hard to get at. While the excavator works, he should be careful to keep the sun's direct rays off the skeleton; and if he leaves it for any length of time (burials have an inconvenient habit of turning up late in the day), he should cover it with moist sacking, cloth, or paper.

Burial Removal. A burial should be carefully and cleanly exposed, photographed, sketched, and recorded with all pertinent information, including its orientation (the directions in which the head points and faces) and position, that is, prone, supine, on its side, extended or flexed, composed or abnormal or in disarray. If the bone is in good condition, you may remove it, piece by piece. But if it is too disintegrated or friable to handle, send for the nearest physical anthropologist or a physician friend who knows about aging, sexing, dentition, skeletal metrics (measurement), and bone pathology. The skeleton is the artifact (of divine manufacture, if you like) that informs us about prehistoric populations and the physical effects of culture.

Bone Pathology. One of the continuing investigations to which bone pathology contributes is the search for the origin of that dread social disease, syphillis. The recovery of syphillitic bone from burials in North, Central, and South America antedating the voyages of Columbus to the New World, coupled with the absence of similar evidence of disease in the pre-Columbian cemeteries of Europe, suggests that Columbus's sailors either introduced syphillis to Europe or superimposed a virulent strain of syphillis upon a mild European strain against which Europeans may have already developed some resistance.

In America it is not only human skeletal remains that were deliberately interred. Dogs were often inhumed as separate burials or with human beings. They should be given the same careful treatment as human bone, for the same reasons. An instance of the kind of discovery that study turns up comes from Alabama, where David Chase of the Montgomery Museum of Fine Arts noted, among seven dog burials at a prehistoric Indian village, two dogs with pathological bone. One of these had had its skull crushed by a blow, probably a mercy killing, since it as well as the second dog was in the advanced stages of hyperpulmonary osteoarthropathy. This is a rare disease occurring in sheep, deer, horses, and lions, and even more rarely in man.

What made this discovery worthy of notice was the curious fact that hyperpulmonary osteoarthropathy has been associated in more recent times with the same area of Alabama where the canine burials were found. A recent study conducted for veterinarians found that the highest incidence of the disease occurred in central Alabama, notably in Lee and Macon counties. Since the canine burials were located only a few miles from the western boundary of Macon County, the possibility arises that the disease has persisted in the same area since prehistoric times.

Removal *En Bloc*

One of the methods occasionally used is exposure of a feature *en bloc* or on a pedestal, a kind of reverse excavation in that the earth is removed six or eight inches below the level at which the feature rests, so that it is elevated. The purpose of such exposure may be either for better photography, where something special about the feature requires a special record, or for exhibit. Some sites are excavated for public viewing; pedestal elevation of a feature, after stabilization, is legitimate scientific showmanship. It is also effective scientific demonstration when features so exposed are left in place for the duration of the project to provide a comprehensive view of the actuality of the site.

Pedestal exposure of burials may be for these purposes or to ready them for removal *en bloc,* that is, undisturbed, for display in museums or because of something unusual about them that requires long indoor study. The excavator will undertake an *en bloc* removal only when he knows what he is going to do with the block. If all the archaeological burials uncovered in America were removed as blocks, museums and laboratories would have become mausoleums with space for little else.

The procedure is to build a wooden frame about the block and drive or slip a steel plate or sheet of corrugated steel or heavy plywood under it, cutting the block off from the underlying earth and providing it with a bottom. Two-by-fours are then driven under the bottom, to be used as a litter for raising and carrying. Steel pipe is easier to drive under the block, but the block can shift and roll on them whereas the frame can be toe-nailed to a wooden litter.

Aside from the carrying arrangement, provision may have to be made for stabilizing the skeletal material. If it is not in too precarious a pile, the glue treatment will serve to preserve the bone and a sheet of plastic, drawn tight across the top of the frame and thumb-tacked, will secure the loose items for moving.

There are more elaborate procedures for stabilizing a loose bone mass that may have to be resorted to. They are, in part, dictated by the necessity of preserving the bone and are thus "old-fashioned" except in rare cases. One procedure is to treat the bone mass and the whole surface of the block with paraffin, of the quality used in home canning, dissolved in gasoline. A typical single burial would require four to five pounds of paraffin dissolved in about 6 gallons of gasoline. But the bone must be dry before this solution is applied or the paraffin-bearing gasoline will not penetrate the bone uniformly. A dosing of the bone with denatured alcohol will hasten the drying, if time is a factor, and will protect somewhat against checking. But the bone positions are not very firmly fixed by this method, and excess paraffin collects on the bone. It is not strongly recommended.

Positive stabilization is accomplished by laying strips of wet newspaper over the remains and moist plaster-of-paris-impregnated strips of burlap over the paper cover, molding them to the contours. When the plaster sets, the whole association is fixed firmly, while the paper cover allows the mold or cast to be removed easily.

Removal *en bloc* is possible with any feature not too bulky to move, but the fact of the matter is that it is really museum business and, if possible, museum technicians should be summoned to do the job. The main concern of the field archaeologist should be to preserve the bone and other organic remains from further deterioration, to record everything in context, and to save what he can for the laboratory technicians.

The foregoing has been based on the assumption that the site being excavated is flat or relatively so. The floors of caves and rockshelters are also relatively flat and are dug by grid plan. But if the cave or rockshelter is elevated above the general terrain, there may very well be at its mouth or opening a talus slope of dirt and rock. This slope will probably contain artifacts, but it should not be excavated as though it were part of the cave fill. Artifacts lost in or debris thrown out of the cave onto the talus will not have the same relative position as material found in the cave fill. The cave fill, which should afford reliable provenience data unless it has been disturbed by pot hunters (an exasperatingly common occurrence), and the talus slope are not to be excavated as though they are the same site geologically. The talus should be cut away until a profile of unmistakable cave fill is reached, or it may even be ignored. As a gradient subject to weathering and wash, it has no validity as a soil deposit unit. But it may produce a number of artifacts valuable in typological or other studies after the priorities of the types have been established by excavation of the cave fill.

HOW TO EXCAVATE MOUNDS

Less than fully manned and equipped crews should not attack mounds unless they are in imminent danger of destruction and no other salvation is promised. The first step, after gridding, should be to trench the periphery of the mound in an arc of, say, a quarter of its perimeter, to expose its "roots," that is, where the mound fill began to be heaped up on the original surface. In many cases mounds have been constructed on previous sites or features. Unless the excavator discovers this early, he may accept as mound-related material artifacts and evidence not pertaining to the mound.

A quarter-arc trench fits in well with one procedure in which mounds are taken down by pie-slice sections. When mounds are so attacked, the next step ordinarily is to cut out the quarter directly opposite. But if it happens that a tomb or other feature is encountered in the center of the mound, it is usually best to excavate the quarter adjacent to the quarter first excavated, so that half a pie section is left standing for zonal study. Many mounds are accretional, their final height and bulk the accumulation of several episodes of burial and addition of fill. These episodes may not show up uniformly over the whole mound, but the excavation of half the mound should reveal evidence of them all.

When haste is called for, a trench may be driven from the perimeter through the center to the opposite side. The taller the mound, the wider the trench should be so that a collapse of the walls will not fill the trench and bury workers. A prominent early mound investigator, Henry Shetrone, was buried under the collapse of a wall of one of these diameter trenches and barely escaped with his life. Diameter trenches are testing and exploratory, not fully archaeological.

The one approach to mound investigation not allowed under any circumstances is the grave robber's shaft, a pit dug from the peak of the mound to the base in a search of treasure. Probably half the mounds in the United States and most of the mounds in Europe and the Middle East—where there was genuine treasure to be looted—have been despoiled by this tactic. It should be considered a felony.

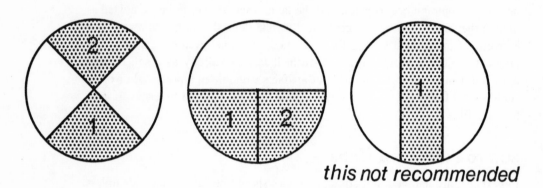

this not recommended

METHODS OF EXCAVATING A MOUND

Every archaeologist, lay or professional, before he opens a mound, should read the account by Thomas Jefferson of his 1784 excavation of a Virginia burial mound in his *Notes on the State of Virginia* (reprinted in *The Archaeologist at Work*, edited by Robert Heizer and published by Harper & Bros., 1959). This was the first scientific excavation of a mound; indeed, it was the first fully scientific excavation done anywhere in the world. It is old-fashioned only in the lucidity and inherent logic of its organization. Few modern workers can match it as communication of method, results, and interpretation.

RECORDING PETROGLYPHS AND PICTOGRAPHS

Petroglyphs, designs pecked or scored into the faces of rocks, and pictographs, drawings on the faces of rocks, require, of course, no excavation, although on rare occasions they may be uncovered during excavation. They are recorded only, and perhaps this note belongs in the section on recording. But the field archaeologist, thinking of them as sites, may expect to find them treated here.

Dr. James L. Swauger of the Carnegie Museum, a leading authority on petroglyphs, particularly in the eastern United States (his main archaeological work was in Palestine), gives the following recording procedure:

"Recording consists of six operations: (1) Sketching the figures of a site

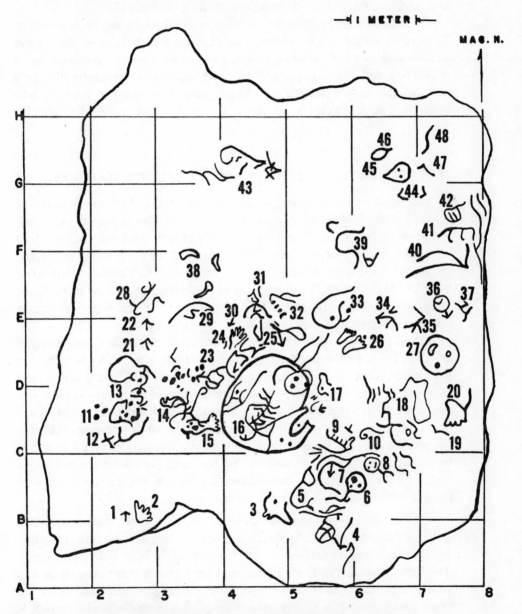

COPY OF FIELD SKETCH OF SUGAR GROVE PETROGLYPHS
Note: Each petroglyph was given a number and identified (tentatively in some cases) as bird tracks, an animal head, human feet, etc.

in relation to a grid whose squares are one meter on a side and which is always oriented north and south, the sketch always made from the south border; (2) Photographing in black and white; (3) Photographing in color; (4) Overprinting, which is a direct print made by rolling printer's ink on a sheet of unbleached muslin stretched tightly over the glyphs of a site; (5) Making latex molds of the glyphs; (6) Making casts from the molds."

The figures are chalked for visibility before drawing and photographing. Pictographs cannot be overprinted or molded; the outlines of the figures usually have to be adumbrated by chalk before drawing and photography. It should be noted that making molds of liquid latex is quite expensive, though it provides the most exact records. Molds have been made in papier-mâché plaster and modeling clay or plasticine, all of which have obvious limitations.

FLOTATION: A TECHNIQUE FOR RECOVERING FINE MATERIALS

Archaeologists, their attention increasingly directed toward the recovery of evidence of the foods used by aborigines, recently began to suspect that much of this evidence—seeds, fragments of stems and fish, small mammal and bird bone—was eluding them because it was too small for the troweler to see and the regular ¼- to ½-inch-mesh screens to catch. The technique devised to avoid this loss is called flotation or, more accurately, water separation. Stuart Struever (*American Antiquity*, July 1968) described the water separation process as used on four sites in the Illinois River valley thus:

"Soil from features is screened and collected on plastic sheets. Samples are hauled to a nearby creek and gently poured into a washtub whose bottom has been replaced with a fine-mesh screen. The tub is held by one person, and its bottom is submerged about 1″ below the surface of the water. As the soil is poured in, the tub is gently rotated in alternating clockwise and counter-clockwise directions, allowing the fine-grained silts and sands to escape. Within a few seconds only the largest inclusions remain; these may include flint chips, bone fragments and plant remains. All represent particles too small to be caught by the ¼″ and ½″ mesh screens at the site, yet are too large to go through the 1/16″ mesh screen in the tub bottom.

"When the tub is dipped into the water, the various raw materials settle at different rates. A second individual, working in rhythm with the person manipulating the tub, uses a small tea strainer to scoop off the bone and plant remains. The latter, sinking at a lower rate than either stone or burnt clay, occur in a momentary stratum somewhat above that containing the stone and other less porous materials. The combined tub manipulation and scooping action is repeated several times until examination of the tub contents indicates that all bone and carbonized plant remains have been scooped off with the tea strainer.

This procedure is simple, requiring only practice in coordinating tub and strainer activity."

The bone and plant remains are later separated in the laboratory by chemical flotation, a zinc chloride solution being used instead of water; the bone sinks in this solution, with a specific gravity of 1.62, while the plant remains float on or near the surface, to be skimmed off by tea strainer. The amount and variety of recoveries by water separation-flotation from hearths and living floors is worth the effort.

DECIDING WHAT TO KEEP

What to keep? All recognized and identifiable artifacts and evidence, of course. The excavator should retain, and enter in the square record by count, all the industrial debris—chips, spalls, cores, and struck stone. Chip concentrations may mean chipping floors; the material found there should be analyzed for place of origin since exotic (nonlocal) stone, traced to the source, may mean that it was acquired by trade or that a new group had entered the area. Moreover, a great deal may be learned about lithic technology from the size, kind, and numbers of the flakes. Fire-cracked stone pieces should also be counted and entered in the record, though they need not be kept unless they are items in an association.

Samples of charcoal should be saved from every concentration where it is found. It is the favorite dating material. But bone, shell, antler, wood, hides, seeds, and all other kinds of organic materials, are equally datable by C-14 test (see the next chapter).

WHAT POLLEN SAMPLES CAN REVEAL

It is a good practice to take a 4- by 4-inch soil core through the profile of a site in case the excavator knows or can contact a specialist in pollen. From the count of pollen varieties, pollen experts can infer changes in vegetation and, hence, climate. Bogs provide excellent pollen samples.

KEEPING THE PARTY INFORMED

It is a wise director who encourages his diggers to announce their finds in a loud and excited voice and thus to draw the rest of the group about for an inspection. Psychologically, the inspection gives everybody a chance to participate vicariously in discovery (the site is a group, not an individual project), especially those who have been laboring in sterile soil. But it is also a way of passing out experience and information, keeping everybody conversant with what is turning up, and teaching and inviting discussion. When the director can make identifications and provide an interpretation, he should do so; if he can't or if he is in doubt, he should be candid about his ignorance or uncertainty, for his own good as well as that of those who are depending on him for guidance. Sometimes students on large projects spend whole digging seasons in their own little sandboxes without ever hearing from anybody in charge about what is being revealed. They log digging time toward credits in field methods, and learn next to nothing about what they are digging. The close-mouthed director who saves it all for his report should be shunned. On smaller projects manned by volunteers, conversation keeps information moving.

CLEANING AND PRESERVATION

Some items may be washed in the field, using water and a stiff brush, but they should decidedly not be cleaned then or later if they show signs of stains or discoloration through use. Paint mortars may still have pigments clinging to them, and sometimes knives and projectile points have been stained by the gum or adhesive used to secure them in handles and shafts. Pottery should be cleaned with a soft toothbrush, but metal should never be cleaned in the field and rarely in the laboratory until it has been examined by an expert. It is not a good idea to be in a hurry about cleaning anything or, for that matter, taking preservative measures unless they are distinctly called for, when Elmer's glue is the safest treatment. Sodden items will very often air-dry into a sound condition, and items already dry that are on the point of pulverizing probably can't be saved, since they have been completely oxidized. Materials for C-14 assay (see the next chapter) should receive no treatment at all; the labs do the cleaning. The desideratum in archaeology is to alter recoveries as little as possible in the field.

THE IMPORTANCE OF *IN SITU* FINDS

The impulse to pick up an artifact as soon as the eye focuses on it is irresistible. But resistance must be taught by exhortation and rebuke. The *in situ* context may triple the significance of the find. Don't move anything artifactual until its place of repose has been evaluated.

SAVING TIME WITH SPADEWORK

The supervisor should not hesitate to use the spade where he has overburden to move, is dealing with a thick fill in which depth provenience is of dubious value, or is in a known sterile stratum. The trowel is for close, careful work; much time can be wasted moving with a trowel dirt that has little archaeological material in it. Still, such dirt should be flat-shoveled and, unless positively known to be sterile, screened.

The techniques, methods, procedures, and household hints discussed in this chapter are universal. There is no such thing as regional or local archaeology so far as procedures are concerned, though there are regional and local conditions to which adaptations are made. The determinant is the site, its geology, and what is found there. The excavator does not use one set of rules in the Northeast and another in the Northwest. What is different is the substance of the prehistory, regional and local sequences, and that can be learned only by study of the regional and local archaeological literature. There is no way to pick it up from a single book.

chapter 8

Establishing the
Antiquity of Finds

THE TWO PRINCIPAL methods of absolute dating in America utilize dendrochronology and radioactive carbon or Carbon 14. Several minor methods have been used, such as the immanent magnetism method, which is especially useful in dating hearths. A sample, about 6 by 6 inches square and 2 inches deep, should be taken of the burned earth under a hearth. Recent studies of magnetism have shown that fire fixes the magnetic orientation of the earth it heats. Since the magnetic pole has shifted through time, the fixed magnetic orientation of a hearth can be compared with contemporary orientation to give a time reading. Therefore, before the sample is encased in plaster and removed *en bloc,* the magnetic orientation must be marked on it. The sample should be placed in a cardboard or wooden box. This dating method will never replace C-14 dating (discussed later in this chapter); most hearths will afford enough charcoal for a C-14 assay. But charcoal does leach out eventually, while the magnetic fixation is permanent.

There is also the obsidian hydration method, which derives a time value from the thickness of the dehydrated layer that progressively accumulates on the surface of fractured obsidian, the "volcanic glass" stone that is of limited distribution in America. It occurs in the mountainous West, from Alaska to the tip of South America and is found east of the High Plains only as occasional trade goods in distinct cultures, such as the Hopewellian of Illinois and Ohio.

None of the minor methods of dating have had much impact on the chronology of American prehistory. The obsidian method is tricky because dehydration rates differ from locale to locale and magnetism measurement dates what can usually be better dated by C-14.

Relative dating methods do not, of course, provide calendar time fixes, and a chronological column of relative dates usually floats, unanchored, in the misty past. Stratigraphy is a relative dating method, as is seriation, to be discussed in Chapter 11. Chemical analysis is useful in certain situations when it is desired to determine whether human bone is contemporary with the bone of extinct animals found in apparent association; if the kinds and amounts of salts and minerals absorbed into the bones are similar, contemporaneity is proved. Such comparative analysis was used to expose the famous Piltdown Man hoax in which a prankster (or charlatan) had doctored the jaw of a modern chimpanzee to look as though it belonged to a human skull cap found in ancient gravels, and had planted it nearby in the same gravels. The fakery upset the study of human evolution for two generations. But the success of the test did not establish the age of the genuine skull cap.

FIXING DATES BY COUNTING TREE RINGS

Dendrochronology (literally, telling time by trees) is dating by comparison with a master chart of the pattern of the growth of trees as determined by the succession of annual rings. It can provide the most nearly exact calendar date of any method, but its use is restricted to the American West, where (1) there are trees of great age to provide the tree ring growth patterns and (2) there has prevailed a long period of aridity which preserved timbers on archaeological sites. The region which fits these conditions is the Southwest and northern Mexico, where dendrochronology has been used effectively to date timbers found in ancient ruins. A master chart was developed for Alaska in the 1940s before C-14 dating had been conceived, but since 1950 (the first C-14 dates were released on January 1, 1950) C-14 has been overwhelmingly the preferred dating method. All attempts to develop a master chart for the territory east of the Rockies have failed, and dendrochronology is meaningless for most of the Western Hemisphere, except indirectly. It has lately become of great importance as a cross check on the accuracy of C-14. (There is no intent here to underrate dendrochronology. As of 1972 it had provided 15,000 exact annual dates on 700 sites where it was applicable.)

Tree rings, the growth in circumference that trees put on annually, vary in width with the kind of growing season; widths are wide for seasons of good rainfall, narrow for seasons of poor rainfall. The succession of wide and narrow rings forms the master pattern. The first trees used in the development of a master chart were the long-lived Douglas firs of northern California. A calendar date can be put on this year's ring and the ring count in wood is the age of the tree, with each ring having a calendar date. (The ring count of living trees is taken by a corer; the trees don't have to be cut down.) The search for older and older trees, alive or in the stump, went on for years, but it soon became apparent that the Douglas firs and the chance finds that could be tied into their master chart had run out of dating potential just before the time of Christ.

In the 1960s, however, researchers came upon a grove of unimposing bristlecone pine trees in the White Mountains on the southeastern California-Nevada border. These trees grow curiously, in a sort of colony which is a family cluster of generations of the same tree. Dendrochronologists were astonished to find ancestral wood in these clusters up to 5000 years old by ring count. The count later was extended to about 7000 years, and there is good reason to believe that a master chart can be drawn up to 9000 years ago. This is of no practical value in dating archaeological remains because logs of this age have not, up till now, been found with remains of this age, although such an association is not beyond the realm of possibility. But 9000 years of wood can be invaluable in checking the accuracy of the C-14 method all the way back to the Pleistocene.

DATING WITH CARBON 14

Carbon 14 is the radioactive isotope of elemental carbon 12. It is formed in the atmosphere by the action of cosmic rays and, as a component of the atmosphere, it is, despite its rarity, absorbed by all living things into their tissue and bone. When they die the absorption ceases, but the C-14 decays, as do all radioactive substances, at a fixed, unalterable rate. The rate is given as what is called a half-life, which means that half of any amount of the substance present will disintegrate in the determined number of years. The half-life of C-14 is 5568 years, and its rate of disintegration is 15.8 atoms per gram per minute.

C-14 is the most apt of materials for solving American archaeological dating problems because its half-life makes it useful up to 40,000 years, the span within which falls all the American archaeological material now known. Only one site, at Lewisville, Texas, has yielded material at that extremity. Lab techniques have been constantly refined until egregious-looking results are no longer challenged by archaeologists, but cause them to re-evaluate their hypotheses.

Nevertheless, C-14 dating rests on two assumptions, and one of these has been proved, through dendrochronology, to be wrong.

C-14 Discrepancy

The first assumption is that C-14 atoms are and always have been uniformly distributed throughout the terrestrial atmosphere. This is certainly true now, and there is no reason why it should not always have been true. But the assumption that the amount of C-14 in the atmosphere has always been at the same level as now is now known to be invalid. Cosmic ray activity, which created C-14 out of N-14, varies with the solar phenomenon known as sun spots. That activity has been less in the past than for the last 2200 years, it appears from the comparison of C-14 results with the dendrochronological annual count.

When the C-14 labs began to run their tests on wood of known dendrochronological age, their results were in agreement for about 2200 years into the past, basically to about the time of Christ. But in dates older than 2200 solar (calendar) years ago, a discrepancy developed: the C-14 dates were less than the calendar year dates; C-14 years were "longer" than solar years and hence the age of the material tested was greater than the test results. The discrepancy increased up to 6000 C-14 years ago, at which age it amounted to about 700 years, so that a test result of 6000 C-14 years meant a real age of about 6700 years. Several laboratories verified the discrepancy and, though the exact value of the discrepancy is a matter of argument between specialists, the order of value is agreed on.

This essential agreement was evident at the meeting of the Twelfth Nobel Symposium on Radiocarbon Variations and Absolute Chronology in 1970. Beginning in 1972 C-14 laboratories began to issue their results, with the correction factor. These corrections will, for the time being in all probability, be given for results only up to about 6500 C-14 years since the amount of the discrepancy has not yet been ascertained beyond that time. Eventually the discrepancy will probably be established up to 10,000 years. Some C-14 specialists believe C-14 results will return to equivalence with solar chronology between 10,000 and 12,000 years ago.

In the meantime the reading of ages obtained by C-14 tests for the time B.C. is in confusion. For twenty years all C-14 results were treated as though directly translatable into calendar dates. For about the first decade of C-14 use, laboratories issued dates B.P., so that the subtraction of the year of the test (say, 1960) from the result gave the calendar year, if the age was B.C., or more than 2000 years. The C-14 result was subtracted from the year of the test if the result were A.D., or less than 2000 years. But this proved unsatisfactory and in 1963 the practice was adopted of using 1950 as the base year.

Thus a C-14 result given as 5000 years B.P. meant 5000 years before 1950 or 3050 B.C.

By reason of the now demonstrated discrepancy, the 3050 B.C. of the above would actually be more nearly 3750 B.C. While all the C-14 dates for A.D. time published in the past twenty years are accurate, all the B.C. dates in the literature are not only inaccurate but their inaccuracy has a substantial effect on estimation of local sequences. Until a table of corrections for C-14 chronological results already published has been agreed on and published, the reporting in the literature will have to be done thus: 5000 C-14 years = 3050 B.C.; + correction factor of 700 years = 3750 B.C. The 3050 B.C. has to be part of the report in order to make possible comparison with previously published C-14 results.

A useful device for correcting C-14 results is the accompanying standard correlation chart. The C-14 dates are marked by lines slanting downward

CONVENTIONAL RADIOCARBON DATES

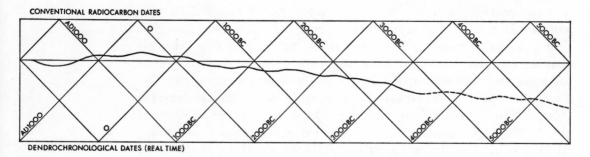

DENDROCHRONOLOGICAL DATES (REAL TIME)

CHART FOR CONVERTING C-14 DATES TO CALENDAR YEAR DATES

from the top of the chart, and the calendar year dates are marked by lines slanting upward from the bottom of the chart. To find the calendar year equivalent of a C-14 date, place a ruler or other straight edge on the chart parallel to the lines indicating the calendar year dates and intersecting the point at which the wiggly line, or calibration curve, crosses the line indicating the C-14 year. Then read the calendar year date at the point where the ruler intersects the bottom of the chart. This date will be the calendar year equivalent of the C-14 date.

Taking Samples

The field worker performs none of the tests by which absolute dating is done; he merely turns his samples over to a laboratory. But "merely" is, perhaps, not the accurate adverb; for he is solely responsible for the application of the result. He must be positive about what he is dating, that is, the association of the datable material and the cultural material. The laboratory is almost certain to provide a good test result. But if it gets into the literature as the date for the wrong cultural manifestation, it can only create archaeological mischief.

Likewise the field worker is responsible for the purity of his sample. Wherefore he collects it with care, not dropping ash, cookie crumbs, or soda on it while he is gathering it, and placing it in a clean container for keeping and/or shipping. The safest procedure to follow is to lift the sample out of the ground with a clean trowel, place it immediately on a fresh, unused sheet of aluminum foil, and fold the foil over it tightly before any pollen or bugs fall into it. This is not to say that laboratories do not thoroughly clean and treat a sample for such intrusions, but carelessness just may create an unsuspected contaminant that produces a result that is worse than useless. When the field worker suspects natural contamination that he cannot control (hair roots are one of these), he should inform the laboratory even though laboratories nowadays treat samples for most natural contaminants as a matter of routine.

Sample Submission

When submitting a sample for dating, it is a good idea to include cultural as well as provenience information about it including, when possible, a guess about the right order of result. This should not be considered an attempt to influence the result (it can't) but to establish a basis for inquiry as to why, if the date seems out of line. To avoid obtaining such a result, it is wise not to spend $160.00 on a C-14 test without having a pretty good idea about what you have been getting into. Although the author has never been asked for full provenience information on a sample, it is the practice of most laboratories to publish, from time to time, summaries of their results with a brief description of what is dated. At that time a certain modicum of information will be requested.

The question remains: where can samples be sent for dating? University laboratories are one possibility, but universities have been dropping their C-14 labs at an alarming rate because of cost and personnel problems and, probably, because of the competition from commercial labs, which provide dates in two or three months. University labs usually take a year or more; the cost is usually only about half that of a commercial lab, but the former are very selective about the samples they accept. You don't just mail a sample in, as with commercial labs.

Our experience with commercial labs has been entirely with Geochron Laboratories Inc., Blackstone Street, Cambridge, Massachusetts, where the test cost for the past several years has been $160 for the first test and $150 for from two to ten tests done within the same 24-month period. The service has been excellent and the results consistent. Geochron was one of the first labs to obtain good results from bone through using bone apatite CO_2, and bone is often the only datable material left on older sites. Charcoal is not completely dependable, since it may be exposed to contamination by percolating ground water carrying C-14 from decayed plants more recent than the charcoal. But the results afforded us by Geochron from both charcoal and oyster shell, a material we prefer because it is not porous or absorbent and the oyster is short-lived, have been in concordance, so far. Some researchers have been disappointed with labs because of what they considered unacceptable results; but, as implied above, unacceptable results may not be the lab's error.

Other laboratories to which samples may be submitted are Teledyne Isotopes, 50 Van Buren Avenue, Westwood, New Jersey 07675 and Radiocarbon Ltd., 4 Tice Court, Spring Valley, New York 10977.

Allowable "Error" in Dating

One final note on C-14 dating is in order. The results are given with a plus and minus "error," as in 5155 ± 120 C-14 years. This is not actual error, but an expression of probability; the chances are two out of three that the age of the tested specimen will fall within the two extremes of 5275 (plus 120) and 5035 (minus 120) years. This may seem rather loose compared with the year-by-year count of dendrochronology, but it is less inexact than it seems. The "error" can be reduced to twenty-five or even ten years by extending the counting time. It has been shown, however, that this extension, which is expensive, does not significantly alter the result. Few specimens will warrant the expense.

Dating by C-14 has provided the chronological structure of American prehistory as we now understand it. Dr. James Fitting of Case-Western Reserve University has called it "the grandaddy of scientific archaeology," commenting, "Rarely has a minor development in one field of study (nuclear physics) had such repercussions as the development of radiocarbon dating slightly over 20 years ago [this was written in 1972] has had on the study of archaeology."

chapter 9

Guidance for Classifying Artifacts

BECAUSE EACH CULTURAL area has its own characteristic artifacts, artifact styles, and sequence of artifacts and styles, an artifactual concordance for this book would have to be itself book-length. What is being presented here is a glossary only, a discursive annotation of the terms not already defined that are at once the vernacular of reading and speaking aboriginal archaeology and the designations of the found items that will have to be put down in excavation records.

ADZE

This is an ax-shaped tool of stone used in woodworking, usually plano-convex in section, that is, flat on one face and convex on the other. It may have been shaped by chipping but was more often manufactured by pecking out a rough blank and then grinding and polishing with a rubbing stone. An adze may have been hafted at the end, like a hoe or the modern "foot adze," or used like a plane for shaving layers of wood lengthwise. Most adzes were made from hard, igneous stone. Bone adzes made of the scapula or shoulder bone of large animals are known from the Plains. Not to be confused with celts or axes, adzes come in sizes from 1.5 to 8 inches or so in length.

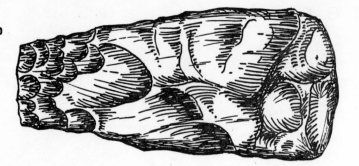

ADZE

ARROWHEAD

The first thing a student learns is not to call an arrowhead everything that looks to him like an arrowhead. The bow and fletched (feathered) arrow does not seem to have been used anywhere in the New World before 2000 B.P. The size-weight test for weapon points demonstrates that bows and fletched arrows could not have appeared east of the Mississippi Valley until after A.D. 1000. The ballistics of the arrow are such that only small, light points can be used on feathered shafts. Larger points can be used on unfeathered shafts, but the heavier the point the higher the trajectory that must be used to attain any distance with a shot; however, a higher trajectory lessens the accuracy and penetrative force. It is entirely possible, even likely, that the bow with unfletched shafts was in use for an indeterminate period, at least in the Southwest where the bow and arrow probably originated, before the invention of the fletched arrow. The bow and arrow should be a trait diffused into America from Asia—the buffalo-hunting Indians of the Plains used short, sinew-backed bows similar to eastern Asiatic models—but the trail between that part of aboriginal America where the bow and arrow appeared and that part of Asia where it was used has disappeared, if it ever existed. But size-weight in weapon tips is not the sole criterion. Many styles and traditions of weapon points

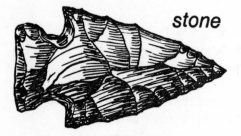
stone

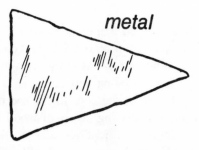
metal

ARROWHEADS

used during the Archaic, when the bow and arrow was almost positively not used, were small enough to have served as arrowpoints. Since the weight of the point also has to be in balance with the weight of the shaft, the diminutiveness of some Archaic points means that the material used for shafts must have been cane or reed rather than solid wood. Only those small weapon tips of stone, bone, or antler that occur in sites known to be of an age subsequent to the introduction of the feathered arrow shaft can be called arrowheads.

ATLATL

This is a length of shaped stick held at one end by the fingers and engaging the butt of a weapon shaft by a hook at the other end. The atlatl is an extension of the arm, and the shaft is cast by an overhand or sidearm throwing motion, with the atlatl being retained in the hand. The shafted projectile launched by an atlatl is called a dart. The simple dart is a single shaft, like a javelin or spear. The composite dart consists of two parts, the foreshaft of about arrow length and character which carries the point, and the back shaft, longer and of larger diameter than the foreshaft, into the forward end of which the foreshaft is inserted in a drilled hole. When the composite shaft is cast, if the weapon point strikes a target and penetrates it, the back shaft falls away. Perhaps as early as 7000 B.P. aboriginal hunters began to add weights to their atlatls, for

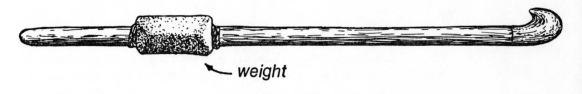

weight

ATLATL

reasons not yet clear to modern investigators and experimenters. Some think the weight gave added velocity and impact to the shaft and others think that it made the shaft more controllable and hence more accurate. Since the Aztecs used the atlatl as an army weapon, its efficiency is unquestionable. Australian aborigines used it with a long cane shaft to bring down kangaroos and wallabies at ranges up to seventy-five yards, according to report. They did not use atlatl weights, nor did the Eskimos who used the throwing stick for casting harpoons because it left one hand free for kayak maneuvering and other tasks. Atlatl weights were usually of stone, though shells were plated together to make weights in the stoneless lower Mississippi Valley. The weights were tied on, perhaps slipped into split sticks, or drilled and slipped on the throwing sticks. The drilled type is called a bannerstone (see below) from a misunderstanding about what these artifacts were when they were first discovered on aboriginal sites.

AWL

The awl was usually made of bone or antler (sometimes of stone), with the unaltered joint of a long bone being used as the handle. Some awls, however,

turkey bone

AWL

were set in wooden handles; you won't find the handle. Bone and antler points were rubbed to needle-point acuity.

AX

The identifying characteristic of an ax is its groove for hafting, which may be full or three-quarters of the circumference. Axes are usually bi-convex in section and are single-bit with the opposite end usually showing use as a hammer. The bit is fine-ground to a cutting edge. The material is usually a dense igneous rock, but sandstone, limestone, and softer rocks were used. There is no standard shape, weight, or dimensions; weights may range from 1 pound to 20 pounds. The blank for an ax was almost always shaped by pecking, with the final shaping done by grinding. Many specimens will still show pecking marks. A very few will be chipped stone, including flint.

BALL

Deliberately shaped stone balls of unknown usage are found in California in early, Archaic age cultures. In the East, particularly among the Iroquois, such balls were used as the heads of war clubs. Some may have been bola stones, some game stones, some ceremonial objects. They are made by pecking and polishing.

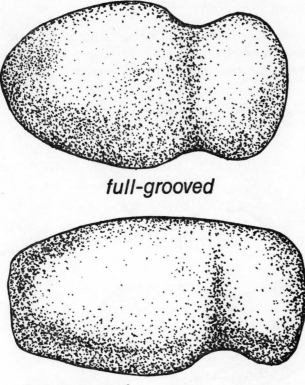

full-grooved

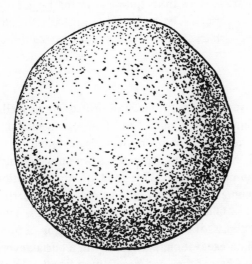

3/4-grooved

AX

BALL

BANNERSTONE

The bannerstone is the center-drilled variety of the atlatl weight (see above). The forms are innumerable; some are barrel-shaped, some prismoidal, some cubes. But by far the most common form is bipennate or winged, the wings

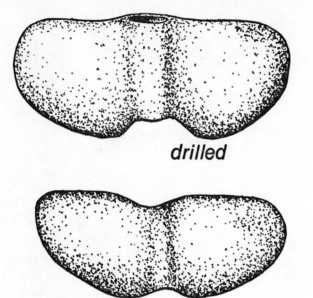

drilled

BANNERSTONES

grooved

being of all geometric shapes from spherical to the long, pointed ones of the so-called whale tail variety. The materials are usually the stones most easily worked by grinding—slate, steatite, fireclay, siltstone, catlinite, etc.

BEADS

Aboriginal beads were most often made of drilled whole shells, parts of shells (as in wampum), animal teeth and claws, stone, compacted or indurated natural clay, ceramics, and native copper. Glass beads found on Indian sites were trade goods. Beads were worn as necklaces, sewn onto clothing, and made into such items as wampum "belts." This kind of ornamentation is at least as old as the Paleo-hunter in America, and as old as Neanderthal Man's Mousterian culture in the Old World. The Hopewell and the later Mississippian peoples used the pearls of the freshwater mussel for beading. When beads begin to appear in an excavation, particularly in a burial, every effort must be made to determine whether they had been strung together in a necklace or had been sewn to cloth or leather.

stone

shell

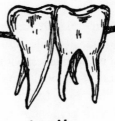

teeth

claws

clay

BEADS

BIRDSTONE

The birdstone is a sometimes nearly realistic, sometimes very stylized effigy of a sitting or nesting bird. No really plausible explanation for them has ever been advanced, but because some of them are drilled lengthwise, they have been conjectured to be atlatl weights. They seem to belong to the Midwest Adena culture, and were made by polishing.

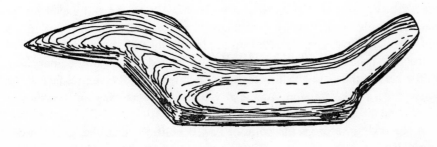

BIRDSTONE

BLADE

The word "blade" has several meanings in prehistoric American archaeology. Bifacial blades are lanceolate, ovate, or triangular pieces thinned by flaking on both sides, with knifelike edges. Most of them are knives or knife-scrapers but many, the so-called cache blades, are blanks or preforms and have never been used. Bifacial blades, often quite beautiful ones, were included as grave offerings in some cultures; they may be designated mortuary or ceremonial blades.

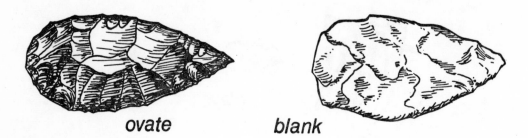

ovate   blank

BLADES

The unifacial blade, sometimes called a lamellar flake or blade or the prismatic flake or blade, is a long, slender, parallel-sided flake struck off a specially prepared stone core. It looks like a table-knife blade in shape, though few are likely to be found in the Western Hemisphere as big as a table knife. In Europe these blades occur in specimens up to 12 inches long that look like bayonets. These are classified as macroblades. Microblades are limited to about 1½ inches in length and about .3 inch in width. While unifacial blades are the best of knives in themselves, they are, in some tool-making traditions, further shaped into drills, scrapers, perforators, etc. The microblade traditions occur in Alaska and along the Arctic Circle to Greenland from about 6000 to 2000 B.P., in the Mississippi Valley from about 3500 B.P. to, perhaps, A.D. 1000, in the Hopewell culture sphere from about 200 B.C. to A.D. 400, and in Mexico during the ceramic period up to historic times. Adventitious unifacial blades that are only descriptively "prismatic" or "lamellar," and not in a unifacial blade tradition, will turn up at almost any site; the mark of the true microblade tradition is the core especially prepared for striking or punching off the blades, the distinguishing features of which are a flat ventral face and a dorsal face ridge. Random unifacial blades not occurring in specifically microblade traditions are best called strip blades.

The body of a projectile point or hafted knife is called the blade, in the terminology of its parts, with the other principal parts being the haft or tang; it is also proper to speak of the blade of an ax, adze, celt, or hoe.

Flint Core and Flake

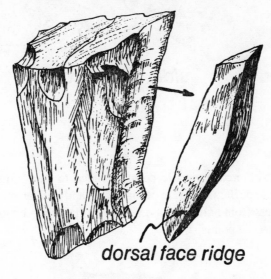

dorsal face ridge

SPECIALLY PREPARED CORE AND MICROBLADE

Other types of blades are side blades and backed blades. Side blades are sometimes bifacial, sometimes unifacial pieces of worked stone approximately the shape of a right triangle which are slotted into the end of a weapon, the perpendicular side being placed in the slot. When side blades are paired on opposite sides of the end of a shaft and a small triangle of stone is inserted in the end, the result is a three-part projectile point. Side blades are recognized only in certain Arctic cultures. The backed blade is not a recognized American aboriginal tool at the moment. It is a prismatic blade of which one longitudinal edge has been snapped off or otherwise blunted to support the finger. Backed blades may also be used in slotted handles; Old World sickles were made of series of backed blades inserted in handles. The kinds of tools and tool categories that have had to be designated blades testifies less to the poverty of the English language than to the lack of imagination and verbal dexterity in archaeologists.

BOATSTONE

Like the birdstone this is an enigmatic artifact thought by some to be an atlatl weight. It is shaped like a canoe, or narrow bowl, being hollowed out in the center. Amerinds ground it into shape. Its occurrence is mainly in the Mississippi Valley.

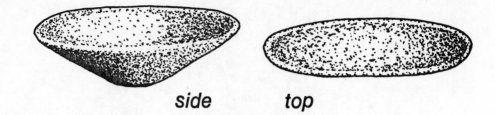

side   top

BOATSTONE

BUNT

A bunt is a blunted projectile point intended to stun rather than to inflict a bleeding wound. Bunts are rare occurrences, and it is sometimes difficult to distinguish bunts from hafted scrapers since both seem to be tools reworked from broken projectile points.

BUNT

BURIN

The burin is an engraving or scoring tool, almost always of flint, that can all too easily be mistaken for a broken blade or chip. It is actually a tiny chisel point made by breaking a thin blade or flake perhaps 1 centimeter thick or less, leaving an incising end; as a matter of fact, those who have not seen one may best picture a burin as a kind of single-toothed implement. Burins are most used in industries that emphasize bone and antler tools.

BURIN

CELT

The celt is another hafted axlike implement shaped by polishing. It is what is ordinarily thought of as a tomahawk head. The bit is broad and slightly convex and usually the blade narrows toward the after end. The celt is not grooved for hafting, and there is ethnographic evidence that celts were actually placed into

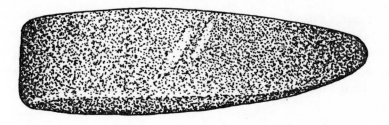

CELT

split saplings which grew around them, to become handles. They are of dense, polishable stone and are, on the average, as handsome tools as American aborigines produced. They were used as tomahawk heads, but this may have been an adaptation of a tool originally used for woodcutting and woodworking.

CHARMSTONE

This artifact is found in several varieties on the West Coast. It is long and cylindrical, of ground stone, with scoring that gives many specimens a phallic look.

CHARMSTONE

CHISEL

Stone artifacts that appear to be chisels, resembling the cold chisel, with chipped or ground bits are occasionally found. They are probably woodworking tools, used as narrow-bladed adzes, as well as to shape softer stones like steatite. Steatite vessels often show the marks of the chisels with which they were hewn.

CHISEL

CHOPPER

The chopper is a hand ax, a tool of some bulk and weight with an axlike cutting edge. It was held in the hand and used for hacking, hewing, splitting, disjointing and, possibly, grubbing and digging. In archaeology a typological distinction is made between hand axes on the one hand and choppers and chopping tools on the other hand that is of fundamental importance in the Old World lower and

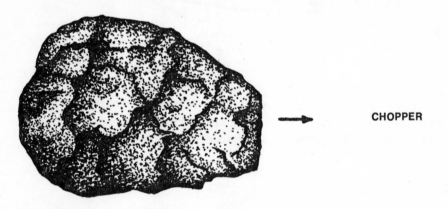

CHOPPER

middle Paleolithic. In those times, from about 750,000 to 40,000 B.P., hand axes of the Abbevillian-Chellean-Acheulean-Mousterian tradition were a universal tool all over Africa, Europe, and Asia to about mid-India. East of mid-India is the region of the chopper and chopping tool tradition, from which the Western Hemisphere received this basic tool tradition. True hand axes are bifacially formed tools, generally almond-shaped, with the cutting edges on the side and the point serving rather like a pick. The chopper is, typologically, a pebble or a single large spall knocked off a pebble or block of stone with a few chips taken out of the working end to edge it up; since this is the only touching up done, the chopper cannot be said to be even unifacial. The chopping tool is unifacial or bifacial. The choppers and chopping tools have broad straight or convex, axlike cutting edges, but there is a type of American chopper with the cutting edge along one side, a kind of slitter. The distinction between choppers and chopping tools is of no consequence in American archaeology and both are called simply choppers. Nor is a distinction made between choppers and hand axes because, though there are many American artifacts that are hand ax-like descriptively, the hand ax tradition per se never reached America, according to prevailing dogma. The pebble chopper was the first tool made by man, perhaps 2 million years ago, with the exception of simple flakes used as tools for cutting; the latter were made all over the New World throughout its stone age, which lasted in some places until 1900. In America the pebble chopper is not always easy to separate from the teshoa, to be described later.

COG STONE

This artifact of unknown usage is found only in southern California and dates from about 8000 to 5500 B.P. It is a stone disc of six inches or less in diameter with vertical grooves around the perimeter and a hole in the center that gives it the appearance of a cogwheel. Archaeologists have no clues to its usage but

front   *side*

COG STONE

it may have been a mace head. Its rarity also suggests that it may have been a ceremonial or cult object. There is a vague possibility it may have been an atlatl weight. Not many citizen archaeologists are likely to find a cog stone, and if one is found outside southern California, something new will have been added to our knowledge.

CORE

Some attention has already been given to cores. Any pebble or block of stone from which chips have been struck is a core. It will be one of two kinds: (1) a preform core, which is in the preliminary stages of manufacture into a tool, or (2) a parent core from which the flakes removed are to be chipped into tools. The specially prepared cores for the removal of lamellar or prismatic blades

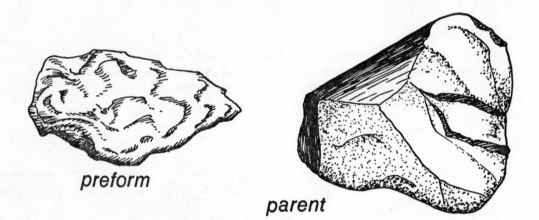

preform

parent

CORE

are the most important of this parent core category, but they are by no means the only kind. All cores from excavation should be retained as semi-artifacts, for study of the chipping planes. In many cases it will be discovered that cores have been converted to use as knives, choppers and scrapers and so are artifacts secondarily.

CRESCENT

The crescent derives its name from its concave-convex shape, which is quarter-moon or butterflylike. Almost always of good material such as flint or jasper and well made, it ranges from about 1.5 to 3 inches in length. It has a

CRESCENT

wide distribution in the Far West, from Nevada to the coast and from Oregon to southern California. Provenience data associate it with an early horizon of big-game hunters but not the Clovis fluted point people. Some investigators have referred to crescentic forms as amulets; and polished or pecked specimens, without sharp edges, sometimes called Stockton curves, are said to have been used in puberty rites. But early crescents are knife-edged and almost certainly were tools. Crooked knives that are more like a dog's leg in shape than crescentic appear occasionally in eastern sites, but they have not been studied as a type and are not known to be related to crescents.

DISCOIDALS

Discs of several varieties are found archaeologically throughout the Western Hemisphere. It would be too lengthy a job here to describe them all or to discuss their uses, putative and known. Suffice it to say they can turn up in excavations of remains dating from about the Middle Archaic onward to historic times, when discoidals were used by the Cherokees in the game of chunkey. The discoidals found in the Lower Hudson are perfectly round, with convex faces, about one inch thick. Whether it means anything or not, in the half-dozen we have recovered each has a single chip out of one face. Since these specimens have been pecked into circularity, it may be that the workmen misjudged and pecked too hard and drove off a flake. But would this happen every time? Our discoidals vary from two to four inches in diameter and have been called manos (hand grinding stones) by some students, but the identifica-

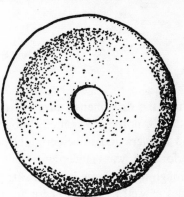
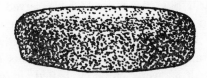

DISCOIDALS

tion seems doubtful since less formally and laboriously shaped manos occur in the same associations. In different eras discoidals take other forms, being concave instead of convex, and hollowed out or holed like doughnuts. One is tempted to think of some of the finer discs as ceremonial objects in some ritual intended to ensure good annual harvests of acorns and grain seeds. They seem to have been made of carefully selected pebbles when these were available.

DRILLS

Drills appear earlier than drilled holes in stone, and they must first have been used on wood; but there is a difference between a wood drill and a stone drill. Wood drills have sharp points as do wood auger bits, to make the penetration which the shaft later enlarges. But a sharp tip would be of no use in a stone drill, which does not do the cutting. This is done by abrasive sand grains

for wood   *for stone*

DRILLS

which the drill merely turns in the holes; wherefore used stone drills have rounded, not sharp points. Probably many so-called drills are really gimlets and reamers and some certainly performed a function like a keyhole saw: a perforation was made and the "drill" was then moved back and forth through it to enlarge it into a slit; holes of any shape could be cut this way, in hides as well as wood. There are tools that have been called drills which are certainly knifeblades reduced by chipping, perhaps in resharpening, until they became as narrow as drill bits; these would have served very handily as keyhole saws. There is no standard size for drills. There are tiny ones an inch long with bits hardly thicker than an old-fashioned pencil lead and used for wampum bead drilling, and six-inch-long drills with bits as thick as old-fashioned pencils. Most drills were probably hafted, in wooden or bone handles, but they need not have been for almost all have broad bases that could be turned with the fingers, like a key on a wind-up toy. The bases are often the same as those of the projectile point made by the same culture, suggesting that they probably began existence as projectile points and, after several resharpenings, became drills. This also suggests that they were used on shafts that were rotated between the hands. When the material to be drilled was thicker than the drill was long, holes were started from either side, to meet in the middle; they didn't always meet, exactly, just as they don't for you and me. Curiously, the drill is much more common in American than in Old World stone cultures. It was almost certainly invented independently by American aborigines.

EAR SPOOLS AND PLUGS

The Hopewellians seem to have been the earliest aborigines north of Mexico to make holes in their ears for the insertion of ornaments. The trait was probably diffused from Mexico by some unknown intermediary. Probably the most famous single artifact ever found in America, the so-called Adena pipe, has as its bowl the effigy of a little man very shortened and gnarled of leg, probably representing a dwarf, who wears ear spools. Though the pipe was found in an Adena culture mound, more than one student privately considers the pipe Hopewellian. The Knight statuettes from a Hopewell mound show both men and women wearing ear spools. The Hopewellian ear spools are of copper or

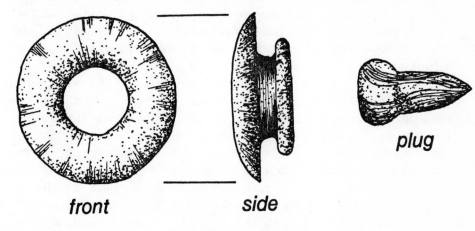

front   *side*   *plug*

EAR SPOOL AND PLUG

copper over wood. The trait appears in post-Hopewell sites in the South, and in the later Mississippian. Ear plugs of copper, shell, and stone look like thick, round-headed carpet tacks. They are found mainly in Mississippian period contexts.

EFFIGIES

This heading is a catch-all for figurines, fetishes, amulets, cult objects, and fakes. There has been a great deal of fakery in artifacts that fall into these classes and about the only way to be sure that artifacts that appear to be representational of man, beast, or bird or symbolic are not fakes is to dig them yourself. And even that isn't always safe. The so-called Bunola head is a case in point. It is a 98-pound sandstone boulder on which had been incised the face of a man with a beard and wearing a cap. The artists were two colleagues of an archaeologist working the Bunola site near Elizabeth, Pennsylvania about 1920, and the purpose was to hoax the expert. But the expert was not hoaxed. He kicked the thing aside and left it lying. In 1955, thirty-five years later, an unsuspecting fourth party, clearing a path to a dock on the banks of the Monongahela, came on the head and quite naturally reported it to some archaeological friends. For the next few years it was passed from hand to hand among art historians and archaeological specialists, gaining notoriety every time one of them had to shake his head in puzzlement. It was Colonial, it was proof that Norsemen had trekked into Pennsylvania, it was whatever imagination wanted it to be. Eventually it reached the ears of a Pittsburgh reporter who on October 25, 1959, wrote a story about it. Among those who saw the story was one of the original artists who immediately got in touch with Dr. James Swauger of Carnegie Museum and related the whole tale of the practical joke that had taken thirty-five years to fool anybody. Had the two artists died in that long interim, or moved out of the area, the Bunola head would still be an archaeological enigma. But hundreds, perhaps thousands of fakes, forgeries, counterfeits, and bogus items are still in circulation and will not be confessed to because they were made by counterfeiters and forgers to begin with. Of all pieces to be suspicious of, effigies are foremost.

A good fake will fool the experts more often than they like to think. But little harm is done except to the purses of those who pay exorbitant prices for the bogus; one more Hopewell bird effigy pipe will not cause Hopewellian theory to be rewritten. But objects outside known styles and contexts are something else. American prehistory during the Archaic and even through the early Woodland is desperately poor in the amulets, fetishes, clan and cult symbols that we feel must have been the basis for the recognizable traditions of later cultures. Amulets are charms worn to ward off evil and bring good luck; fetishes are objects believed to have or exert powers by reason of their materials of manufacture or their shape or through thaumaturgic incantation. The distinction may not have been as clear in the aboriginal mind as in the minds of the compilers of dictionaries.

At Croton Point, in the lower Hudson territory, there is a clay formation within which water action long ago produced strange little forms called "clay babies." School classes make visits to the clay banks every year and bring home the "cute" ones. Fancy can see many anthropomorphic, zoomorphic or, perhaps, mystic shapes in those smooth little compacted clay nodules. We find them occasionally in our shell midden sites miles from Croton Point, from which they must have been deliberately transported. Who can divine what was the world of the supernatural evoked when an aborigine came upon one of these little images on the beach, washed out of the bank? Did he think of it as of an ancient race and time of fairies or "little people"? Since these "clay babies" were carried away, we must assume they were not regarded as evil and to find one must have been regarded as good luck. Amulet or fetish? Or both? That strangely shaped stones and other naturally occurring objects would have been picked up when encountered by chance, as omens, tokens, talismans, "medicine," is implicit in the example of the "clay babies." There are authenticated instances of the addition of a touch of line or dot to a natural object, usually a stone, to accentuate a resemblance to an animal or human being; and probably there is many another instance in which the resemblance was sufficient in the eye of one beholder if no others. There is no design, art style, rhyme or reason to this kind of value-seeing because it is private and adventitious; somebody chanced upon an object which had superstitious or "medicine" meaning at that moment. The excavator looks for these things but is not too gullible about accepting them.

metal

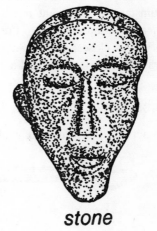

stone

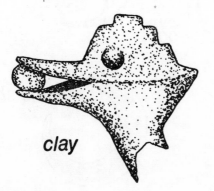

clay

EFFIGIES

The term "effigy" is meant to cover such objects as are representational and recognizable to some degree to the excavator as well as to the people who made them. The "clay babies" are not effigies; a natural stone with a dot for an eye in the right place, to give it the appearance of a bird, animal, or human being, might be. Archaeologists class as effigies any imagistic executions, such as pipes whose bowls are done in anthropomorphic and zoomorphic forms or are decorated with faces, etc.; pestles, whose ends have been carved into bear heads and other animals; and combs whose handles have bird or other such representations. There are also effigy pots, flints, beads, figurines, and statuettes. Though much of this is art, the archaeological classification—American archaeology is almost Philistine in its avoidance of artistic appreciation—is based on intention, and the intention of most effigies seems to have been clan, cult, ceremonial, or mystic invocation. Realistic animal representations are probably clan symbols and fetishes; more fanciful figures and motifs, such as the Weeping Eye and Long-nosed God, double-headed serpents, and the like are icons from cultural myths or cult mysteries.

Effigy flints attract the faker, since the flintsmith practiced in pressure flaking—which can be done with a common nail—can execute amazing designs. But fakes and counterfeits should not be of any concern to the digging citizen archaeologist whose collections are assembled only from his digging, not from commerce in artifacts. Needless to say, no archaeologist would, under any circumstances, mix what has been dug with what has been acquired by other means. Because they are the rarest of archaeological finds and the ones that bring us closest to the Amerind "soul," effigies demand the taking of extraordinary care in regard to their provenience.

FISHHOOK

Amerinds made quite conventional-looking fishhooks for angling.

bone

haliotis shell

FISHHOOKS

GORGE

The gorge is a fishing implement, usually constructed of a pair of sharpened bone splinters or pins tied at the end of a line which acts as both a lure and a hook. The gorge is easy for an unfortunate fish to swallow, since the pins go down like a worm, but once inside the mouth they open up, when the line is pulled, into an anchor-shaped double hook. But there is another class of implement which, it has been suggested for lack of other plausible usage, is also a gorge. It is the polished stone plummet, shaped like a carpenter's or surveyor's plumb bob. Some of these are quite large and they could not have been

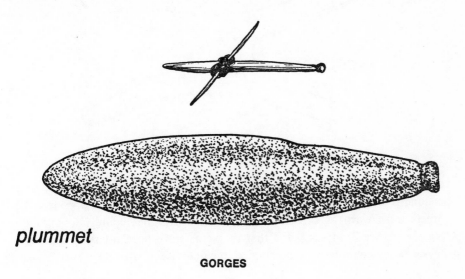

plummet

GORGES

swallowed by anything but trophy-sized fish, but there were trophy-sized fish in those days. Plummets are grooved or have a little turret-top for line suspension. They are shaped like long radishes or beets and are smooth and rounded of surface, hardly the kind of gorge that it would seem a fish could not disgorge; yet they hardly seem designed as pendants and nothing we know of Amerinds shows them to have needed plumb lines. Plummets are most likely to be found in late Archaic sites of the Northeast, but they also occur in the late Archaic of the lower Mississippi Valley and in the Northwest.

GORGET

The gorget has no relation to the gorge. It is a stone ornament or insignia of rank or authority worn at the breast by suspension from the neck. It is usually rectangular or subrectangular, flat, and two-holed so that it will hang with the length horizontal. When there is only one hole, so that the length would hang

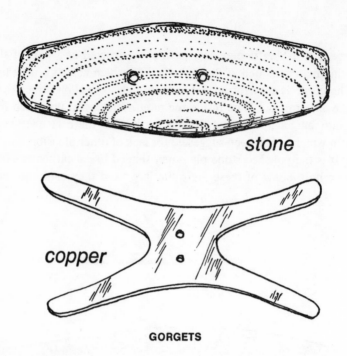

GORGETS

vertically, gorgetlike artifacts are called pendants. The material is usually slate or stone relatively easy to polish and drill. That all items that appear to be gorgets were worn as breast badges or ornaments has come into question recently. It has been suggested that they may have been atlatl weights, and they certainly could have so functioned, the holes being used for tie-on thongs.

GOUGE

The polished stone gouge, presumably a wood-working chisel, has a limited distribution and occurs most frequently in the middle Archaic of the Northeast, in association with plummets. It is a long, tapered, semicylindrical implement with a broad groove or hollow at the U-shaped, scooplike working end.

GOUGE

HARPOON

Strictly speaking, the harpoon head is a projectile point. It is usually regarded as a specialized fish spearing implement. Made of bone or antler with multiple and often elongated barbs, it may or may not have a hole in the base for the line that enables the caster to play the fish or animal after the head has been set.

HARPOONS

HOE

The hoe varies considerably in execution and may be of well-chipped stone or a piece of naturally flat stone with the edge chipped or ground or even scarcely altered stone, but can be separated from choppers and other axlike implements by the "shine" imparted by digging. Probably some hoes were root-grubbers, but differences in usage can hardly be detected by the shine. Also, it takes a while for a stone implement to acquire a polish from use. As field tools, hoes are likely to occur as single, isolated finds.

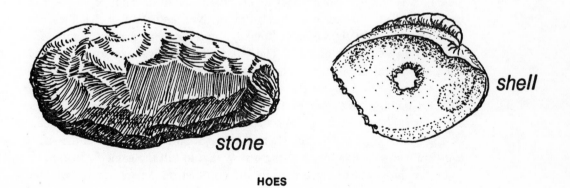

stone

shell

HOES

GRAVER

The graver is usually a short, sharp spur on a flake or on another tool, commonly a scraper. Perhaps gravers were used for perforating thin material such as hides and leather. Paleo-hunter scrapers often have graver tips at their corners, sometimes two or three. The interesting suggestion has been made that they were scarifiers used in tattooing. But I have seen demonstrations of leather-cutting in which these tiny tips sliced through leather like razors. As with so many Amerind tools that appear to be simple and single in purpose, gravers are probably misnamed and misunderstood, with different uses in different eras and areas.

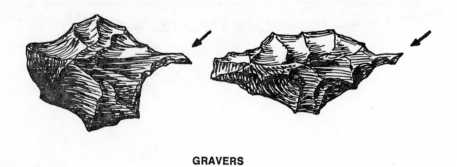

GRAVERS

KNIFE

There is little than can be added to what has already been said about knives. The simplest flake is a good knife. In an experiment conducted by archaeologist Fred Kinsey of Franklin and Marshall College, the carcass of a raccoon was completely butchered with a single flint flake about one square inch in size without any damage to the edge at all. The report is that its one disadvantage was that it became very slippery. Prismatic or lamellar blades, as has been explained, are specially struck flake knives, and the fact that they are often found without signs of edge breakage does not mean they were not used; it means they were not misused. The bifacial blade knives are not as good as flake knives but are better for heavy work, such as stabbing. Either bifacial knives were often made in the form of projectile points or projectile points had an auxiliary use as knives; they frequently show evidence of edge use as knives and repeated resharpening. A projectile point on a short handle instead of a projectile shaft is a knife. There is ethnographic evidence from the African Bushmen that the points of the arrow used to kill the game were used to make the throat cut to bleed the kill and do other on-the-spot incisions. The two uses go hand in hand when a hunter is traveling light.

A form of knife that might puzzle the novice, but only once, is the ulu or ulo, the so-called Eskimo woman's knife, but known in the Northeast as the semilunar knife because of its half-moon shape. The ulu, made of metal, is still used by the Eskimo. The Amerind semilunar knife is of ground slate and usually has a ridge for a handle across the diameter. The cutting edge is on the curved side, and it is ground sharp. The semilunar knife belongs culturally with plummets and gouges, though it is of wider distribution and it outlasted them.

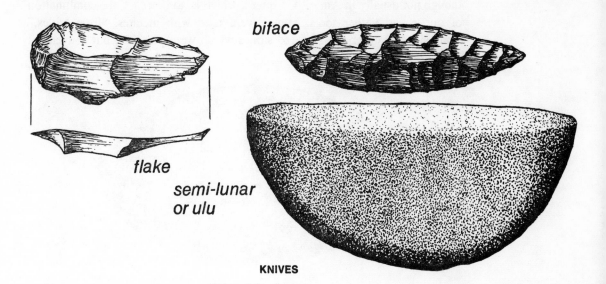

biface

flake

semi-lunar or ulu

KNIVES

A knife that the student is more likely to run into in his reading than on a site, unless that site is western Paleo-hunter, is the Cody knife. It is another of the crooked or bent-bladed knives, a square-based blade with the cutting edge at a 45-degree angle across the vertical axis of the blade.

The student, after he becomes knowledgeable about an area, will be able to recognize its indigenous forms of the knife, the tool that has to be present in one variety or another wherever general living activities took place.

CODY KNIFE

MANO

The word itself is Spanish for hand, and the best definition is that a mano is the stone held in the hand in milling or grinding against another stone or other surface. It is, therefore, called a grinding stone or a muller and sometimes, though not usually in America, a quern, which is, to be exact, the combination of upper and nether tools. Manos were used with metates, "little tables," stone slabs or other flat-surfaced stones which were portable; but convenient

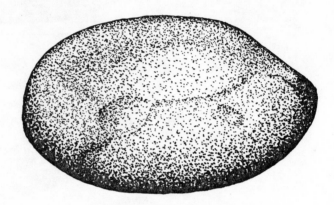

WELL-USED MANO

outcrops of bedrock were often used as the nether stone of the mill. In the lower Hudson large metates are most often large cobbles. If pebbles were to be had, a suitably sized pebble was selected and evidently became a valued implement, since manos are often found with one or both faces reduced to flatness by wear; well-used manos look rather like oblate bars of soap. Most of those found in the lower Hudson are obviously not one-use implements. They show hammerstone development at one or both ends and sometimes on the sides, so that the side indentations give them a "waisted" look. It is likely that these manos were nut-cracking as well as nutmeat- and seed-grinding stones and were used in processes beyond our suppositions.

MORTAR

The mortar and pestle are, like the mano and metate, the two parts of a grinding mill. Mortars and pestles of stone are far from uncommon, the mortars often being deep concavities in bedrock and just as often large cobbles dished out by wear, but it is probable that even more were made of wood, the mortars being hollowed out logs and the pestles baseball bat-like lengths of tree branch or sapling. Some stone pestles are merely cylindrical pebbles and

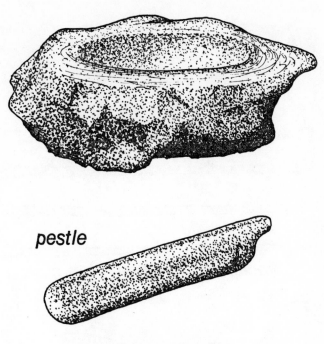

pestle

MORTAR AND PESTLE

others are almost as exactly rounded and sized as a section of steel pipe. The stone mortars and pestles were prized implements, the pestles sometimes being effigy-decorated; and the author has seen a boulder mortar ten inches thick worn down to a hole in the bottom. Few mortars are still lying around awaiting discovery; large, unwieldy, and not portable, they were found on the surface by the settlers who first cleared the fields and who treated them with very little respect. You are as likely to find a stone mortar in a masonry dry-stone field wall as on a site.

PIPE

The Amerind smoking pipe probably had its origin in the shaman's "sucking tube," usually a bird bone, which is naturally hollow, through which evil spirits causing illness were "sucked" out of the patient by the medicine man. The first pipes used in smoking were hollow, cigar-shaped tubes of stone. The blocked-end tube pipe, a hollowed-out tube of stone or fire clay with the distal end closed except for a perforation, which seems to have been contemporary with the tubular pipe, could hardly have been a smoking pipe and must have been medicine equipment. As smoking caught on culturally, the elbow pipe came into favor, first with the bowl at an obtuse angle to the stem and then with the bowl-stem angle sharpening to a right angle as in most mod-

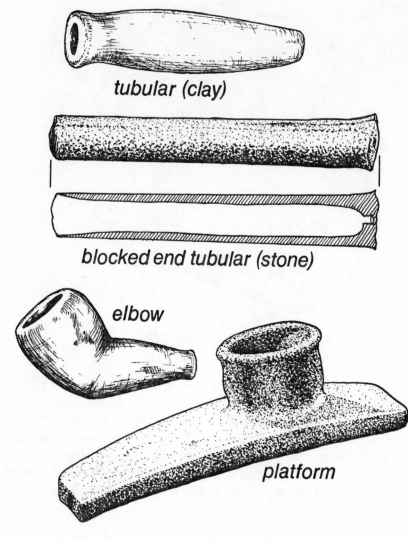

tubular (clay)

blocked end tubular (stone)

elbow

platform

PIPES

ern smoking pipes. The first pipes were of stone, and stone pipes continued to be made up to the time of white contact; the public generally seems to believe they were the only type made. But ceramic pipes appeared in the East as early as about A.D. 700, and pipe-makers took full advantage of the plasticity of baked clay to model an astonishing variety of shapes, all of those in which stone pipes were made, including effigies, and to incorporate decorations. Stone pipes are, perhaps, deservedly more highly thought of. Many are sculptures of artistic merit. The platform pipe is a pipe bowl, often an effigy, set on a thin, broad base; the stem must have been an inserted hollow reed, for the platform is almost never long enough to have been used as a mouthpiece. The excavator will have no trouble recognizing pipes on his site except, possibly, for fragments of straight or blocked-end tubes.

POTTERY

Because of the innumerable variations—all of which have cultural significance—in shape, size, decoration, finish, tempering, and method of manufacture—ceramic pottery is the most nearly inexhaustible subtopic in American archaeology even though its use spans no more, probably, than a tenth of the duration of American prehistory. The three basic methods of manufacture were modeling, molding, and coil-winding; the pottery wheel was not known in aboriginal America. A modeled vessel was made simply by shaping a lump of plastic clay. The molded vessel was made by shaping it to a mold, usually a basket. In the coil-winding method the vessel was built up by laying thin fillets of clay on top of each other, like the coils of a rope. Modeling was probably the first method used, coil-winding the most widely used; in both, the clay was further processed and the vessel shaped by thwacking the outside of the vessel with a stick or paddle while an anvil of stone or wood was held inside the vessel where it was being thwacked. In coil-winding the stick or paddle was usually wrapped with twined cord, and the impact of this corrugated surface on the surface of the pot seems to have been very effective in bonding the coils together. The practice continued even when the decorative, or at least patterned, design of cord marking ceased to please, and began to be smoothed or buffed out.

Probably the earliest ceramics had no aplastic, that is, tempering material, in their clay at all except by chance. Not much of that type is likely to be found; it deteriorates too rapidly. It is sometimes called clay-tempered, but clay-tempered pottery is actually that in which the aplastic is fragments of previously fired clay. This kind of temper performed well enough the function of tempering, which is to induce into the plastic clay hard, nonshrinking material to which the clay can cling and which prevents shrinkage to the point of cracking.

The first pottery known in the United States has been found in Florida; it was tempered with grass or other vegetal fibers, which usually burned in the firing. In the Southeast ceramic pottery preceded the use of soapstone, which is the reverse of the sequence in the Northeast, where steatite vessels were used for several centuries before ceramics. It seems thus to have come about that steatite grits began to be used as tempering material. In the Northeast the first pottery and the pottery of several subsequent stages was tempered with grits of other kinds of crushed stone, which made for quite thick walls, and heavy, clumsy, easily broken vessels. It was not until fine sand came into use for tempering that thin-walled vessels could be made. In the Midwest crushed shell is an early tempering material; in the East it is late. Tempering material has chronological meaning to the student who knows the pottery of his area.

Surface treatment is not to be confused with decoration. Cord-marking is a surface treatment, and so is net-impressing, fabric-impressing, brushing, and stippling. Net impressions and fabric impressions may have been acquired during a step in manufacture; the pots, while still plastic, may have been held in bags of netting or fabric for a final shaping. Brushing, with the frayed ends of twigs or switches of stiff fibers, and stippling, produced in some unknown way, bring nothing so plausible to mind.

Something has already been said about the decorative techniques of punctating, incising, and dentate stamping. In the Northeast the use of these techniques was stiff, reiterative, and unimaginative. In the Midwest incising in large, free curvilinear motifs characterized Hopewell pottery of what is thought to be ceremonial vessels, as distinguished from utilitarian vessels. In the South complicated stamping of designs like the filfot cross and checking follows what seems to have been the diffusion of Hopewellian influence, although Hopewell was by no means the only inspiration. Painted and slipped pottery, the slips being used for design effects, are endemic to the Southwest. Pottery is scant and very late in California, and was not made in the Pacific Northwest—curious in view of the fact that it is about 3000 years old in Alaska—or in the Northern Plains and much of the buffalo-hunting Plains Indian territory.

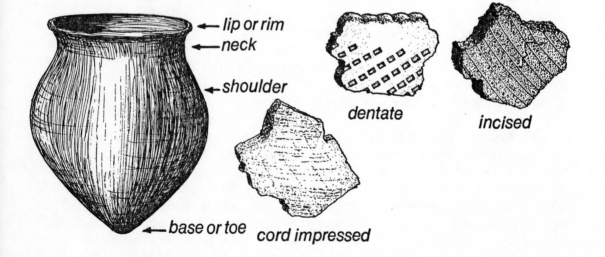

POTTERY

No authority knows everything there is to know about Amerind pottery; the experts claim no more than regional knowledge and even the regions are, in the areas of proliferated traditions, hardly more than state-wide.

POVERTY POINT OBJECTS

The "objects" were pieces of baked clay, used, as previously noted, as stones for boiling water; and Poverty Point, named for a site in Louisiana, is the culture in which these objects appeared in such numbers that they had to be given a place on trait lists and in the literature of artifacts. It has been calculated that they were made by the millions in the stoneless Mississippi Valley and originated with the late Archaic Poverty Point people before the transition from boiling with stones to ceramic pots. It must have been an easy transition because Poverty Point objects are ceramic. They have been sorted into several varieties, most of which are roughly spherical in shape. The

POVERTY POINT OBJECTS

varieties must have some kind of validity since the same varieties occur on widely separated Poverty Point sites. Baked clay objects occur in California in the alluvial delta of the San Joaquin and Sacramento rivers, where there is an abundance of clay and an absence of stone, as in the alluvial Mississippi Valley. But they also occur a continent's width away, at Sapelo Island off the Georgia coast. Where they occur they occur in such numbers, whole or in fragments, as to corroborate their common, everyday use. But why such use would cause standardizations in such a diversity of shapes beyond a generalized sphericity remains enigmatic.

PREFORM

Strictly speaking, all stages of worked stone between the unworked block or pebble and the completed artifact are preforms: cores (except for those used as parent material for flakes and flake blades), quarry blanks, and cache blades. Most often what is meant is the form just preceding the finishing details, notches, stemming, fluting, etc. It will be apparent to anybody who gives the matter a second's thought that all broad-bladed artifacts have to pass through a stage in manufacture in which the core is reduced to relative thinness and that in this stage it must have a relatively symmetrical shape— triangular, ovoid, or lanceolate. In this final stage and shape, the preform is a usable tool, and one sometimes wonders why Amerinds ever elaborated on it

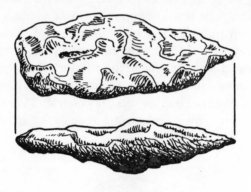

PREFORM

in the production of projectile points and knives. Curiosity, the human urge to experiment, and the desire to "show off" or try one's skill to its limits, must have been the stimulants. These qualities do not leave data behind.

For a discussion of the methods used in working preforms, see Chapter 4.

The word "preform" is just coming into use and is not found in the literature before about 1965. Although it is more categorical, it is no particular improvement on "core" and "blank" to the ear.

PROJECTILE POINT

Used alone, this phrase almost always means chipped stone weapon heads. These date from as early as 15,000 B.P., and the evidence strongly points to a wholly autochthonous development of chipped stone projectile points in the Western Hemisphere south of Alaska.

The plane form shapes of stone projectile points fall into a few simple classes: stemmed, side-notched, corner-notched, basally notched (rare), and the shankless or haftless, plain blades of lanceolate, ovoid, or triangular shape. Within these classes there are perhaps 100 combinations of variations in features, dimensions, and total configuration of attributes that include workmanship, material preference, and edge treatment. Since a few points with

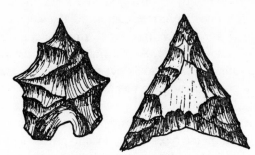

basally-notched

shankless

antler

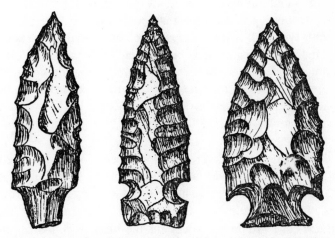

stemmed side-notched corner-notched

PROJECTILE POINTS

fluted faces have been found in California, the only type that may be said to have nationwide distribution is the Paleo-hunter fluted point of generalized Clovis lanceolate outline. Other types, somewhat more specific, have regional distribution, such as the Kirk and LeCroy points found from Alabama to Maine and Michigan, and Lerma points, found from the Carolinas across the South into Central America. Side-notched and corner-notched points are styles rather than types, and are often difficult to break down into types and varieties. Thus there are regional, areal, even local "types" of points, with the upshot that there are, at a guess, 300 "type" names in use by American archaeologists for points from Alaska to Tierra del Fuego. Among these are many types differently named but of descriptively similar form; there are also different types with the same name. To further complicate the situation, types from one region which look very much like types from another may be thousands of years apart in time of usage. And a final twist is the fact that points were made one at a time by crude tools out of un-uniform materials, with the consequence that a point intended to be made according to one holotype may, in execution, look like another.

The excavator of American prehistoric sites must try to acquire a working knowledge of the projectile point types of his locality, area, and region; otherwise his projectile point finds will be only artifacts instead of cultural clues. A good way to acquire this working knowledge is to consult published catalogues, read archaeological journals, and study collections. Not that the citizen archaeologist cannot learn much from the first point he picks up. It can tell him more quickly than any other single clue where he is, chronologically, and what kind of cultural material he can expect to find. Projectile points can even refine the time placement of that other time maker, pottery. Some projectile point types fall within comparatively narrow time spans and hence can serve as index artifacts, dividers between cultural eras. Old World archaeologists do not understand the American archaeologist's constant dependence on point types, which have no such importance elsewhere in the world. But the stone projectile point is the only kind of tool in use by practically every Amerind culture for the past 15,000 years that has fine and discriminate attribute variability.

Two details to watch for are saw-tooth serration of blade edges and grinding of bases, notches, and blades. The practice of serrating blade edges dates from the early Archaic period in the East but arrived late, during the last 2000 years, in the Southwest. The serrated edge probably accelerated bleeding. Blade-edge grinding partway up the blade is found on almost all fluted points and some slightly later big-game hunter types; when the student is called on to decide, by attributes alone, whether a point is early or late, he should instantly look for edge and basal grinding. The big-game hunter points will normally be dulled by grinding on sides and base, while early Archaic styles are ground on the bases and in the notches. No good explanation for basal grinding that satisfies most students has ever been advanced, but the reason for dulling the blade edges of lanceolate points and the notches of Archaic styles is obvious: to prevent cutting the lashings by which the point was bound to the shaft.

A third attribute that seems not to correlate with either time horizons or cultures is edge-beveling. Once it was naively believed that the beveling of projectile points on opposite edges gave a shaft torque in flight. A single test exposed this as nonsense, but a pragmatic student demonstrated that the beveling is merely a dexterous way of sharpening edges by the removal of a single long flake. That may not be the whole explanation, but it is a sufficient one until the practice proves to be something more than a sporadic occurrence.

The attributes of chipped stone points mentioned above are only a few of the many that determine types and varieties; they are only the more patent of those that are not incorporated in the plane form. One that might not be noticed at all, at first glance, is that some stone points are not chipped but ground into shape. This group is small even in the cultural facies where ground points are found, the same facies that includes plummets, gouges, and semilunar knives. Ground points are usually of slate but rubbed points of siltstone or sandstone may turn up willy-nilly; it may be that it was simply easier to make a point out of the piece of stone at hand by rubbing.

Projectile points were made in much lesser numbers of bone, antler, and native copper. Bone points were made occasionally in conventional stone point shapes and in long, stilettolike blades, as well as barbed harpoon heads. Antler points were usually long and conical, like the tip of a rapier. The malleable, 99-percent-pure native copper could be beaten into almost any shape, with broad, thin blades favored; but some copper points were made of rolled copper sheets in the shape of the antler tips. All of these points have their place on cultural trait lists and copper points are cultural diagnostics, but none of them have the bread-and-butter usefulness of stone points in cultural differentiation. That usefulness has been far from exhausted by students, who have been slow to realize their potential.

SCRAPERS

Any artifact that can serve as a knife can serve as a scraper and it is hard to say sometimes just whether an artifact is a scraper, a knife, or both. Any flake is a scraper, as it is a knife, as soon as it is used for one or the other or both chores. Large flakes or spalls struck from the outside of pebbles (called teshoas) were particularly effective because the pebble rind is harder than the interior. They were easily knocked off by a hammerstone blow. But scrapers are also formal tools, and of the formal scrapers the snub-nosed ones are very distinctive-looking.

Scrapers are usually classified as side scrapers, end scrapers, and side-and-end scrapers. Side scrapers are so called because the scraping edge is along the side of a blade or spall, and the supposition is that they were used to rake crosswise, from left to right or vice versa. But it need not have been; the scraping motion could have been toward the user. While many end scrapers, of which the scraping edge is across the width dimension of the spall and almost always convex, were probably used with this motion, the snub-nosed scrapers, among others, appear to have been pushed away from the user. Snub-nosed scrapers were made on thick spalls with the working edge, always convex, retouched by the removal of narrow, parallel ribbon flakes, giving it a steep bevel. The Paleo-hunters made large, heavy, snub-nosed scrapers up to two inches or more in diameter, usually trapezoidal in shape, and with one or more "graver" spurs on the working edge, usually at the ends. As has been pointed out, these tips will slice through hides or leather like glass; could they have been used to sever tendons and ligaments? Or to puncture? Or make cutouts for, say neck holes and armholes in capelike garments? Clearly the Paleo-hunter scrapers were tools used in a sequence of operations or in work where certain contingencies could be expected to occur. Later snub-nosed scrapers were smaller and had no graving spurs.

Whether the Paleo-hunter scrapers were hafted cannot now be determined. They are large enough to have been hand-held and are much too thick for attachment to a handle to have been likely. But their probable descendants, the little thumbnail snub-nosed scrapers, must have been slotted into a handle of wood or bone. Because of their size and inconspicuous flakelike appearance, resembling buttons, thumbnail scrapers are the easiest of all formal tools to overlook in excavation. Archaeologically, they may be a clue to what happened to the Paleo-hunters, at least in the East.

Many a flake scraper has been thrown in the bag with the industrial waste, to be looked at one day when there is time—and there never is. The oversight is forgivable except in the case of hafted flake scrapers, in which a corner chip has been removed from a flake to form a little haft for slipping into a handle slot.

snub-nosed   **end**   **side**   *thumbnail*   *hafted*

SCRAPERS

There is something homely and familiar about these little throwaway trifles, like used razor blades. More formal hafted scrapers were made from projectile points with the tip broken off, the blade being reworked into a convex scraping edge. One wonders why this was not done more often than the number of such tools that turn up indicates. Probably it was much easier to pick up or strike off a flake for the task of the moment.

Though the snub-nosing of heavy scrapers pretty well ceased with the Paleo-hunters, scrapers of the same bulk, probably for the same purposes, changed only somewhat in form to what are called plano-convex or turtleback scrapers (that is, scrapers with one flat and one humped side). Why was such bulk necessary, when any edge was an efficient scraper?

The trouble with scrapers is that the name is a file card title, not a tool named for a known function. The underlying assumption is that most scrapers were used for hide-dressing and perhaps they were, with various kinds of scrapers used for various stages of the work. Many may have been used for woodworking; the special type called the spoke shave, a flake or blade with a half-moon concavity, was certainly a shaft scraper or shaver; a type called a scraper plane, as big as half a brickbat, may have been used for the same general purpose as an adze. But the fact is that we do not know what tasks Amerinds had to perform or how they used tools to perform them. Microscopic studies of edge attrition have given insight into what wear does to stone, rather than the mechanics of tool use. Experimentation is fine, and if anybody has a bright idea, he should try it.

WHISTLE

A class of hollow tubular bones with one or more perforations like flutes is called whistles. They may have been musical instruments, signal sounders, or shaman's equipment. They appear about the mid-Archaic, and are almost the only surviving musical instruments, if that is what they are, since drums

WHISTLE

quickly deteriorated; drums are known, of course, ethnographically. Rattles, often made of turtle shells, gourds, and hooves, may be regarded as rhythm instruments, but they were definitely medicine paraphernalia. Probably bones were clashed together; a rare artifact, a notched rib bone, may have produced patterned sound by being scraped and struck with another bone. One strange example of a music producer reported in the literature is a flint "bell." It is a thin, long flint blade which, when struck with a baton, gives off a pleasantly resonant note. You might try any such blades found for sound quality.

The foregoing list of artifact headings may appear to vacillate between the two extremes of being too general and too specific, but the odds are that, as the excavator recovers material, he will be able to apply either the big or the little end of the telescope thus provided to the decisions of classification. The objective of the list is to make him think about his finds pragmatically and independently. Taxonomy—classification and typology—is no more than consensus based on plausibility; because an investigator can classify an artifact as a knife or scraper, he is not thereby relieved of all responsibility for explication, i.e., analytical interpretation of a particular artifact in a given context. What we know about Amerinds is only a modest fraction of what there is to know, and a good deal of what we think we know is provisional, not necessarily true but true within the present limitations of information.

In any event the list does not pretend to be exhaustive. There are dozens of items not mentioned: tally sticks and shell spoons, inscribed stone tablets and textiles, finger rings and arm rings and the whole inventory of forms made of copper by the Old Copper culture and its relatives, shaft wenches, the use of sheet mica, conch shells and hairpins, cups and atlatl hooks, tinklers and pottery trowels, among others that have not been itemized. Nor could all the types within classes be alluded to; there must be at least twenty types of hammerstones and almost as many types of celts. It is impossible to put all there is to know about archaeology within the confines of a single book. This is why archaeology is not a fad, and does not pall; there is always more to learn.

chapter 10

Cataloguing the Finds

THE BASIC ON-SITE RECORD for an excavation consists of the field book, a log, an inventory, a portfolio of sketches, and a coordination of the results of the group digging campaign. The author has tried two methods of putting together a field book, and is prepared to recommend one for volunteer groups.

Our first approach was to require that each digger report with a clipboard on which he had two or three copies of a form, which we had adapted from a form used on a site in the Near East. The form was designed to record the artifacts, features, and stratigraphy of one excavation unit, that is, one five-foot square. When the square was completed, the form was turned in and the compilation of all such square records became the field book.

This method can and should work when the members of the digging party are either paid workers or have paid to work for college credit and can be expected to appear every day and to work a full six or eight hours or whatever the schedule calls for. But it is not appropriate for groups of volunteer archaeologists, adults with the usual obligations of adults nowadays, both family and professional. In our group these obligations kept taking the personnel away, quite often unexpectedly, and the author, as coordinator of operations, found himself with a handful of incomplete or confusing square records and too many missing ones. This experience suggests that even on the most carefully run project, this loose-form sheet procedure will have its drawbacks.

THE FIELD BOOK

We have since switched over to the maintenance of a single field book in which each worker records his finds as he makes them, or records them before he leaves for the day from notes taken during the progress of the work. There is something about making a find that inclines a digger toward redoubling his efforts, so that you can't get him out of his hole and away from the "hot" spot to do his recording; such doggedness is tolerable if notes are taken immediately. One salient advantage of the single field book is that no matter how many workers dig in a square they all use the same square record.

This field book should be the responsibility of the director, who keeps it in custody and must be grim about maintaining it. If he is, the book will shortly become dog-eared and smudged, despite its polyethylene cover and normal care and protection. But the marks of hard usage and the evidence of pluralistic authorship are the cachet of honest records made on the spot, by muddied, sweating hands, in April drizzle or July's heat. One of our more fastidious diggers remarked one day, "So that's why you call it a field book, it's got field all over it."

The pluralistic authorship results in a decided unevenness in internal appearance; some workers are draftsmen and artists and their records could be reproduced facsimile; others can neither draw, print, nor write legibly, and their records are, well, strictly for the record. But then records are not kept for art's sake, and the homelier a field book is the more trustworthy it is; a crisp-looking field book was never compiled in the field.

The type of notebook the author uses for field notes is the copyrighted "Engineering and Science Notebook" available at most stationery suppliers, with facing pages of graph paper which has half-inch squares subdivided into smaller squares and conventionally lined paper. The square-ruled page is used for plan and profile sketches and drawings requiring scaled dimensions. The lined page (the lines serve no particular purpose but that is the way the book comes) is used for outline drawings of finds and for notes. The recording procedure we use is an adaptation of the records suggested by Robert F. Heizer in his standard *A Guide to Archaeological Field Methods.*

PLAN SQUARES AND PROFILE DRAWINGS

In the upper left-hand corner is outlined a five-foot excavation square, one macrosquare to the foot, where finds are noted, by serial number, according to their horizontal location. The smaller, aliquot division squares are measurement units, and the exact placement of each artifact is determined according to these. The serial number identifies the outline of the find drawn on the opposite page, beside which is placed a note on what it is, its material and color, and its depth below surface and height above the sterile base if there is no observable stratigraphy; diggers are encouraged to add any other significant observations about the find or its provenience, such as its probable association with a nearby find. After the finds have been entered into the permanent catalogue or register by serial number, that serial number is placed within the outline in the field book.

The plan square uses only half the width of the page, and is usually sufficient for the entry of all finds; if it proves not to be, there is room beside it for another square. The author has never seen a square with more than two dozen recordable artifacts so that he has no idea what he would do if he ran into squares like the two test squares dug by Coe at the Hardaway site, previously mentioned, from which he took over 1500 artifacts. That's about five books full.

Below the plan square is the profile drawing for noting in the depth of finds by the serial number used in the plan. The profile drawn is that which is exposed at the beginning of excavation of the square. Once in a while a profile of the square at the midpoint has to be included because the stratigraphy begins to change.

In addition to the excavation unit date, there should be an overall grid plan on which are noted other features present: trees, balks, and such details of locality. Also, after completing a trench, an excavator should draw the long profile. Special situations that spread over more than one square have to be given special drawing and notation treatment. All features should be drawn in detail, if not with skill, and numbered consecutively.

THE IMPORTANCE OF INTERPRETING WHILE DIGGING

It is unfortunate that the members of most digging groups do not jot down in plain language the observations and hypotheses that occur to them if they stay alert to the unfolding story as the trowel turns the pages. The truth is that the artifacts will reveal themselves if the diggers are concentrating their attention on the fine print of texture and color of earth and nonartifactual occurrences; they are as obvious as pictures in a close-printed text. The digger who does not keep his mind working as well as his trowel is going to find that his eyes aren't working all that well either. But the digger who does use all his faculties is going to notice things, think things, and hypothesize things, some of which are valuable or provocative or invite investigation. These should be pencilled down on the proper page as a memo to all, including the director.

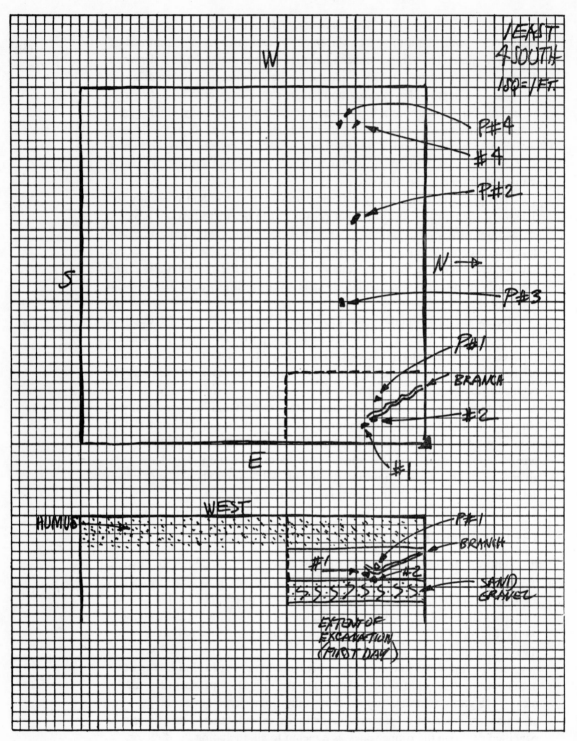

RECORDING FINDS IN THE FIELD BOOK
Plan Square and Profile Drawing on One Page

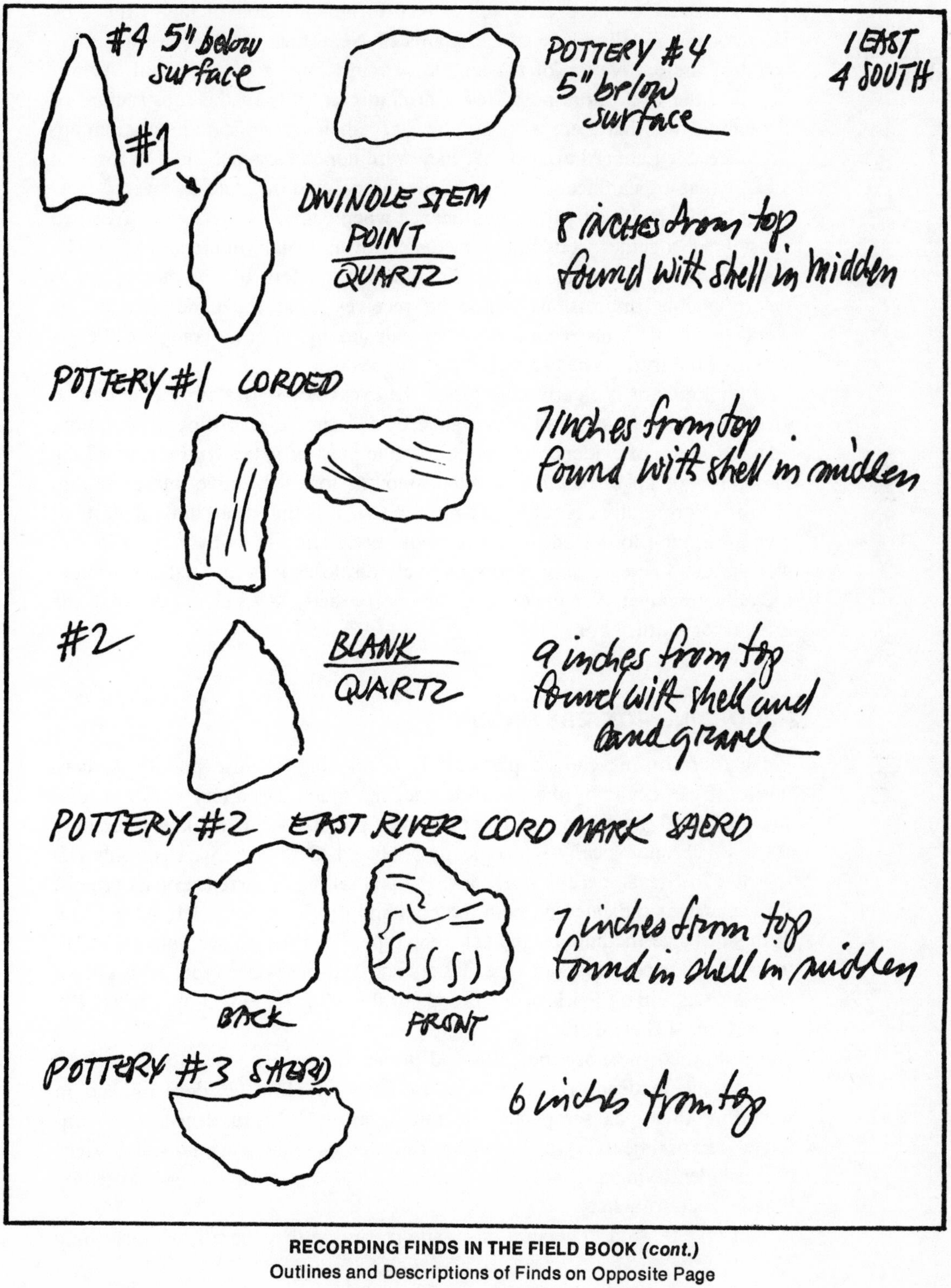

#4 5" below surface

#1

POTTERY #4
5" below
surface

1 EAST
4 SOUTH

DWINOLE STEM
POINT
QUARTZ

8 inches from top
found with shell in midden

POTTERY #1   CORDED

7 inches from top
found with shell in midden

#2

BLANK
QUARTZ

9 inches from top
found with shell and
sand gravel

POTTERY #2   EAST RIVER CORD MARK SHERD

7 inches from top
found in shell in midden

BACK   FRONT

POTTERY #3 SHERD

6 inches from top

RECORDING FINDS IN THE FIELD BOOK (cont.)
Outlines and Descriptions of Finds on Opposite Page

The need to interpret as well as record finds was convincingly argued by Sir Leonard Woolley, one of the giants of Near East excavation, in his account of the excavation of the temple of Nin-Khursag at Al-'Upaid. Admitting that the excavators possessed a ground-plan only of the substructure of the temple and that there were no physical remains to indicate its original appearance, Sir Leonard argued that they were nonetheless obligated to form an idea of that appearance. The excavators, he pointed out, had uncovered facts which, while possessing little significance when considered individually, when considered together constituted evidence from which inferences could be made. Sir Leonard concluded: "If the field-worker fails to give due weight to the intangible impressions which he receives from the conditions of his work, . . . then . . . his record, however painstaking, is not a complete preservation of the truth as he has seen it."

Sir Leonard is clearly saying that the excavator senses more than can be given a proper weight and importance by the simple recording, description, and placement of evidence. What he sees the need of is the synthesis of *all* the particulars of an association in what amounts to a subjective interpretation; but the interpretation is subjective only in that it is that of an individual mind giving meaning to not only what is in the association but why it is all in that association. The excavator who sensitively discloses it is the first and usually the only perceiver ever to see an association exactly as its elements lay in the ground for centuries or millennia.

RECORDING POTTERY FINDS

Potsherd recording can be particularly perplexing because pottery is diagnostic, it can occur by the handfuls and, inasmuch as pottery sites are relatively late and the occupation layer in which pottery occurs is likely to be thin, it can be chronologically-typologically confused. Ordinarily we treat only rim sherds as artifacts, except where a sherd is a telling occurrence or its type is. Provenience is indicated on both the plan and profile serially, P1, P2, P3, but in this instance the number indicates the type. P1, for instance, may be an interior-exterior cord-marked type; P2 a smoothed-over-cord type, P3 a known type such as Piping Rock open-corded. In the notes these will appear as "P1, int.-ext. m., 4 sherds, etc."

And then there are the chips and pieces that have apparently had casual use, on the evidence of edge wear or damage. How far does one go in recording them, as scrapers, perforators, knives? It's a decision of conscience. Experiments have shown that repeated use may leave no visible signs of it; so identifying a casual or informal artifact is not always as easy as telling blonde from brunette.

It may be said in general of on-site recording that there is no such thing as a superfluous notation or observation, but there is such a thing as obtuseness and irrelevance.

In short, everything notable is to be set down in the field book, toward the clearly understood end of an eventual synthesis of found relations and recognized associations into the impossible, the understanding of a whole culture. The field book is the reporter's notebook; out of it he must write his story.

RECORDING MISCELLANEOUS DEBRIS

It would be misleading to infer that recording consists of entering in the record only artifacts and features. What about tips of projectile points and jags out of blades or cores about industrial debris, about fire-cracked rock, about nonrim pottery sherds, and about bone and unworked stone found in cultural situations? It is a common practice to sack these by square and by stratum within the square, without recording individual pieces, which would be such a maddeningly tedious task as to drive the amateur archaeologist into another avocation. The sacks are then stored at the lab for study and analysis. But routine is not law and sometimes not even an excuse. There are associations where any or all of the above may be critical and should be recorded as carefully as though they were artifacts. And there are, moreover, specific research objectives that require the exact placement of, for instance, chips. Investigators inquiring into flint-smithing techniques will want every flake, for the pattern of the fly and fall of the flakes. It is not possible to know, when a site is opened, what situations will be encountered. In a dozen excavation units the occurrence of fire-cracked stones will be sporadic and infrequent; suddenly they will increase in numbers and the digger begins to suspect a hearth area, of which the fire-cracked stones are the only evidence.

RECORDING BURIALS, FEATURES, STRUCTURES

Burials, features, and structures, being complex artifacts, require more elaborate records. The kind of record taken of burials is shown in the accompanying recording form. The drawings and photographs that should be part of burial records have already been alluded to.

Features and postmold structural outlines are best shown in sketches and photographs, with their placement shown on site maps. There is no standardized form, like that for burials, that is regularly used for recording features and structure patterns. The illustrations on pp. 191-192 show how both are handled.

ARCHAEOLOGICAL BURIAL RECORD

1. Bur. No. _____ 2. Site _____ 3. Excavation unit _____

4. Location _____ of datum _____ to _____

5. Depth from surface _____ 6. Depth from datum plane _____ to _____

7. Stratification _____

8. Matrix _____ 9. Condition _____

10. Bones absent (or present) _____

11. Sex _____ 12. Age _____

13. Pathology _____

14. Type of disposal _____

15. Position of body _____

16. Left side _____ Right side ____ Back ____ Face ____ Sitting _____

17. Position of head _____ side ____ Back, ____ face, facing _____

18. Orientation _____ 19. Size of grave _____

20. Associated objects (itemize) _____

_____

_____

_____

_____

21. Remarks _____

_____

_____

_____

22. Exposed by _____ 23. Recorded by _____

24. Photo _____ 25. Sketch _____ 26. Date _____

FORM FOR RECORDING BURIALS

Photography is an auxiliary to recording, supplementary rather than comple-
mentary; it confirms what the excavator has found or observed and makes it
all the more vivid and more convincing. The camera is an eyewitness, whose
retinal images assume permanency when the negative is printed, and so it
becomes a critic, which is why archaeologists are at such pains to plumb,
level, and true up their work before calling in the photographer. The experience of Helmut de Terra and Tepexapan Man of Mexico and the object lesson
of that excavation are well known.

In 1947 when devices for detecting subsurface objects based on resistivi-
ty as used on World War II mine detectors were first coming into use in archaeology, de Terra conducted investigations in the Valley of Mexico in what
had been the bed of a late Pleistocene lake that was still in existence, though

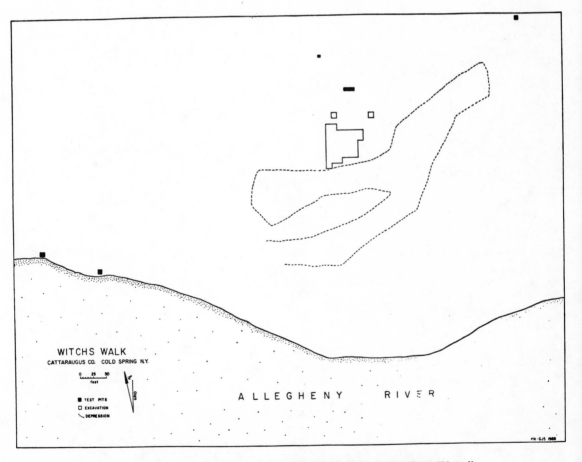

RECORDING WITCHS WALK NO. 1 SETTLEMENT PATTERN (Plate I)
Note: Dotted line indicates old river bed.

drying up, as late, perhaps, as 12,000 years ago. He was trying to locate bones of Pleistocene animals, using the detector device more or less experimentally. These devices cannot tell the user what is beneath the surface, only that something is there which differs in hardness from the soil matrix. Some mammoth bones had been found in the general vicinity of the village of Tepexapan, and when another "anamoly" was found, workmen were instructed to begin digging down to it. For some reason de Terra was away from the site when the anamoly was reached. It proved to be not a mammoth femur but a human skull, the rarest kind of Early American find in the literature of archaeology.

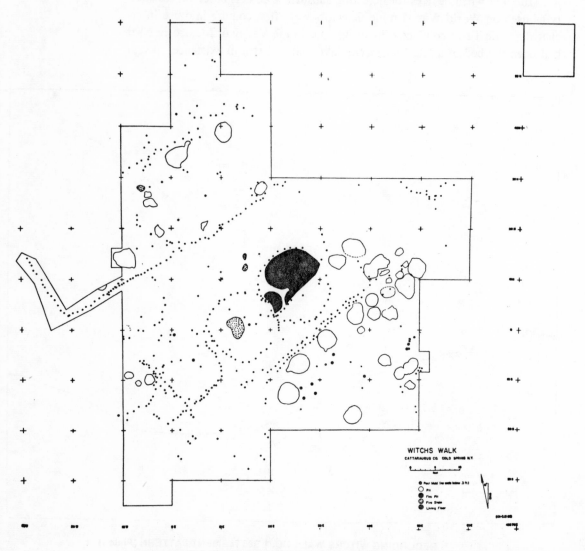

RECORDING WITCHS WALK NO. 1 SETTLEMENT PATTERN (PLATE II)

In their excitement the workmen exceeded their instructions and, instead of awaiting de Terra's return, uncovered the skull. It was this situation that de Terra, wanting not to disturb it further, had photographed immediately, and these photographs were the ones used in announcing the discovery of the remains of an 11,000-12,000-year-old mammoth hunter. It was within de Terra's discretion at the time to have "faked" the excavation by cleaning it up and giving it a look of having been approached with full knowledge of what lay five feet under the surface. It is to his credit that he did not.

The climate of opinion at the time was hostile to Early Man (though 11,000 years is hardly "early" by 1973 standards), and when de Terra's report reached its professional audience, the hostility against the idea found an easy target in the photographs. The late Glenn Black, who had never come closer to the Tepexapan excavation than the Angel site in southern Indiana where he worked for over thirty years, threw de Terra's claims for modest antiquity contemptuously out of court and summed up the professional consensus of rejection with the withering, "The photographs show an incredibly sloppy excavation."

Thus a first-class find, which would meet with only hospitality today because of the paucity of skeletal evidence of American Early Man, was condemned to archaeological exile, where it remains today, not on the facts of provenience but on an interpretation of photographs. *Caveat archaeologiensis.*

To learn how to take good archaeological photographs, the beginner can do no better than to consult *Archaeological Photography* by Dr. Harold Simmons. The excavator will discover soon enough that his first and foremost problem will be to get the right amount of light on a profile that faces north, or into a pit overhung by trees in leaf. Good stratigraphy will blanch out under too much sunlight, and will show only as a nondescript pile of dirt under too little. Because the layers of genuine stratigraphy differ in absorbency and reflectivity, it is usually better to take shots of profiles when they are moist, after a rain or a wetting them down by hand, which can be a chore when no water source is close by.

What cannot be stressed enough is that the photographer who works a site should be an archaeologist himself and should do his own developing. He will, as an archaeologist, understand what the photograph was taken to illustrate, so that he can use the necessary tricks of developing technique to bring out and enhance what is important in concept and detail. The canny developer can get a great deal into, and out of, a photograph.

The archaeologist's role in photography, strictly defined, is to decide what pictures he wants and what is the subject of each picture. He should know for what purpose the picture is to be used, whether simply for record, or for printed or oral reports. The impetuous archaeologist who does not synthesize data in his head as the site develops may very well find, when the time comes to deliver his report, that he has a great many pictures in his files that he doesn't need and not all of those he does. The staple shots are of stratigraphic profiles, of features, and of artifacts *in situ* when these have something to contribute to cultural or geologic evaluation; and, of course, the landscape photographer gets in his innings in taking panoramic site views.

The photographer should have two cameras, or the group should have two photographers, because two kinds of pictures have to be taken: black-and-whites for development into glossy prints for publication, and colored pictures for development into slides for lecture reports. The subjects of color pictures should be selected and composed even more carefully than for black-and-whites. An overillustrated lecture with diffuse, pointless slides is certain to put an audience to sleep.

OFF-SITE OR LABORATORY RECORDING

On-site recording is primary and original; off-site recording is rearrangement of that data for custodial and study purposes. The principal secondary record is a catalogue or register of artifacts in which these are entered serially, the entry consisting of a sketch of the artifact, its accession-identification number, material, nature, location as to square and depth, and a note as to association with other artifacts or features, if any. Museums usually prepare a file card for each artifact with the above and some additional information—but museums have clerical staffs. The efficiency of separate cards, which can be lost or misplaced, is questionable; anything in addition to the register is an elaboration that the citizen archaeologist has little use for.

The entry of artifacts found over the weekend in the site register is made by us on the following Wednesday. At that time there is also prepared what we call "scattergrams," which show the placement of artifacts that seem to show relationships or associations. These are an attempt to work out both vertical sequences and horizontal associations. They are not really records but fall, rather, into the preliminaries of study and analysis, and they serve to help us in sorting for the purpose of boxing the collection. A scattergram is a grid plan on which is entered the placement of artifacts and features which appear to have some relationship to each other, the relationship being defined by the design of the "scatter" of provenience. In most instances these are simply trial arrangements to see what ideas they suggest. Even when they are not put down on paper as such, they are concepts or hypotheses based on field book notes.

BOXING THE FINDS

The reason for doing scattergrams at this stage is, as indicated above, to provide some kind of guide to the temporary storage of artifacts for study. It seems the most routine of tasks to dispose of materials once they have been catalogued and marked with a catalogue number: you just put them in a drawer or in a box to be stacked on a shelf, don't you?

Yes, you use drawers; we have a museum-type bank of drawers of various depths where materials from sites under active excavation are stored. But to heap everything from a site together in one or two drawers would be to create haystacks in which it would be too difficult to find the needle we wanted. Therefore we categorize finds and put them in clear plastic boxes of appropriate sizes, which cost $.40 apiece but are worth it. "Putting the stuff away" after cataloguing is usually the least routine of tasks, for the categories keep changing and being added to or subtracted from as the recoveries accumulate. Let us examine the present state of categorizing for the Piping Rock site, already alluded to, on the former estate of the late Joseph M. Patterson, owner and publisher of the *New York Daily News*; the estate, called Eagle Bay, is slated for development by builders. We have boxes for:

1. White contact materials: a rusty jackknife, a rodent-gnawed candle, a kaolin pipestem, an 1859 silver quarter, some wrought iron nails, etc.

2. "Exotic" materials—flakes of jasper, chalcedony, crystal quartz, colored flints—that could not have come from the lower Hudson.

3. An assembly of traits that are 200 miles from any known similar association, including a little steatite platform pipe, a broken, partially holed gorget, a native copper awl, projectile points of a type called Jack's Reef corner-notched, and a distinctively cord-marked pottery. This trait assemblage is known as Kipps Island and occurs on the Lake Ontario plain, with nothing like it reported between there and Ossining, thirty-five miles upriver from New York City.

4. A collection of about 30 "dwindle stem" points, a type the stems of which contract or dwindle to a pointed or almost pointed base, the series including two types of contracting points that appear in the literature as separate types, Poplar Islands and Rossvilles.

5. A collection of early Archaic point types, with dates elsewhere from 7000 to 10,000 B.P., and including one possible Paleo-hunter fluted point, found on the old, leached-out soil level.

6. The collection of points which fortuitously appear in one undisturbed spot almost directly above each other in an orderly and conventional sequence.

7. The collection of materials from a pit: points, pottery, bones, scrapers, flakes.

8. The collection of miscellaneous types of projectile points.

9. The collection of minor tool types, drills, thumbnail snub-nosed scrapers, strip blades, perforator-tipped flakes.

10. The collection of bifacial blades and preforms.
11. The collection of cores.
12. The collection of flakes or fragments showing casual use.
13. A dozen boxes of pottery by specific types or wares not yet typed.

The heavy stone tools (choppers, manos, axes, pestles, etc.), are kept loose in a drawer.

This categorization contrasts with the sorting of items at the Montrose Point, Dogan locus, etc., a spread of midden shell about an acre in area, the depth of shell varying from one foot to four feet. There are considerable expanses of this midden built up over about 3000 years, where nothing occurs on, in, or beneath the shell but bone scraps and flakes. Instead, concentrations of material are found at loci in which there are evidences of campfires. The Dogan site material is therefore boxed by campsite, with four such loci having been uncovered so far. When we began to excavate, we had no idea this was going to be the structure of the site. We now know that it is a collection of tiny sites, or campfire loci, and that the materials from each locus, none of which have yielded voluminously, are associations, the nature of which has to be determined by study-analysis.

Recording, then, is not mere cataloguing, filing, enumeration, alphabetizing, and neat storage. It takes the new-born data delivered from the matrix of the earth and begins the process of giving it useful, meaningful existence. When thorough records have been made, the physical objects could vanish and the archaeological significance of a site could be derived from them, unless the artifacts are of material or workmanship different from anything known or recognized previously. Site re-creation begins with the record.

chapter 11

Main Currents in
Archaeology Today

STUDY-ANALYSIS OF the evidence excavated from an archaeological site is a two-phase process: (1) the study and analysis of the artifacts and the evidence considered by themselves and (2) study, analysis, and interpretation of the total collection. Interpretation may be considered rhetorically a separate phase, but it is generated so spontaneously—rather like the aroma of food when it is being cooked—that it is inseparable from study-analysis.

When an excavator, at the completion of his dig or at any time during the dig that he feels the necessity of formulating an impression of his site, lays out his material either *in toto* or by classes on the lab table, the first task is identification. Chapter 9 was devoted to the shape of implements as defining function so that the beginner can recognize them by class as they come out of the ground. In study and analysis the task becomes the further recognition of styles and varieties within classes, since these are the real clues to cultural and chronological placement.

It has been previously stated that projectile point styles are the principal diagnostics for preceramic time, that is, for both the Archaic and the herd-hunter eras (but not, of course, for the earliest, pre-stone projectile point epoch) and that pottery styles are the diagnostics for the ceramic horizon. In projectile points it is necessary, for these to be culturally meaningful, to recognize not only that a specimen is side-notched or corner-notched, stemmed or haftless, but the varietal attributes of shape, size, manufacture, material, secondary usage, and the repetitive combinations in which these occur. Similarly with pottery: it is not enough to know that a sherd had come from a vessel made by coil-winding that had been malleated by a cord-wrapped paddle or stick. A score of other attributes—tempering, firing, vessel shape, rim, decoration, interior treatment, etc.—enter into the classification of wares (genus), types (species), and varieties (subspecies).

FINDING RELEVANT ARCHAEOLOGICAL LITERATURE

But where is the excavator to acquire the needed information; where can he see the types with which he must compare his own? Not in museums. It can be said without qualification that no museum in the country will have on display, correctly identified, the range of projectile point types, pottery, and other artifacts the excavator needs as comparative material. The anthropology departments of some colleges and universities are repositories of up-to-date materials from local sequences, but they may not be convenient of access. The one dependable and the best and most current source of description, illustration, and cultural information is archaeological literature: monographs, full-length books, and periodicals.

This literature is not to be had in the nearest library unless that library is very large or specialized. But nowadays most libraries are under the charge of professional librarians who not only know how but are very happy to work up bibliographies on specific subjects. These bibliographies will probably be meager but each item will itself include a bibliography, and the list of titles of interest and relevance will almost instantly increase by a factor of ten. The list will inevitably contain the periodical that covers the area or an adjacent area. Alternatively, the excavator may write either his state library of the Library of Congress for bibliographic leads.

To print herein a list of area and regional periodicals would be to disseminate information more inaccurate than useful. Such periodicals frequently change editors and publishers and the addresses to which subscription inquiries may be sent, or they drop out of existence or suspend publication for long periods disconcertingly. But once one has made contact with the literature, he quickly discovers where to turn for material. There are, however, many standard, in-print items which it should be helpful to mention.

The most famous of all artifact digests is H. Marie Wormington's *Ancient Man in North America,* Denver Museum of Natural History, Popular Series No. 4. It began originally as a compendium of Paleo-hunter cultural information but has gone through several editions, each containing new material, and it now includes, in summary, a broad spectrum of artifact types, especially projectile points (Wormington is an authority in projectile point classification) from the Paleo-hunter to middle Archaic period. The book is especially valuable because it will introduce the reader to classic names, key cultures, and type sites from all over the North American continent.

Southwest. The first of what can be called catalogues of projectile point types was *An Introductory Handbook of Texas Archaeology* by Dee Ann Suhm and Alex Kreiger, Bulletin 25, The Texas Archaeological Society, Austin (1954). It has since been revised, with added material, and contains virtually all the established projectile point types occurring in the Southwest from Louisiana to California and from the Great Basin to the Valley of Mexico.

Southeast. The Southeast is served with equal comprehensiveness by Cambron and Hulse's *Handbook of Alabama Archaeology, Part 1, Point Types,* published by the Alabama Archaeological Society, University of Alabama.

Middle South. Robert Bell's *Guide to the Identification of Certain American Indian Projectile Points,* Special Bulletin No. 1, The Oklahoma Anthropological Society, Norman (1958), covers the Middle South and the Mississippi Valley. It was revised and issued as Bulletin No. 2 in 1960.

Florida. Florida is a special case in the Southeast and has its own catalogue, Ripley Bullen's *A Guide to the Identification of Florida Projectile Points,* Florida State Museum, Gainesville.

West Virginia. Bettye Broyles, in her 1970 *The St. Albans Site, Kanawha County, West Virginia: Second Preliminary Report,* West Virginia Geological and Economic Survey, Morgantown, has described 11 Archaic types for the region between South Carolina and Ohio.

Northeast. The Northeast has depended for many years on William Ritchie's *A Typology and Nomenclature for New York Projectile Points,* State Museum and Science Service Bulletin 384, Albany. A new edition, with the same bulletin number and the addition of new types, was issued in 1971. The types listed are found from Pennsylvania to Maine and their names are the vernacular of northeastern archaeology. The bulletin, however, is in need of revision.

Ohio. For the Ohio-Illinois region *Ohio Projectile Point Types,* published by the Archaeological Society of Ohio, Newcomerstown, is useful.

Upper Midwest. Edward Wahla's *Indian Projectile Points Found in Michigan* makes a beginning for point typology.

Northern Plains. In 1970 the Montana Archaeological Society in Missoula began printing in its journal, *Archaeology in Montana,* a series of projectile point types from the Northern Plains, filling in the sequence for post-Paleo-hunter times.

West Coast. The point types for California and the Northwest are scattered through dozens of site reports. For the Northwest, however, much information can be gleaned from B. Robert Butler's "The Old Cordilleran Culture in the Pacific Northwest," *Occasional Papers of the Idaho State College Museum,* Pocatello, 1961, and from L. S. Cressman's "Cultural Sequences at The Dalles, Oregon," *Transactions of the American Philosophical Society,* New Series, Vol. 50, Part 10, 1960.

The total of point types listed in the above sources will run, probably, in excess of 250. Another 50 to 100 are scattered through various other reports. Nor is this likely to be an end to point typology. The projectile point is highly variable and, when the kind of material it is made of is taken into consideration, it becomes a true index artifact. What happened even in the slow evolution of conservative cultures was that there was a drift away in small details from a prototype, so that a type is actually a chronological reality, the shape plus other attributes, made for a longer or shorter period within a certain tradition of projectile point making. A site collection of points, when a type is present in sufficient number, will show a variability of specimens ranging from the prototype to a new type toward which the makers were tending. Every type evolved a new type, and the typologist is always in a quandary about where one type ends and another begins.

Projectile point identification is not a cut-and-dried procedure of superimposing a point on a point illustration and finding the two congruent or not congruent. It is a study of all the attributes and contextual data. Again and again, Amerinds evolved point shapes similar to those already made by other Amerinds thousands of miles away, because there are only so many that can be made. Small side-notched points were being made by eastern Amerinds during the late Archaic that could lie unnoticed in a collection of points of Plains buffalo hunters of 500 B.P. About 9000 to 10,000 B.P. Amerinds at the tip of South America were making a type called the fishtail, with rounded, rather than angular shoulders, and a flaring stem. Points with this same outline evolved out of angular shouldered prototypes in Pennsylvania and New York about 3000 B.P. They are the Orient fishtails of the Miller Field site report in Chapter 13. No expert would confuse the two if he handled them but it is possible to confuse them were the illustrations of some South American fishtails to be compared with illustrations of some Orient fishtails.

The study and analysis of projectile points should include their technology (whether they were made by direct or indirect percussion, pressure flaking, or combinations, and whether they were made directly from the block or from spalls), size range, probable use and combination of uses from use evidence, the type of stone used, and the origin of that stone. Some types were made of anything at hand while others were made, by preference, of only one kind; for instance, the fishtail points found in the lower Hudson are usually of Pennsylvania jasper. If that kind of stone does not occur in the area, the conclusion is that the point-makers were either visitors (as we believe the fishtail makers were in the lower Hudson) or they obtained the preferred stone by trade or by travel to its source.

STUDY-ANALYSIS OF OTHER LITHICS

Lithic artifacts and lithics generally are subject to the same kind of study as projectile points. Artifacts shaped by pecking, abrading, or grinding, and by use pose somewhat different problems in technology, but basically the study of lithics consists of ascertaining the function by form and evidence of use, determining the cultural implications of the use of the specific materials and technique, and of shaping cultural hypotheses about the presence, association, and numbers of lithics on a site. *These are, in appropriate adaptations, the lines that all archaeological study follows.*

POTTERY STUDY-ANALYSIS

The student of pottery is not so fortunate as the student of projectile points in the sources he can readily consult for typological comparison. There are no catalogues of pottery, though Dr. James Griffin established at the University of Michigan Museum of Anthropology in the 1940s a repository for pottery types of the eastern United States where samples are kept for examination; type descriptions of these were published on pages suitable for loose-leaf notebooks by the University of Michigan Department of Anthropology. But no single center could cope with the pottery variations of even the eastern half of the country. The student can only begin a long search of the literature, full of bad photographs and misleading drawings, for his ceramic complex clues.

What is beginning to be realized is that the longer the period of pottery-making the more localized in type and variety pottery becomes. Sooner or later the archaeologist has thrust upon him the necessity of becoming his own expert in the pottery of the vicinity he is working. But with 1000 or 2000 sherds from the site he has just excavated spread out on a table in utter confu-

sion, how is he to bring order out of this wreckage? Obviously he is not ready
to begin consultation of the literature for comparatives because he doesn't
know what he has.

To deal with just such a puzzlement Edward Kaesar, a specialist in the
pottery of the most deranged archaeological area in the world, metropolitan
New York, has provided the following instructions.

THE CERAMIC STUDY
Edward J. Kaeser

Of the various types of material recovered in archaeological excavation
ceramics are usually the most sensitive in interpreting cultural change. The
following is a suggested method for ceramic analysis which might aid in the
determination of cultural identification of potters inhabiting sites scattered
over large areas and, in the case of sites exhibiting long occupation, periods of
occupation by the cultural group or groups present.

Methodology

(1)

After the sherds are washed and dried, they must be marked individually
with a field or catalogue number. If sherds are too small or friable to mark,
they can be placed in polystyrene bags marked with a number on gummed
tape. This marking must be done to avoid mixing with artifacts from other
squares, or collections from other sites under analysis.

(2)

Spread out the cleaned and dry sherds on a large table. A quick scan of
the spread out sherds will enable you to distinguish gross differences of the
sherds. These differences will appear as: (a) surface finish; (b) paste; (c)
temper; (d) firing; (e) vessel shape.

Make a chart listing these same differences as titles, widely spaced for
additional differences or traits such as: protuberances which may appear as
nodes; and appliqués, such as faces, corn, etc. These differences can be added
to vessel shape traits.

(3)

There being no understanding at the moment whether these differences
will later turn out to have cultural or temporal meaning the sherds should be
separated into piles based on the easiest recognizable categories: surface
finish; paste; etc. and counted. This tabulation should appear next to the
descriptive title on the chart.

We begin with the first gross trait on the list, surface finish. *Surface finish* must be observed in some detail to determine the range of surface treatment techniques. Once these techniques are determined, if the surface of the sherds are not too eroded and the impressions were made on the clay when it was not too wet or too dry, details will be observed for further subdivision; for instance, in the recognition of fabric impressed design, the various weaves used by the potter such as: plain plaited; twilled twining; plain twining; etc.

(Suggested Ceramic Tabulation Chart Form)

Gross Traits

Surface Finish	
Cord Marked	
Fabric Marked	
Net Marked	
Brushed	
Incised	
Punctated	
Cord-Wrapped Stick Stamped	
Dentate Stamped	
Scallop Shell Stamped	
Plain	

(Continue with next gross trait)

Paste	
etc.	

The local Indian used Dogbane or Indian hemp (a common milk weed) to make cordage for fish nets and fabrics. The individual fibers were twisted together to form these cords. The specific twist appearing impressed on sherd surfaces can be recognized by comparison with our modern cordage as s-twist, right-hand twist, left-hand twist.

Vessel bottom sherds may exhibit woven mat or fabric impressions, as the result of being forcibly pressed downward on a cloth or mat during manufacture.

Proceeding to the next trait on the list, *paste*, we may subdivide it into compact or poorly consolidated or laminated paste. In texture paste may be described as fine, granular, clayey, gritty, flakey, hard, soft, or any other adjective which will describe the visual character of the clay. Method of manufacture, whether coil constructed if coil separation is evident on sherd edges or possibly the paddle and anvil method used.

Under the *temper* the subdivisions will be:

Grit or granular mineral; list the kind, size, water worn or crushed and the amount.

Shell; state whether marine or fresh water shell, and the amount. Shell tempered sherds often exhibit holes left by leached out particles leaving negative impressions of the type and size of the particles.

Vegetal; a rare occurrence in coastal New York. Appears as hollow molds of disintegrated vegetal matter, not always intentional inclusions and sometimes the result of uncleaned clay used in the vessel production.

Firing; to determine the method of firing, the surface and core colors of the sherds must be examined to determine the degree:

Oxidizing fire, which is the most complete and well controlled firing method, is signified by constant color throughout the sherd thickness, with fire clouds rare.

Reducing fire, recognized by black core and lighter colored surfaces due to low temperature fire or lack of oxygen or draft. Fire clouding on surfaces of vessels is common.

Analysis of paste, temper and firing is important, since these are sometimes the only usable diagnostic traits for recognition of pottery series or type when sherd surfaces are obliterated, as often happens when pottery is found in association with burials or other significant features, or when only crumbs of sherds are recovered.

Vessel shape may be subdivided into a possible five (5) categories.

Body: wall thickness; neck constriction; shoulders.

Bottom: conical; rounded; flat.

Is bottom thickness constant with vessel walls?

Is bottom formed from pan-cake like piece of clay with coil pinched on to periphery of clay disk to build up vessel wall?

Collars: incipient or channeled; true applied collar.

Rim: flaring (in, out); straight; castellated.

Lip: flat; rounded; tapering; crenelated; interior surface decorated.

Ceramic traits taken singly may have little value except from a purely descriptive standpoint; as such they are often utilized in preliminary site reporting where a conclusive analysis is not possible. It is the combination of these traits, paste, temper and shape, in both exterior and interior surface treatment, that becomes important in the comparative study and as an aid to understanding the cultural development, popularity and change of ceramic wares within an area throughout time. Ceramics having in common surface finish technique, paste characteristics and composition, and vessel shape represent the longer period of use and the wider geographic range of a ceramic series, wares or styles. Further refinement within the series will allow the separation of vessels, by their repeated distinctive differences in decorative technique and motif and associated characteristics forming the types within the series, into types of chronological significance.

This data having been tabulated, to show the trends of pottery types in the ground and their possible chronological implications, the stratographic evidence is analyzed, through the use of field notes, published site reports, profiles of squares, etc., and comparing the data with that established by analysis with other sites.

What comes out of following the above procedure will be something like the following type description by Robert L. Stephenson of pottery found at the very intensively occupied Accokeek Creek site on the Potomac River directly across from George Washington's Mount Vernon estate. Stephenson had 58,298 sherds to make sense of typologically. He reduced these to eight "wares," of similar manufacture, paste, and tempering, within which were sixteen types. The description given below of the Moyaone Cord Impressed type of Moyaone ware will tell the student what he has to look for in pottery analysis and how to describe what he finds.

MOYAONE CORD IMPRESSED
(New type name)

Summary Definition

The type Moyaone Cord Impressed is a coiled pottery with cord-wrapped paddle malleated surfaces often smoothed over, smoothed interior surfaces, and of a gray, brown, buff, or reddish clay, tempered with extremely fine-grained sand often mixed with some coarser sand and occasionally with crushed quartz. It has a compact, fine-grained texture but is always gritty and slightly friable. Vessels are small, rarely ranging to medium small, with globular bodies, rounded bases, and flaring, straight, or slightly inverted, rims (see the accompanying profiles). Decoration is confined to the rim area and consists of any of several variations of cord impressions. Rims are sometimes thickened by application of a strip of clay.

Type Description

Method of manufacture.—Coiled with paddle-malleated surfaces. Coil breaks are rare but present.

Paste.—Temper is predominantly fine and with minute flecks of mica. The sand gives the sherds a distinctive, gritty feel and the mica specks often produce a slight glitter. A minority of the sherds also contain small quantities of coarser sand or crushed quartz.

Plastic is a fine-grained, compact, well-mixed clay.

Hardness in Moh's scale is 2.0 to 2.5. Medium.

Texture is soft, smooth, and compact. The extreme fineness of the sand is quite distinctive and readily discernible to the feel, giving the sherds a texture like that of gritty powder.

Color.—Exteriors are predominantly light gray to gray-brown but range from almost black through brown, gray, and reddish-buff to tan.

Interiors are about the same as exteriors but sometimes a shade darker or a shade lighter.

Core color is usually the same as the surface but occasionally a little darker or lighter. A distinct core color is seldom perceptible.

Firing.—Moderate temperature, usually evenly fired in an oxidizing atmosphere with no smudging. Sometimes uneven fire-clouding or over-all smudging is apparent.

Surface treatment.—Exterior surfaces are predominantly malleated with

RIM PROFILES OF MOYAONE WARE (interiors to left)

VESSEL PROFILES OF MOYAONE WARE

PROFILES OF MOYAONE WARE

a cord-wrapped paddle leaving cord marks usually vertical to the rim but sometimes horizontal, diagonal, or criss-crossed. A substantial minority of the surfaces are partly or completely smoothed after cord roughening.

Interior surfaces are carefully smoothed. Rarely are fine tool striations, either vertical or horizontal, to be seen.

Vessel form.—Lips are rounded but often flattened or wedge-shaped. Rarely do lips have cord markings along the top or diagonally along the outer edge.

Rims are usually flaring with a neck constriction. Sometimes they are only slightly everted, inverted or straight. Rarely a strip of clay has been added around the rim to thicken it. Rims are usually low, ranging from 10 to 35 mm in height or but 10 to 15 per cent of the vessel height.

Bodies are usually globular but rarely are hemispherical or cylindrical. Bases are rounded.

Thickness of the vessel walls range from 5 to 10 mm but usually is 6 to 8 mm. Thickened rims range to 10 or 12 mm as do basal sherds. In proportion to the vessel size the sherds are moderately thick.

Lugs are absent.

Decoration.—Technique: decoration is confined to the rim area and lip and consists of horizontal, vertical, or diagonal cord impressions either stamped or rolled onto the vessel or applied as a single cord.

Designs are usually simple, vertical cord impressions around the rim or 3 to 5 horizontal cord or cord-wrapped dowel impressions encircling the rim. Rarely are diagonal cord-wrapped dowel impressions found and complex designs are absent.

Other.—Mending perforations are rare but present.

Vessel size.—Predominantly small, ranging to medium. Maximum diameters are usually 8 to 12 cm rarely up to 20 cm. Depths are usually 10 to 15 cm rarely ranging up to 20 cm. Orifices are usually about the same as, or slightly smaller than, maximum diameters. Depths are slightly greater than diameters.

Sample size.—189 rim sherds, 710 body sherds, 78 basal sherds, and 6 reconstructed vessel sections. Body and basal sherds of all three types of the Moyaone ware are lumped together here as they are indistinguishable.

Temporal position.—Late Woodland.

When the student has found in his collection what he believes to be a type, he will not, of course, enter it into the literature as a new type until he has referred to the literature to learn whether that type or a similar one has already been found and described, either as a type or a ware. Among classifiers the two extremes are the lumpers, who prefer to stuff as many things into a taxonomic bag as it will hold, and the splitters, who find any difference sufficient excuse to create a new category. With pottery it is better to be a lumper. You won't make quite as many mistakes.

The study of pottery begins with the examination of the paste, or plastic, and the tempering material, or aplastic. The tempering material was included to prevent excessive shrinkage and subsequent heat cracking of the clay. In the very beginning vegetal fibers, grass, stems, etc. were used in modeled pots, made out of a lump of clay, as a child might make a pot. The mechanical fallacy is simple to see; the fibers served as tendons to bind the wet clay together but disappeared on firing. Soon afterward in the learning process, hard clay fragments probably from broken vessels were tried as tempering. In some areas crumbs from old steatite pots were used. Clay tempering was followed by coarse sand tempering and by grit, coarsely crushed rock. The adoption of fine sand and finely crushed grit represented the final improvement in material.

The first manufacturing technique was modeling, but the vessels so made had to be small. The second technique was coil-winding, the method used in Moyaone ware, and it continued in most of America outside the Southwest and areas of Mexican influence, until after contact with the white man, as long as any native potters were left. Since vessels broke along coil lines (usually, but not always), this method is easily detected in sherds which will show the positive and negative impressions of the coils often on the same sherd. Molding is the technique of building up a vessel inside a mold, usually a basket. The limitations of the method are obvious; no shape that would not slip easily out of the mold without destroying it, if it were a useful artifact of itself as is a basket, could be made. There is no reason why molded vessels could not have been built up by coil-winding and doubtless some of them were. The potter's wheel was never invented in America, but methods were in use in the Southwest and Mexico that approached it. They are best studied in the ethnographic literature (for example: Alice Marriott's study, *Maria, the Potter of San Ildefonso,* published by the University of Oklahoma Press in 1948). Pottery kilns do not occur outside the Southwest and Mexico but some well-fired ceramics were made, by a means not yet established, all over pottery-producing America for the last millennium of its prehistory.

The technique employed for studying the surface marking and surface decoration is to take impressions in modeling clay. Scrutiny under low-power magnification will reveal details of the implements and materials used to effect the imprints: cord-wrapped paddles and sticks, nets, fabrics, shell edges, fingernails, reeds, combs, corn cobs, styluses, stamps and "brushes," the frayed ends of sticks. The markings are often the result of the manufacturing process, but when they are clearly decorative a whole new study area in design opens up. It must be pursued through the literature.

By inspection, with the aid of magnification from 2 up to about 20 power, the excavator can assemble the necessary information for report description of his site collection of pottery, temper, paste, surface treatment, etc. If he becomes a pottery enthusiast, like many excavators, he is advised to acquire *Ceramics For the Archaeologist* by Anna O. Shepherd, Publication 609, Carnegie Institution of Washington, Washington, D.C., 1961. Lines of investigation of pottery are pointed out therein to keep him busy for a lifetime.

STUDY-ANALYSIS OF OTHER TRAITS

Because the lithics and pottery of a site will be the main preoccupations of the excavator's study and analysis, and because the line has to be drawn somewhere in this book, other study subjects will not be discussed at length. The reader will recognize some of them in what follows. If an excavator does a good job on the lithics and pottery he will have acquitted himself honorably, but every cultural trait is its own curriculum. All investigations lead to their literature and most will lead to the door of the specialist; burials to the osteologists and physical anthropologists, faunal remains to zoologists, plant remains to the botanist, soil problems to the pedologist, and many another problem to the chemist, physicist, the glaciologist-geologist, the metallurgist, and even the engineer and architect. What was done by man in the past was done no less than today under the natural laws we have learned since then and can now apply to the evidence he left behind.

THE TRAIT LIST

Stone tools and pots are artifacts, but the making and use of them are cultural traits. The description of a cultural unit begins with the list of all the traits that excavation shows to have been associated with it. After the excavator has identified, studied, and analyzed his recoveries, he draws up a trait list. Having compared his projectile point types and/or pottery with those of other sites in the area he may already know with what cultural unit or phase he is working. Or he may find that the trait list he has compiled differs significantly from that of any so far reported. In which case he has something new.

The following is the sketchy trait list for a cultural unit of what we call in the lower Hudson Valley the Twombly tradition. It is sketchy because we have found the characteristic Twombly side-notched projectile points at four sites including Twombly Landing, but these are all shell midden riverbank camping sites, representing a term of residence of probably only one month out of the year. We have not been able to find the sites away from the Hudson shore where, presumably, these people lived the rest of the year. We do know that there existed such a cultural tradition and we do know when. At Twombly Landing the diagnostic side-notched points were associated with Vinette I pottery, the first pottery in the Northeast; at another site upriver, on Montrose

Point, they were associated with steatite potsherds. Therefore the point makers were in the lower Hudson Valley during the steatite period and they were still here when ceramic pottery was introduced. Their residency in the lower Hudson falls within the half a millennium between 3500 and 3000 years ago. These dates make them contemporaries of the Orient fishtail point makers (about whom there is more in the Miller Field report of the next chapter) at whose sites both steatite and ceramic pots have been found. But fishtail points are found by us on lower Hudson sites only by ones or twos, while the Twombly side-notched points are found in clusters. Hence the Twombly point makers were probably residents and the fishtail point makers were visitors from Long Island or the Upper Delaware where their habitation sites, with burials, have been excavated. Because of the sketchiness and known incompleteness of our trait list we do not call this group a "complex," but merely an identifiable cultural group.

**TRAIT LIST OF THE
TWOMBLY SIDE-NOTCHED POINT MAKERS**

1. Chipped Stone:

    Projectile points: Twombly side-notched

Small—1 to 1¼ ", base to tip	25
Medium—1½ to 2", base to tip	20
Large—2" and over, base to tip	4

    Knives

Ovoid, biface	3
Ovoid, uniface, with retouch	2
Subrectangular, biface	1
Subtriangular, biface	2
Lanceolate, biface	2
Ovoid blade, stemmed with single shoulder	2
Strip blade, uniface, no retouch	5
Casual flake, showing edge use	37

    Scrapers

Plano-convex	2
Flake end scrapers, with retouch	10
Blanks or cores showing scraper use	10
Blade fragments showing scraper use	8
Hafted, reworked projectile point	1

    Drills

Reworked projectile point	1
Narrow, thick blank with gimlet tip	2

Perforator or graver
    Flake with needlelike tip   1
Strike-a-lights
    Blade fragments showing battering   3
Industrial materials—all of local origin
    Black flint, quartz, sandstone   500

2. Polished Stone
    Axes
        Fully grooved
            Sandstone   1
            Trap rock   1
    Gorget
        Half, two-hole, soapstone   1
    Pendant
        Long, narrow rectangular "clay-baby"
        or natural clay concentration with groove
        for suspension by string   1
    Pestles
        Cylindrical (may be intrusive)   1
        Pebble, slightly worked   1
        Gyratory crusher type   2

3. Rough Stone
    Metate-mortars: large cobbles, 12″ diameter
    with one flat face in which has been worn a round
    indentation 3″ in diameter   2
    Hammerstones
        Combination mano and hammerstone   3
        Pebble   5
    Choppers
        End   3
        Side   3
    Teshoas   10

4. Steatite
    Pot fragments   2
    Gorget (see above)

5. Bone and Antler

Antler flaking tools	4
Tine drilled lengthwise as though for tubular pipe	1
Bone needle or awl with polished tip	5
Bone fragments, mostly deer, usually split	150
Bear canine	1

6. Ceramics

Vinette I—interior and exterior cord-marked	30 sherds
Bead—small, nipplelike perforated object broken around edges	1

7. Subsistence

Habitation: temporary camps on bank of river at oyster beds
Food: Shellfish gathering (oyster, hard clam, bay scallop, ribbed mussel, whelk); hunting (deer, small game, bear); gathering (nuts, roots, seeds, as shown by manos, pestles, metate-mortar)
Hearths: small fires (for cooking only?) laid on surface, without pit or stone enclosure

8. Negative (absent) traits

Evidence of shelter

Net-sinkers, fishhooks, or other fishing gear (Apparently no special gear was needed to take fish as wanted.)

Smoking pipes (The drilled antler tine could not have been smoked; it may have been a shaman's sucking tube.)

Atlatl weights

Adzes or other heavy woodworking tools for manufacture of dugout canoes

Burials (None of the lower Hudson oyster gatherers buried their dead in or near shell middens, though it would have been easier to scoop out a grave in loose shell than in the hard clay subsoil. Jettisoning of corpses, or of skeletons after exposure, into the river is a possibility.)

Chipping floors (Very little stone work was done by these people at these sites except perhaps for dressing down a preform or rough blank.)

Sooner or later in his reading the excavator will encounter references to the McKern system or the Midwest taxonomic method. The reference is to the cultural classification system proposed in 1939 by W. C. McKern in an article in *American Antiquity* titled "The Midwest Taxonomic Method as an Aid to Archaeological Culture Study." The method is the classic genus-species-subspecies-variety taxonomic order or hierarchy applied to cultural units. The order runs thus:

> Period
> > Phase
> > > Aspect
> > > > Focus
> > > > > Component

In the McKern system the four sites where we found the Twombly side-notched camps (Twombly Landing, Dogan Point, Crawbuckie Beach, and Parham Ridge) are each a component in a Haverstraw focus, lower Hudson aspect, coastal phase, of the early Woodland I period. It is very reassuring to be able to fit something you have found into so plausible a system of established and understood reality. It is wholly reasonable that five or six or perhaps twice that many bands of a culturally and socially-genetically related group resided for ten or more generations in this area, which constituted the focus of their habitation and activity. But this focus must have been at the same cultural level as that of its neighbors; it must, therefore, have had the same cultural aspect. Considered within the cultural state of the whole region, this aspect had defining characteristics that set it apart from the regional aspect, or phase. And all this was in existence within a period of time which has been recognized by the name Woodland. The Woodland begins with the advent of pottery and it applies to, or was meant to apply to, the forested United States east of the prairies within which pottery was thought to have appeared more or less coevally.

But the McKern system broke down under the impact of archaeological fact. Ceramic pottery was being made in Florida, southern Georgia, Alabama, and probably along the Gulf Coast 4500-4000 years ago, whereas it did not make its appearance in the Northeast quadrant, the true Woodland region, until about 3000 years ago. Nor was the early pottery of the South—molded or modeled and fiber-tempered—at all like the grit-tempered, coil-wound Woodland pottery. The southern early pottery is believed to have come out of Mexico along the Gulf Coast. There are still archaeologists who believe Woodland pottery came out of Asia, though there is absolutely no excavated evidence to corroborate such an origin. (About that origin nobody at the moment has a persuasive theory.)

In addition to the two-pottery discrepancy there was the no-pottery problem. Some cultures apparently never adopted the trait of pottery making until as late as 2000 B.P., or the middle Woodland under the McKern system. But the objections to it were more than these, and the McKern system is now out of fashion, but not entirely. For the Woodland pottery area it is just as applicable as it ever was. For the northeastern United States—that is, from Ohio to Maine in the North and Ohio to the Carolinas in the South—the early, middle, and late Woodland, with subdivisions as required, are decidedly current terminology. For the South the middle Woodland is applicable because middle Woodland (Hopewellian) pottery influences spread from Ohio and Illinois as far as Florida, but there were in the South phases of early Woodland pottery in the Mexican-influenced pottery tradition. There is no late Woodland in the South; again Mexican influences seeped in and the late Woodland of the South and the Mississippi Valley is the Mississippian period.

As unsatisfactory as the Midwestern taxonomic method proved to be for the length and breadth of midwestern and eastern prehistory, it still has a modified utility; when rightly applied, using proper criteria, it can be and has been used everywhere. You will find the terms component, focus, aspect, etc. employed with the same meaning McKern gave them in reports from Peru to Alaska. It is a system of reference points, rather like the grid layout of a site but, like the grid, it does not parallel or reflect the underlying cultural reality.

CULTURAL-HISTORICAL INTEGRATION

In 1958 the University of Chicago Press published a significant volume, *Method and Theory in American Archaeology* by Gordon B. Willey and Philip Phillips, that was a finalization of ideas which had been originally presented by them in articles published as early as 1952. One of the authors' key concepts was "cultural-historical integration," their term for what they felt should be regarded as "the primary task of archaeology on the descriptive level of organization." As these authorities pointed out, cultural-historical integration had traditionally been concerned with the reconstruction both of space-temporal relationships and contextual relationships. "Operationally," insisted the authors, "neither is attainable without the other. The reconstruction of meaningful human history needs both structure and content."

The structure begins with the following outline of developmental stages in sequence of early to late.

1. *The Lithic:* This stage brackets together the early stage of

"unspecialized" core and flake industries, which Willey and Phillips were the first to recognize almost twenty years in advance of the Ayacucho Valley excavations, and the later stage of biface blades including lanceolate points, both fluted and unfluted.

2. *The Archaic:* This is "the stage of migratory hunting and gathering cultures continuing into environmental conditions approximating those of the present," roughly the Holocene, or period after 10,000 B.P.

3. *The Formative:* This stage is defined by "the presence of agriculture, or any other subsistence economy of comparable effectiveness, and by the successful integration of such an economy into well-established, sedentary village life."

4. *The Classic:* "The American classic stage is characterized by urbanism and by superlative performance in many lines of cultural endeavor."

5. *The Postclassic:* Confined to Meso-America and Peru, this stage "is marked by the breakdown of the old regional styles of the Classic stage, by a continued or increasing emphasis upon urban living and, inferentially, by tendencies toward militarism and secularism."

The reader will immediately recognize that this system applies to the prehistory of North and South America outside of Meso-America and Peru with decreasing appropriateness. Effectively, only the first three stages were attained outside the "Classic" areas of Mexico-Central America and Peru, and the first three stages are not any better resolved than by the McKern system. But Willey and Phillips did direct attention to a principle that the reader will recognize as innovative and practical; it is the tradition. Willey and Phillips used the diagram on p. 216. In it the components are single sites which are the habitational locations of people who participated in the same specific culture in the same area at the same time. This specific culture, described by its trait list, is called the phase. The phase existed at a level in time called the horizon and is the particular expression at that time of a cultural continuity called the tradition. The tradition is central to the understanding of cultural evolution, process, and development. It is axiomatic that all culture bearers had ancestors, culturally as well as genealogically, and begot descendants, culturally as well as genealogically. Populations, and the cultures they make and use, are linear through time; it is therefore impossible to observe, study, and interpret cultures, either of themselves or as human behavior without recognizing the sequential linkage or concatenation, that is, the time chain.

Once the historical or time-flow nature of culture was recognized systemically, it became clear that what was coming out of the ground was not the locally peculiar expressions of generalized time-level cultures but a series of what are now called cotraditions. The Paleo big game hunters and the early

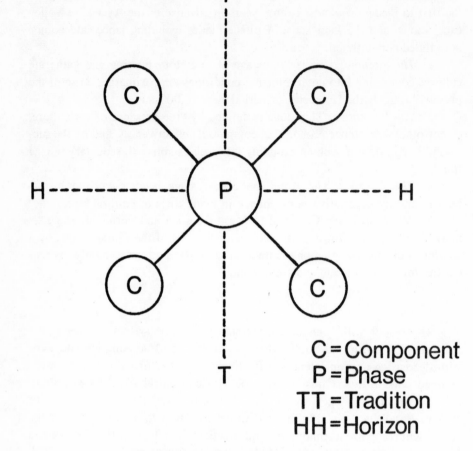

C = Component
P = Phase
TT = Tradition
HH = Horizon

KEY CONCEPTS IN MODERN ARCHAEOLOGY

Archaic of the South were cotraditions in one region, as the Paleo-hunters were cotraditional with the Archaic pattern Desert culture in another. The reader will certainly hark back to the earlier pages of this chapter to an even more exact example of cotradition, the Orient fishtail and the Twombly side-notched point makers, both of whom visited the banks of the lower Hudson during the steatite-first ceramic pottery period. Two cotraditions make interpretation difficult enough; the existence of four, as we believe was true of the lower Hudson during this period, seems almost a prank played by Amerinds to confuse the overearnest, uptight student of the enigmatic past.

An understanding of both the McKern and the Willey and Phillips systems will give the beginning analyst a sense of balance and orientation.

Seriation is not a theory, though it is founded on plausible assumptions, but a study-analysis technique for reaching certain conclusions about change in culture through time. It is used in some cases in an attempt to discover the sequence of phases (in the Willey-Phillips definition) at an unstratified site of some depth. And it is also used to describe the onset, climax, and decline of artifact styles, principally pottery.

The procedure is to plot the provenience of the style or class of artifacts under study on a depth chart. If the site is expressive of the full range of the phase, the subject artifact type (usually a diagnostic one) will occur infrequently at the bottom, will then wax in popularity toward 100 percent of the recoveries of that class, and will then dwindle toward extinction in top levels. The result is said to be a "battleship-shaped curve," that is, pointed at both ends and broad in the middle.

The example of seriation on p. 218 is from Kraft's Miller Field site. It will be noted that both the numbers of fishtail points and their percentage of the whole collection of points increase upward. The percentage is 51 in the D zone, 80 in the C zone, 83 in the B zone and, though the numbers have decreased, the percentage is 93 in the A zone. This is a classic seriation pattern, as are the patterns of the minor types present, the Perkiomen and the Koens-Crispin. These minor types are diagnostic of earlier phases, and they should appear as they do. The "other Archaic" types do no more than indicate that the site had some visitors who left behind casual points that were mixed into the site material. It is not even necessary, to shape a seriation pattern like that of the fishtails, for the camping group to have increased in numbers. The numerical increase in fishtail points indicates only that the fishtail point makers were the only people to use the site and they used it regularly, for several generations, though in all probability the use was seasonal only. Such regular use would prevent any zonal buildup.

But these nice, symmetric seriation curves will not occur at every site, or even at most, though one can always do depth charts and fancy he sees the battleship. Real seriation requires class specimens in such quantity that the percentages are not skewed by a few examples. It works best on village sites where potsherds occur by the bushel.

Presented on p. 219 is linear seriation of projectile point types excavated by W. Fred Kinsey of Franklin and Marshall College at the Kent-Hally site on Bare Island in the lower Susquehanna.

Had this figure been done in seriation curves, it is clear that no type curve would have been completed. The stemmed points cluster heavily at the bottom, which would mean that Kinsey had only the upper half of the theoretical curve; thus the site was not a phase-inclusive habitation site, in that occupation by the stemmed point makers did not begin and end there. Nor is there any certainty

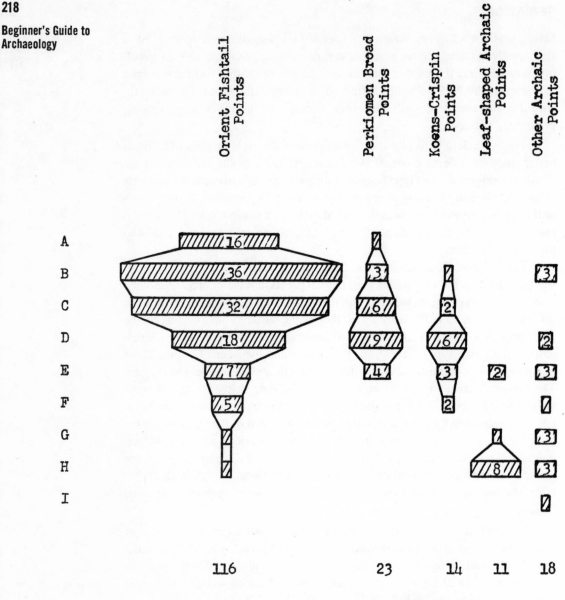

EXAMPLE OF SERIATION FROM THE MILLER FIELD SITE

about how the majority of the stemmed points happened to accumulate at the bottom; the gravitation-migration downward through living soil, explained in Chapter 4, would do just this, so that there would be fewer points at the top than at the bottom. There is at least a fifty-fifty chance that the distribution of projectile points at Kent-Hally owes more to nature than to culture. Seriation is such a

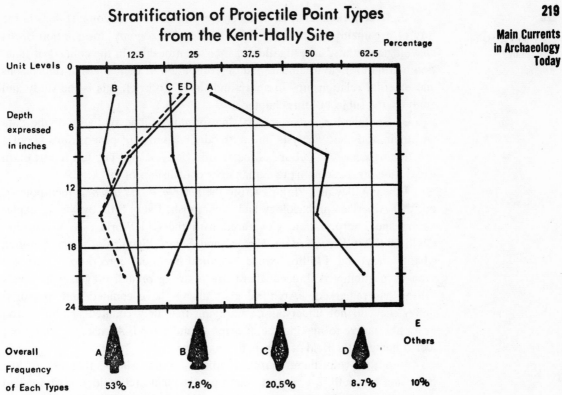

Stratification of Projectile Point Types from the Kent-Hally Site

LINEAR SERIATION OF PROJECTILE POINT TYPES AT THE KENT-HALLY SITE

logical, scientific-looking way of handling materials that otherwise make little sense that it has been badly abused.

Coe calls seriation like the Kent-Hally graph (Kinsey only presented it and did not use it to interpret the site) "clerical exercises" and adds, "Seriation has meaning only when it can illustrate the relative use, or popularity of two or more styles of a given product at one time in a single community." This means it cannot be used to interpret sites where cotraditions or traditions of different time levels are found. It is wise to remember this dictum both in using and in reading about seriation.

THE "NEW ARCHAEOLOGY"

Willey and Phillips break archaeology down into three steps, which the reader will have no difficulty in adjusting to what has gone before. They are:

1. **Observation:** Field work, that is, survey and excavation, or what is herein called discovery.

2. **Description:** That is, "almost everything the archaeologist does in the way of organizing his primary data: typology, taxonomy, formulation of archaeological 'units,' investigation of their relationships in the context of function and natural environment, and determination of their internal dimensions and external relationships in space and time." In brief, this is the study and analysis, the subject of this chapter.

3. **Explanation,** or processual interpretation: The synthesis of the data and their study and analysis into a "model," a series of propositions about a functioning whole—a culture, a social unit, or a society. The full report of an excavation aims at coming to explanatory conclusions of this kind.

When Willey and Phillips wrote their *Method and Theory,* they pointed out that American archaeology had accomplished very little by way of explanation and interpretation. Compared with the Old World (see V. Gordon Childe's *What Happened in History* and Stuart Piggott's *Ancient Europe*), what Willey and Phillips called "cultural-historical integration" had not even been attempted. Indeed, there was a strong prejudice against it. James Fitting has remarked, "Archaeologists always have counted and measured things they do not understand," implying that they counted and measured as an alternative to making the attempt to understand. Archaeologists do not feel at home in the field of reasoned conjecture.

Into this void there marched boldly, in the 1960s, that era of the explosion of youth, a group of young professional archaeologists who called their movement the "new archaeology." They advocated and, in many arresting instances, demonstrated effective new ways of achieving explanation. Two of their most significant books are *New Perspectives in Archaeology,* edited by Sally R. and Lewis R. Binford, and *Explanation in Archaeology* by Patty Jo Watson, Steven A. LeBlanc, and Charles L. Redman. The Binford-edited work is a case-book in the application of the "new archaeology." Any student will profit by reading it. The Watson-LeBlanc-Redman book is concerned with how scientifically valid propositions may be arrived at, and may not be everyone's cup of tea.

The "new archaeology" now dominates the scene in America, its disciples owning the editorial desks of professional journals and occupying the academic podiums from which the indoctrination of the next generation is directed. The change will certainly be permanent. But the fact is that the new archaeology does not have anything to work with until the field work has been done and "cultural-historical integration" has been accomplished, that is, local sequences worked out, phases fitted with trait lists, and the relation of sites to the environment understood. Explanation and interpretation have always been ultimate archaeological objectives, but all too few archaeologists have had the courage to attempt them.

chapter 12

The Making and Unmaking of Archaeological Doctrine

EXPLANATION AND INTERPRETATION are best defined as the answers to the cultural-historical-anthropological problems that the excavator had in mind, if he followed the recommendations already given herein when he began to dig his site, and to the problems that framed themselves during the digging. They are best explained and interpreted by illustration.

A much quoted example of explanation-interpretation in the "new archaeology" is that by William A. Longacre, excavator of the Carter Ranch Pueblo in east-central Arizona, dated A.D. 1050-1200. After recognizing 175 design motifs on 6000 potsherds recovered from the pueblo, he defined two clusters of design attributes or details, one of which was associated with a group of rooms at the north end of the settlement and the other with a group of rooms at the south end. Assuming from ethnographic analogy that pottery making was a tradition that passed down the female line, from mother to daughter, Longacre deduced that the community was matrilocally organized: that is, postmarital residence was "in the vicinity of the wife's female relatives" and inheritance of real property, both the residence rooms and the

221

right to be buried in either the north or south cemetery, was through one or the other lines of matrilineal descent.

The foregoing summary is unfair in that it reduces a major excavation to apparently one proposition. Several other lines of evidence from the excavated data of rooms, kivas, cemeteries, and storage pits contributed information to the support of that proposition. Put in another way, it was that these Hopi or Zuni lived in A.D. 1000 very much the way the Hopi and Zuni were living 800 or even 900 years later. Thus Longacre had a model with which to compare the synthesis of his excavated data. What he dug need not have been similar to the historic model, but it proved to be.

This was intensive explanation and interpretation, assisted by the most modern of techniques, including a computer analysis of sherd frequencies, and a great deal of knowledge of the descendants of the people who had inhabited the site. Is it possible to arrive at explanations and attempt interpretations of a more extensive nature with less concentrated data? Our work in the lower Hudson Valley is offered as an example.

CHANGING INTERPRETATION OF DISCOVERIES
ON THE LOWER HUDSON

All but two of the sites excavated by the author in the lower Hudson Valley, Winterich and Van Cortlandt, had *in situ* shell heaps as principal features; and there had been heaps at Van Cortlandt but they had been scattered by all manner of vehicles, from plows and wagon wheels to bulldozers, since this site was the barn lot of the estate of the Van Cortlandts, original Dutch patroon grantees of about 1650. These sites are far from exhausting the oyster midden site resources of even the east side of the Hudson for a stretch of only ten miles.

The local explanation of all this shell was that it was the refuse of "clam bakes" (though clam is extremely rare in the area), firemen's picnics, and beach parties. Only one archaeological survey of the lower Hudson had even been conducted and reported, by a party from Vassar College, Poughkeepsie. The survey this far south had apparently been by small boat from the water, since only that shell visible from the river side was noted, though it was recognized as archaeological. There are a few references to shell heaps in minor local historical papers; the deposits were assumed to have been late prehistoric, the refuse of the riverine gathering activities of the Indians whose villages had been located along the river when the white man first made contact here. That oysters had been so plentiful once and do not grow in the lower Hudson now was attributed to the Hudson's notorious pollution, although pollution could not have been ecologically critical until the 1920s at the earliest. During historic times periods of intermittent oyster beds in the Hudson have been recorded but the periods were short and the beds were used mainly as a source of spats, which were transported elsewhere to attain commercial growth.

How the Old Explanation Was Demolished

When we began to dig oyster shell middens, all archaeological doctrine for the Northeast decreed that the harvesting of marine shellfish by Amerinds had not begun until about 2000 B.P., by which time they were living in permanent, though part-time villages. The "model" for shell-heap archaeology, then, was that shell middens were the persisting refuse heaps of resident riverbank people who did a great deal of fishing and shellfish gathering, along with hunting, and that the waters of the estuary provided such a reliable food supply that permanent part-time settlements could be maintained near the river.

Not one detail of this model is factual. But it took the first eight years of digging before we began to see the outlines of the true model through the cobwebs of old dogma. During that time we discovered:

1. There were no villages or settlements using structures at any of the shell midden sites; we have never discovered a structural postmold at any shell midden site. Indeed, the middens are seldom in locations where a house of any size, to say nothing of a group of houses, could have been situated.

2. The occupation evidence was concentrated in small "hot spots" of, usually, not more than thirty to fifty square feet—obviously the sites of small, single-band camps.

3. The shells were not deposited in one large heap or spread, as they would have been had they been the refuse of a single settlement. Instead the shell spread was an accumulation of smaller heaps deposited on, around, and beside each other, often with soil layers separating one from another, showing lapses of time.

4. The artifacts were not typologically of one phase and were, moreover, of phases much earlier than 2000 B.P.

5. There was little pottery and this was early, Vinette I and types earlier than 2000 B.P.

6. There was no gear specifically designed for fishing—no net sinkers, fishhooks, or fish gorges—and there were very few fish bones in the naturally preservative shell. If fish were speared, they were speared with the same projectile points used in hunting. We did not doubt that this was so, since the lower Hudson was the richest fishing grounds in the Northeast, but the midden depositors could not have been a fishing people; they were forest hunters and gatherers who made periodic visits to the Hudson shores.

How a New Explanation Was Begun

Our model now was that the middens had been accumulated by the visitations of small, family-sized bands, probably during the early spring, through thousands of years of, mainly, the Archaic period. This was such a contradiction of the doctrinal model that we needed at least one date to substantiate it. But C-14 tests cost $600 during the 1950s and we were loathe to invest that amount in so flagrant a heresy. Then we heard that Minze Stuiver, director of the Yale Radiocarbon Laboratory, was engaged in a project of dating any kind of phenomena that related to the postglacial rise of the sea and, if he accepted a sample from us, would charge $35. The price was certainly right, if our middens were pertinent. And Stuiver agreed they were. He accepted a sample of charcoal from the GO horizon at Croton Point in 1962 and had the result back to us in May of 1963. It was eminently satisfactory. The GO horizon was 5863 ± 700 C-14 years old; with the correction factor, that is a true age of about 6500 years, well within the Archaic. At the time Croton Point was the oldest C-14 dated site in New York, and the oldest C-14 dated Archaic site in the Northeast.

The old model had been refuted, but what we had was not by any means a new model. And we had little enough to start with; as the reader will recall, the GO horizon has produced no diagnostic artifacts. When we came down to it, all we did have were the valves of oysters, about which we knew nothing. The direction of our environmental studies, then, was indicated.

The GO midden oysters were very large and heavy, and many of them, by count of their plates of annual growth, were from 30 to 40 years old, which meant that conditions in the lower Hudson about 6000 C-14 years ago were favorable for oyster growth for at least that long a span of time. But in what way had they been so much more favorable than they are now?

Our oyster research disclosed that oysters, though a marine animal, live only in estuaries where there is an input of fresh water. The salt content of the open ocean is 35 parts per thousand, but oysters like water no saltier than 22 parts per thousand and they can survive in water down to about 11 parts per thousand. When the water freshens beyond that, they die, and the lower Hudson today is less than 11 parts per thousand, except in certain deep holes for short periods. Water temperature, which we once thought might be an inhibiting factor, proved to be a neutral influence at our latitude. Oysters do best at 70°F., but they can function from 40 to 80 degrees. Beyond those temperatures they close their valves, slow down their metabolism, and wait for better times.

The answer to what was different about the lower Hudson 6000 C-14 years ago was, therefore, that it was saltier. But why?

We tried half a dozen theories and finally came up with what is undoubtedly the right answer: it was saltier because it was deeper. The fresh water input being constant on the average, a deeper basin would allow more sea water, with its higher salt content, to wash in with the 3- to 4-foot tides. That gave us an answer to why oysters do not grow in the lower Hudson today and have grown here for only very short, widely spaced periods since about 2000 B.P.: silting has kept the estuary basin too shallow.

But why was the lower Hudson deeper 6000 C-14 years ago than it is today? The search for an answer took us into the subject of sea level rise concerning which, in the early 1960s, much work was being done. It was generally agreed that Wisconsin III had, at its climax 19,000 years ago, lowered sea level by about 420 feet. By 12,000 B.P. the level had recovered to about 220 feet below present, though much of the broad Atlantic continental shelf was still dry and very habitable land. By 6000 C-14 years ago sea level was only 40 feet below present level. (This reading has been arrived at through several lines of investigation, but for the lower Hudson it is proved by C-14 tests of cores taken from a 94-foot-deep deposit of peat directly across the river from our area of sites. This deposit is shown as Ring and Salisbury meadows on the Haverstraw U.S. Geological Survey quadrangle. The 40-foot-deep level of a peat core was dated at about 6000 C-14 years ago.) The rate of rise was especially rapid, then, between 12,000 and 6000 B.P.; it was about 180 feet or 3 feet a century, and it outran or at least kept pace with the rate of silting. The estuary very probably was salty enough during this entire time span to have supported oyster beds.

At Croton Point we had noticed that the top of the GO midden was a 3- or 4-inch layer of fragmented and decayed shell intermixed with humus. This could only be a soil stratum, a layer created when the GO midden lay exposed as a surface and subject to weathering and soil-building. How long the period had been there was no way to calculate but we kept the fact in mind when we began to dig the midden at Twombly Landing, about fourteen miles downriver from Croton Point and on the west bank.

Whereas the bottom of the GO midden at Croton Point (it was about 30 inches deep) was only about 8 feet above mean tide level of the Hudson, the Twombly Landing midden was on a shelf at the top of a virtual bluff 100 feet above present water level. At high tide there was no beach at all at the base of the bluff. The Twombly Landing midden produced plenty of identifying material of a phase we called the Taconic stemmed-point tradition. Most of the shell had been deposited by the Taconic people, over a period ranging from about 5000 to about 4000 C-14 years ago. The early occupation was established by C-14 tests on a hearth for which Yale gave a date of 4750 C-14 years ago and Geochron a date of 4730 C-14 years ago. This was not quite the earliest occupation of the site by the Taconic people, so we estimated it at 5000 C-14 years ago. But there was positively no GO midden under the Taconic.

By interpolation of data from the peat core at Salisbury Meadow, sea level at the time the earliest Taconic shell was being deposited was 27 feet below present level. Between the GO horizon period and the Taconic period there had been a rise of 13 feet; therefore, this had to be the reason for both the absence of a GO midden and the placement of the Taconic midden on a 100-foot-high bluff to which it must have been an arduous climb to carry baskets of oysters and other burdens. The GO midden had probably been on dry land at present beach level, and the 13-foot rise had covered this land and left the bluff the only camping spot in the vicinity.

But there was another factor to be considered. The Taconic people seemed to be a new people in the area. Despite the lack of diagnostic material in the GO midden, we were certain the GO people were not the Taconic people. But if the Taconic people appeared in the lower Hudson more or less simultaneously with the 13-foot rise, it was probably more than coincidence. What best explained this was that the Taconic people had been living farther out on the coast and the rapid and critical rise had, by inundating their former living space, pushed them inland into the lower Hudson. And why not? The oysters also returned to the lower Hudson and with them, at Twombly Landing, at the edge of New York Bay, was an extensive marine shellfish fauna: hard clam, bay scallop, ribbed mussel, and whelk. The Taconic people had simply followed their accustomed habitat upriver.

Yet there was, on the dates we had, an 850- to 1000-year hiatus between the GO and the Taconic middens. Had there been no oysters in the Hudson for that length of time? Or had the GO midden been someplace else because the oyster beds of 5863 C-14 years ago had been somewhere else? With the soil horizon on top of the Croton Point GO midden in mind, we thought it more likely that there had been a real period of oyster absence, by reason of shallowing. What would best account for the facts we had was that sea level rise had come to a halt or near halt about 5800 B.P., silting had shallowed the estuarial basin, and oysters had had to abandon the area. Then, some time before 5000 B.P., the sea had resumed its rise, the basin became deeper, oysters re-established themselves, and the Taconic people arrived to eat them.

In the meantime we had found another GO midden, about four miles upriver from Croton Point and almost its duplicate, in that it was about eight feet above river level, was exposed in the riverbank, was being rapidly eroded, and was topped by a weathered shell and soil stratum. In this stratum we were happy to find Taconic points. The sequence, deduced from Croton Point and Twombly Landing, was therefore corroborated. But the date on the GO midden, kindly provided by the Lamont Laboratory, which was then specializing in shell dating, was 5650 ± 200 C-14 years. Thus the hiatus was reduced to about 650 years.

But this midden, the Dogan Point locus on Montrose Point, was much more extensive—there is almost an acre of shell spread—than the tiny remainder of midden at the Kettle Rock locus on Croton Point where the GO horizon had been discovered. As we dug into it we quickly ran out of GO midden, but within 15 feet we came on a small, leached-out hearth, lying on the old land surface under the shell deposit, with a slate knife and a notched point of red shale in association. There being too little charcoal in the hearth to date, shell from directly above the point was submitted to Geochron. Test result was 5155 ± 120 C-14 years. The notched point was therefore older than 5155 years.

About 20 feet farther on, we came to another interesting association, three stemmed points, probably not Taconic, in the ancient humus that covered the original clay till surface. Geochron dated shell from this humus and in association with the points at 5075 ± 160 C-14 years.

The next dated locus was 35 feet farther inland. It was a living floor of about 30 square feet with a hearth in the center. Five projectile points and several knives and scrapers were recovered. Three of these points were within the typological range of the notched point dated older than 5155 years. Two of the points and a scraper were in touching association, as though they had been set down by hand. Shell lying on top of this little assemblage was dated at 5095 ± 110 C-14 years.

We now had a consistent series of three C-14 dates—5155, 5075, and 5095—on shell lying directly on the former land surface and outside of but adjacent to the GO shell deposit. This, then, must have been the approximate period when oysters returned to the Haverstraw Bay area. The hiatus had been reduced to almost exactly 500 years, the difference between the 5155 of the red shale point and the 5650 of the GO midden. But the important fact was that there had been a hiatus in oyster production in Haverstraw Bay. And we had a point type that, being older than this hiatus, was probably associated with the GO midden, the red shale side-notched type, even as we had the Taconic points in association with the post-hiatus shell.

Here were two elements of a model. But the Dogan Point locus also provided us with a third.

Between the red shale point locus, with its 5155 date, and the non-Taconic stemmed points, with their 5075 date, lay the most intensively occupied area of the site, producing a medley of point types. One of these was a Taconic stemmed; since the average of 5155 and 5075, the dates bracketting the locus, is 5115, this seemed confirmatory of the time placement we had already determined for Taconics. But the most numerous type at this locus was a small, narrow, simple triangle, at bold variance with the elementary Taconic stemmeds and the rather more technologically sophisticated notched points. The triangle points were named the Shattemuc tradition, from an Algonkian name for the tidal Hudson, meaning "river that runs both ways." They might have been of the same horizon as the Taconics, and finds elsewhere at

Dogan Point did show they were contemporary with Taconics, but one of them was among the five points found on the floor that dated older than 5095 C-14 years; therefore they belonged with the GO midden horizon as well.

Three projectile point traditions, as distinct as three different languages or three different races—from whence had they come into the lower Hudson?

The origin of the Taconic people has already been surmised; they were dwellers in oyster-producing estuaries when the coastline was farther east and they had been nudged farther into the Hudson by the encroachment of a rising sea. Since their ancestral homeland is now fathoms deep under the Atlantic, the proof of their existence by excavation was impossible.

The origin of the Shattemuc people is also speculative but much more susceptible to eventual proof. Their "triangles" are not all rectilinear-sided. They often tend toward pentagonoid and lanceolate. In short, they are very plausible as reduction in size and simple variations in blade shape of the lanceolate points of the Paleo-hunters of caribou who roamed the Northeast as late as 10,500 B.P. It is hardly likely that these thoroughly competent hunters died out as the deciduous forests and white-tailed deer became established in the region. It is much more likely that they adapted to the new milieu and maintained themselves as well in it as they had maintained themselves in the vanished taiga. There is a Paleo-hunter site in New Jersey less than 100 miles from us where these small "triangles" occur among the more conventional fluted lanceolates, showing that the conventional lanceolates were tending toward them. We do not lack good typological evidence of this post-Paleo hunter tradition; what we lack are datable occurrences of it. And it is our problem. Although these Archaic triangles occur rather widely in the Northeast (and here alone at that time level), they are most abundant in the lower Hudson. It is a strong tradition here, and a long one, for triangular points persist into historic times, and the tracing of it through almost 10,000 years can probably be done nowhere else. But we are happy with it; it seems to be all ours.

The origin of the notched-point people has already been outlined in another context; they drifted with the deer and deciduous forests from the Carolina piedmont and, as it now seems, from West Virginia. Almost all of our excavations, we noticed from the beginning, produced two or three points strange to the then established typology. With the publication of Coe's Carolina finds and, later, Broyles' Saint Albans sequence, these points no longer seemed strange. Broyles actually identified a half-dozen points from Twombly Landing and Piping Rock as being MacCorkles, a type she established at Saint Albans; they date at about 8800 B.P. Our conclusion was that the southern Archaic had begun to infiltrate the lower Hudson directly and immediately on the spread of deer and deciduous forests into the area, if not somewhat before. Because the conclusion was based on a handful of points and no C-14 dates, it did not attract many adherents. But in 1969-70 a group of nonprofessional diggers on Staten Island began finding hearths with a surprisingly wide range and significant numbers of Carolina and West Virginia early Archaic point types in association. They were authentic specimens of these types, not mere resemblances, and a series of C-14 dates from the hearths confirmed contemporaneity; they ranged from 7500 to 9500 B.P. The presence of the southern early Archaic in the lower Hudson could no longer be denied, and we had good ancestry for the GO horizon notched points. Since early Archaic points have been found on oyster midden sites, it is even possible that their makers gathered oysters. We have no evidence of association of shell and early Archaic points but in 7500 to 10,000 years the shell may very well have entirely decayed.

The Current Explanation

Our new model now was:

1. The Paleo-hunters, who were roaming the Northeast 12,000 years ago, had left behind a viable tradition, the Shattemuc triangle tradition.

2. The southern early Archaic notched point makers had made their way as far north as the lower Hudson by about 10,000 B.P. and become a regional cotradition. The GO midden people of 5600 C-14 years ago were of this tradition, as were the Twombly side-notched people of 2000 years later. The two traditions lived peaceably side by side, but apart, without competition and without influencing each other noticeably.

3. At about 5100 C-14 years ago the Taconic stemmed point people began to move up the valleys of tidal rivers, not only the Hudson, but the Delaware, the Susquehanna, and lesser streams. They increased and multiplied and kept moving inland with the notched point people retiring before them. But the evidence we have is that the Shattemuc people were not intimidated or disturbed. They held their own as a local cotradition.

This was the situation about 5000 B.P., with the Taconic and Shattemuc peoples holding sway in the lower Hudson for the next 1200 to 1500 years, with few changes of any kind being archaeologically discernible, even in oyster production.

By 4000 B.P. the Taconic stemmed point had changed somewhat; the blade was still narrow and the workmanship rough or casual, but the stem expanded from the blade to the base. The Shattemuc triangles tended toward the pentagonal, but this tendency had always been present. Exactly when the Twombly side-notched points put in an appearance we can't say, but it must have been about this time; they apparently came from upriver and mark a return to the area of the notched point tradition, but from a different direction. And now a fourth tradition makes the scene.

At about 4500 C-14 years ago, in Coe's Carolina sequence, there occurred a large, broad, stemmed point type called by Coe the Savannah River. It was either an immediately popular type or was associated with an immediately popular idea of some kind, or its makers were a vigorous and restless people. As a generalized style—heavy, broad of blade, and stemmed—it spread into West Virginia, Ohio, New York, and Massachusetts. Further, it went through a series of comparatively rapid modifications, of intense interest to, but not yet explicable by, archaeologists. Slightly modified, it became the Koens-Crispin of New Jersey and the Snook Kill of New York. In Pennsylvania it initiated what is called there the Broad spear tradition of the "serpent head" Lehigh type, the bulbous-bladed Perkiomen, the quadrangular-bladed Susquehanna and, finally, the narrow, sleek, round-shouldered Orient fishtail. All of these types, except the Savannah River itself, have been found on the lower Hudson riverbank sites, but only by ones or twos. Nothing suggests that any of these people were ever permanent residents of this area; they were, it seems, visitors.

Why they were visiting is not clear from anything left behind; it may have been that they were missionaries or medicine men of a religious cult; or they may have been, as one archaeologist called them, "canoe Indians" who lived on the shores of streams and spent a great deal of time in water travel; almost certainly they were not traders or raiders. They might have been emissaries. Or, then, they might merely have been hungry.

What our model needs, in the final event, is an explanation of the attracting power of the lower Hudson, and the answer is probably food. From this lengthy but still sketchy construct of cultural history now coming to a close, at least half a dozen typological strains that are not yet understood have been omitted, as has the whole of the ceramic period, which is still in confusion in the lower Hudson. Which is to say that the profusion of cultural materials has been organized herein but far from exhausted. The lower Hudson was visited throughout the length of human occupation by groups from hundreds of miles away, and whatever the reasons were, one of them must have been that it was an unfailing and rich source of food. An arm of the sea thrust deep into a woodland environment, the food supplies it afforded were not affected in the least by drought, climatic reverses, or cyclic scarcities. If late frosts killed off the acorn, nut, and berry crops, if drought cut the harvests of vegetal foods, if the deer were thinned out by heavy winter snows, if streams dried up, there were still fish and shellfish in the Hudson and waterfowl overhead. There must have been times of hunger in this area; there need never have been starvation. Anybody who could stagger to the Hudson's shores could find a meal there. It is therefore not too unlikely that the lower Hudson was a place of mystical significance, hallowed ground, like the pipestone quarries of Michigan, where hostilities ceased and all tribes tolerated each other in times of common need and adversity.

This is what explanation-interpretation strives for, the understanding of the flow of human life, its quality and its purposes.

The reader who lives in Seattle, Washington or Tampa, Florida may object that the foregoing tells him more about the lower Hudson than he has any possible use for. But it is not really about the lower Hudson; it is about the archaeology of Seattle and Tampa and every other place inasmuch as it demonstrates what archaeology does. The details of the story will not be the same in every area, but the story itself will be, a succession of peoples and their evolving cultures related to their needs and the environmental potential in satisfying them. We gathered what evidence we could and made of it what we could, in human history and human behavior. The digger from Seattle and from Tampa will find himself doing the same thing, running into the same *kind* of problems, doing the same *kind* of research, and finding the same *kind* of solutions. The basic data of archaeology are always what is found and that varies from place to place, but the activities that produced the data were motivated by basic human group motivations, which do not, on the precivilized level of most of American prehistory, vary from place to place. Every topographically "natural" area like the lower Hudson will reveal to the persistent digger another lower Hudson story.

chapter 13

Writing Good Reports

MANY—PERHAPS MOST—citizen archaeologists view the writing of a report for publication of the sites they have excavated, studied, and analyzed with foreboding. In consequence, the report does not get written, and the work becomes just another unprosecuted hijacking of the treasures of American prehistory. Or the data is turned over to somebody else to write, and becomes his by adoption, with the parent's name tacked on as junior author. The writer always gets first credit.

While it is true that the translation of data into the cogency and persuasiveness of a good report requires another order of competence than that which produced it, there is a basic conventionality of design in reports that, like the rules of any game, from hopscotch to chess, can be learned by watching a performance, with commentary. Once the design is learned, writing a report will become almost like filling in an application form for a job.

The two reports that follow are examples of the basic report design. That they are both on work in the East grows out of the often stated endeavor of this book. The reader is by now familiar with the typological names, phases, and general cultural succession of the East; it will not be necessary to introduce, hastily define, and laboriously describe the elements of a whole new regional archaeology. It would be very bad form to bring on stage, in the last chapter, a whole new cast of characters. The reader should be able to follow the sense of the two reports, not as specimens contrived for his instruction but as episodes in a narrative of which he already has a grasp. Thus he will not only have absorbed a text on methods and theory; he will have, vicariously, done archaeology.

The first report, by the Weinman brothers, both non-professionals (though Paul does work out of New York State Museum and is the author of *A Bibliography of the Iroquoian Literature, Partially Annotated*), is on a limited site which yielded few materials and posed no difficult problems of interpretation. The structure of it, therefore, is not obscured by necessities of elaboration or extended discussion. The student can emulate it line by line and paragraph by paragraph and produce a useful summary public record that almost any editor of a state or regional archaeological journal will consider printable. This report appeared in the New York State Archaeological Association journal, the *Bulletin*, in July, 1969. Following the report are explanatory notes by the author, keyed to the numbers in the superior reference marks, which have been added to the article.

THE MOONSHINE ROCKSHELTER*
Paul L. Weinman, and Thomas P. Weinman

The Moonshine Rockshelter (Cox29)[1] is located approximately 75 yds. to the north of, and 25 ft. above, Greens Lake in the Coxsackie quadrangle, 6 mi. northwest of Athens, New York.[2] We picked the name "Moonshine" after being informed by the shelter's owner, Carmen Liquori that a bootleg liquor still had been operated there during Prohibition. We found no direct or indirect evidence of this during excavation.[3] We wish to thank Mr. Liquori and his associates for permission to excavate, as well as Dr. Robert E. Funk and David Wilcox of the State Science Service and Anne Finch for their help in the work.[4]

The aboriginally occupied area lay along 5 faces of a small cluster of continuous rectangular block remnants of Onondaga limestone. These were in a stepped pattern, set at right angles to each other. The overhang was very slight, being no more than 3½ ft. deep and 4 ft. high in any place except along the northern-most block where it was 8 ft. high but only 2½ ft. deep. The vertical faces of the various blocks ranged from 7 to 10 ft. in height.[5]

*Site
Description*

Although the protected area beneath the overhang would probably not have been adequate under usual conditions, the site had the added attractions of being protected on all but the southern side by rock faces, and of having a

---

*Excavated during September, 1968.

large, flat, living floor with no immediate talus slope. Furthermore, the large quantities of eastern Onondaga flint interbedded within the shelter rock provided raw materials for tools, while the adjacent Greens Lake and rolling countryside were sources for fish, game and nuts.[6]

During the excavation of 11 five foot squares,[7] we found that the artifacts were concentrated along the southernmost block and along approximately 25 ft. of the adjacent east-facing wall. The percentage of artifacts was highest beneath and just in front of the overhang, dropping to nearly zero less than 10 ft. in front of the escarpment. Unfortunately, several large boulders of limestone had been bulldozed into what probably would have been productive squares in the southernmost end of the shelter.[8]

STRATUM I[9]

Stratum I was a dark brown material composed of a mixture of humus and finely broken down limestone, varying from a sandy texture outside the overhang to a loose powder beneath. Numerous fragments of flint, both worked and unworked, and limestone were mixed throughout. For the most part, stratum I was 10 in. in thickness, although it ranged from 8 to 15 in. A small number of historic items such as glass and nails were discovered almost to the bottom of the stratum.

The major, if not the entire, Indian occupation of this stratum was representative of Transitional[10] times as characterized by the Orient phase. Two whole Orient Fishtail points[11] and the base of a third were recovered as well as 2 other points which were short (36 mm and 33 mm) and broad (21 mm and 20 mm) with the typical fishtail flaring bases. Although within the morphological range of Orient Fishtail points, these last two may some day be separated into a subtype, if found in abundance elsewhere.

In this stratum were found five untyped side-notched points which, as Dr. William A. Ritchie has noted (personal communication,[12] 1968), have been found on Long Island Orient sites, specifically Jamesport (Ritchie, 1959) and may well represent a form used in developmental Orient times during the terminal Lake Archaic or very early Transitional. These 5 points were fairly well-made, medium in length and width, having broad side-notches and concave to convex bases. In length they ranged from 40 to 56 mm with an average of 47 mm; in width from 20 to 23 mm with an average of 21 mm; in thickness from 7 to 9 mm with an average of 8 mm. An eleventh point was a short, crude lobate-stemmed untyped variety with sharp shoulders.

Other artifacts found in stratum I were: a finely chipped rectangular-bladed knife with an Orient Fishtail base; 7 triangular to ovate knives, 3 of which were very fine and thin and one of which may have been a point; 17

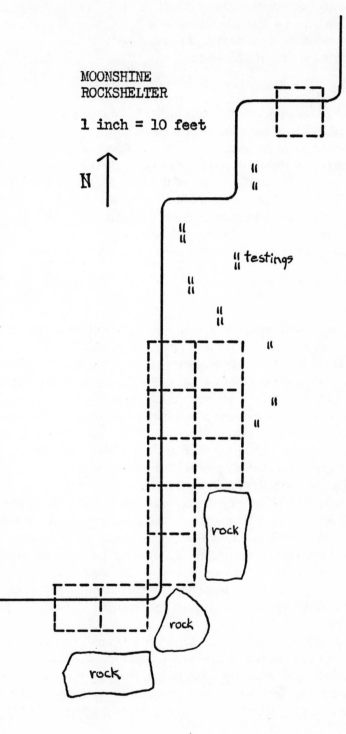

MOONSHINE
ROCKSHELTER

1 inch = 10 feet

N

testings

rock

rock

rock

crude ovate to triangular knives or knife blanks; 6 flake knives; 1 straight drill; 2 small side scrapers; 39 variously worked flint fragments; a single worked slate piece; 4 quartzite and 1 flint hammerstones; a granite and a sandstone anvilstone; a quartz crystal piece; a quartzite anvil-hammerstone; a polished bone awl tip and a flint core.

Although the large amount and variety of flint chipping debitage of eastern Onondaga flint mined from the parent rock, in context with the 9 tools (hammerstones, anvil-hammerstone, and anvilstone) used in chipping, are strong evidence for the use of this site as a workshop station, slightly less than 40 percent of the flint artifacts were of this Onondaga flint. Sixty percent of the other flint artifacts (all Normanskill flint) had their source at nearby Flint Mine Hill and other related quarries. Several specimens were of Kalkberg flint which was obtainable within 10 mi. north of the site.[13]

Deer and turkey bones, evidence for hunting, were also found in stratum I.[14]

The only other available reports of the Orient phase in the middle Hudson Valley are those from Lotus Point (Ritchie, 1958), which is about 5 mi. south of the Moonshine shelter on the Hudson, and the Dennis Site (Funk, n.d.)[15] near Troy on the Hudson some 35 mi. north. Both of these sites produced the characteristic steatite vessel fragments, though only Dennis yielded Vinette I pottery, which is often found on Orient sites. At the Moonshine Rockshelter steatite and pottery did not occur. Taking this into account, along with the equal proportion of side-notched to fishtail points at the shelter, and noting that these probably earlier side-notched forms were not found at Dennis and Lotus Point, we feel justified in calling the stratum I occupation at Moonshine an early developmental stage of the Orient phase. The absence of pottery and steatite at this particular site does not necessarily mean that the Orient inhabitants of the shelter did not have these containers. If the shelter were primarily, if not exclusively, a fall-winter camp, the heavy stone bowls or fragile Vinnette I pottery may have been too burdensome for small, mobile hunting parties to carry around. The extreme rarity or absence of both items in back-country stations has been demonstrated by Funk (n.d.) for the Hudson Valley.

Ritchie (1965) has dated the range of the Orient phase on Long Island from 1043 B.C. to 763 B.C. We believe that the Moonshine occupation would fit into the earlier phases of this span, taking into account the time which may have passed if the traits of the Orient phase diffused into the middle Hudson Valley from the Long Island area where they are best-known.

Stratum II was a tan to brown soil composed of leached and compacted humus and powdered limestone intermixed with numerous fragments of limestone and flint which had broken from the rock wall. Fortunately, it was thickest (5 in.) beneath and in front of the overhang along the east-facing wall where most of the artifacts were uncovered. Stratum II pinched out at the northern and southern extremes of this wall and within 10 ft. outside the same overhang.

At the top of stratum II we found 1 Normanskill type projectile point;[17] a narrow stemmed point similar to those found on some River Phase sites; a red slate Snook Kill[18] point; 3 quartzite hammerstones; a knife fragment; and an ovate knife. Because of the thinness of this upper zone, no stratigraphic relation can be suggested between the diagnostic points of the River and Snook Kill phases. However, at the base of stratum II were a Vosburg[19] projectile point, a notched slate bannerstone wing and a side scraper. If nothing more, this does suggest a confirmation of the generally accepted relationship of Vosburg to later periods such as the River and Snook Kill phases (Funk, 1965).

Deer, bear and turkey bones were found in stratum II.

Archaeology

Stratum III was a compact yellow-brown sand of untested thickness. The sole artifact which might be associated with this stratum was a flint object found directly on the junction of strata I and III where there was no stratum II. This piece has a striking resemblance to preforms for Clovis points[20] found at Kings Road (Funk, Weinman and Weinman, 1969) and West Athens Hill (Funk, n.d.), both Paleo-Indian sites. Made of Normanskill flint, it is fluted on both sides, 29 mm and 27 mm from the base. It is 8 mm thick and 37 mm long from base to the hinge fracture which is 10 mm above the end of both flutes. The sides are roughly parallel to each other as well as being parallel flaked. Except where the flutes had been driven from the center, grinding is evident on the base and along the entire length of one side and 5 mm of the other. Unfortunately, the absence of any other diagnostic artifacts and the lack of convincing stratigraphy lead us to no definite conclusion on its significance. However, accepting the probability that it is a Paleo-Indian artifact, when considered with the Cumberland point found at the Dutchess Quarry Cave (Funk, n.d.), it is only the second known piece of evidence for rockshelter habitation or visitation by Early Man in the Northeast.

Surprisingly, no features were found at the Moonshine Rockshelter, although 2 definite postmolds were discovered several inches apart nearly 5 ft. from the overhang in the middle of the occupied area along the east-facing wall. These were 4½ and 5 in. in diameter and extended 14½ and 16 in. into

Conclusion

the ground, well into stratum III. They may be evidence of supports used for a skin or bark windbreak leaning against the escarpment. There is no means of ascertaining to what occupation the post molds could be attributed.

Apparently the Moonshine Rockshelter was inhabited, possibly in the fall and winter, because of a unique combination of factors—shelter, abundant flint, nearness to a source of fish, and within a good hunting and gathering region. Individuals, or at most, a few people stopped for a very short time at the site during Vosburg, River and Snook Kill phases times as shown from diagnostic artifacts found in stratum II. Stratum I evidenced the most intensive occupation during very Late Archaic or early Transitional times by spasmodic visits of single Indian hunters or nuclear family groups.

Aside from the limited amount of information concerning the aboriginal occupations, we did learn that an uninviting-looking overhang may well have been used by primitive man and that such sites should not be ignored in archaeological surveys.

References

Funk, Robert E.

1965.   *The Archaic of the Hudson Valley—New Evidence and New Interpretations.* Pennsylvania Archaeologist, v. 35, nos. 3-4. Gettysburg, Pa.

n.d.   *Recent Contributions to Hudson Valley Prehistory.*

_____, Thomas P. Weinman and Paul L. Weinman

1969.   *The Kings Road Site: a Paleo-Indian manifestation in Greene County, New York.* The Bulletin, No. 44. New York State Archaeological Assoc. Rochester, N.Y.

Ritchie, William A.

1958.   *An Introduction of Hudson Valley Prehistory.* New York State Museum and Science Service Bulletin. 367. Albany, N.Y.

1959.   *The Stony Brook Site and Its Relation to Archaic and Transitional Cultures on Long Island.* New York State Museum and Science Service Bulletin 372. Albany, N.Y.

1. The site designation, according to the quadrangle numbering system, assigned in the New York State site register.
2. Almost always in short site reports and very often in long, monograph-length reports the site name and location constitute the opening statement. There is no standing rule barring other kinds of leads if they are, in the journalistic sense, good

ones, but the site name and location have to be introduced in this direct fashion in an early paragraph.

3. Prior historic use of the site. Most sites do not have such colorful skeletons in their closets, having been cornfields, lawns, or woodlots.

4. Acknowledgments usually appear at the end of the report, but the reporter should be scrupulous about paying them.

5. This is an obligatory description of the site as a locus.

6. An obligatory placement of the site within its environment. In longer, more ambitious reports, this placement can run to pages or even a chapter.

7. Obligatory statement on extent of work.

8. This whole paragraph describes special site conditions.

9. Usually there is at least a paragraph here on the internal geology-stratigraphy, but there seems to have been nothing remarkable at Moonshine except two discernible zones. These have been treated as strata, with the recoveries from each stratum assumed to be time-associated and the strata themselves time-separated, later on top, earlier underneath. The writers then list, identify, and read the archaeology of each zone.

10. The short period between the nonceramic Archaic and the Woodland pottery era, when soapstone vessels were in vogue.

11. A reference is missing here. It is Ritchie's *A Typology and Nomenclature for New York Projectile Points*, one of the projectile point catalogues mentioned earlier and the one in which the Orient fishtail type is formally described. Most readers of the NYSAA *Bulletin* know this, however, and do not need the reference.

12. Personal communication probably means conversation. Paul Weinman and Dr. Ritchie (now retired) worked at the time in the same building. The phrase also covers correspondence. Authorities are frequently thus consulted interpersonally. The points referred to probably belong to the Twombly side-notched type, mentioned in the previous chapter, which had not then been recognized.

13. Recognition of flint source is actually study-analysis. It derives from a knowledge of lithic sources in the area and region obtained by reference to geologic studies and knowledgeable specialists. The authors, veterans in the archaeology of the upper Hudson, have long been familiar with the flints they name. For instance, the apple green of Flint Mine Hill flint, herein also referred to as Coxsackie and Deepkill flint, has to be seen only once to indelibly impress the memory.

14. The bone recovery was meager and of food animals so common on eastern Woodland sites that an experienced excavator soon learns to identify them. But a total assemblage of bones from a site should be turned over to an expert because he may find something of significance. Even experienced excavators would not know the difference between a caribou and an elk astragolus, or between the jaws of a northern and a southern vole, but it would be of critical importance if a caribou's astragolus and the jaw of a northern vole were found on a site, since that would mean a Canadian biotic province environment.

15. The reference (Funk, n.d.) means that the work cited has not been published but is in manuscript. At the time of the report, Dr. Robert Funk was acting New York state archaeologist and a colleague of the Weinman brothers with whom he frequently both dug and published. But this is not an unusual case of "it's whom you know." Most citizen archaeologists soon learn the advantage of a friendly working relationship with a professional of stature to whom they can turn for consultation, and as often as not the information and guidance they receive is based on new current information that has not yet reached the literature. The (Funk, n.d.) reference is Funk's doctoral dissertation, which is certain to have a strong influence on New York State archaeology when available. It is therefore good study-analysis to cite it, but frustrating to the reader, who cannot see it for himself. Hence it is incumbent on the report writer to give a short summary of the relevant

material with, if there is a concise one, a quotation supporting the point being made.

16. The areal extent of stratum II should have been given.

17, 18, 19. The reference again should be *The Typology and Nomenclature*. Normanskill points are dated at about 3750 years ago, Snook Kills at about 3500 years ago. Vosburg points range widely in date from about 4500 to 5650 years ago. They are the notched points of our GO midden. Thus the contents of thin Stratum II confirm that it is in true stratigraphic position and is uncontaminated and undisturbed.

20. There is no Stratum III as a culture-bearing zone. If the preform is Clovis, that is, Paleo-hunter, then the time range represented by Stratum II is from, conservatively, 10,000 years ago to the 3750 years ago of the Normanskill points, surprising in view of the thinness of Stratum II.

The Moonshine site poses many questions for study and analysis, principally why the curious thinness of Stratum II, if it is the accumulation of some 4500 years, and why there is no cultural material representing that 4500 years. The reasons may be cultural—the area was very sparsely populated; or geologic—the overhang was destroyed by a rock fall during Clovis times and was not restored until later erosion of the rock face; or environmental—the surrounding area was in very heavy forest and not food productive. But the materials are too scarce, the stratigraphy too simplistic, and the site itself too marginally useful for any explanations that will stand tests of probability on the weight of evidence. The authors of the report have set down what came out of the site, identified it, interpreted it within the strict archaeological-anthropological limits of the meager data, and provided an excellent model of what is fundamental in site reports, that reports on more complex sites build on and expand.

The Miller Field site, on the banks of the upper Delaware, was excavated by Herbert Kraft, assistant professor in anthropology at Seton Hall University. He directed a numerous crew of up to thirty students of a summer field methods course and was partially supported by the National Parks Service. This report is a condensation of a monograph, *The Miller Field Site, Warren County, N.J.*, published by the Seton Hall University Museum. The reader should have no difficulty discerning the same skeletal structure as in the Weinman report or in recognizing the relation of the two sites.

THE MILLER FIELD SITE IN NEW JERSEY AND ITS INFLUENCE UPON THE TERMINAL ARCHAIC AND TRANSITIONAL STAGES IN NEW YORK STATE AND LONG ISLAND.

Herbert C. Kraft

Damming up a river is not the ideal way to foster archaeology, but the proposed construction of the Tocks Island Dam and Delaware Water Gap National Recreation Area have stimulated renewed interest in the prehistory of the Upper Delaware River Valley. The work conducted in this area to date has profoundly altered our views of the archaeology not only of New Jersey and Pennsylvania, but especially of Long Island and New York State.

The U. S. Corps of Engineers has developed plans for the construction of an earth-filled dam 160 ft. high to span the Delaware River from the Kittatinny Mountains in New Jersey to the Pocono Mountains in Pennsylvania. The water level behind the dam (to be located about six miles north of the Delaware Water Gap) is expected to rise to a height of 110 ft. The resultant lake will shoal off near Port Jervis, about 37 miles away. In some parts this man-made lake will be one and one-half miles wide, and the National Park Service expects to have about 100 miles of shoreline for a variety of recreational and conservational purposes.

The flooding of the Upper Delaware Valley will destroy numerous historic houses, inns, forts, and much of the Old Mine Road, one of the nation's oldest highways. The prehistorian will lose a great deal because numerous significant Indian sites are located on the flats and terraces of this beautiful valley. These Indian sites run the entire chronological gamut from Paleo-Indian to historic times.

The Miller Field site is one of the archaeological sites threatened with inundation. It is located 10 mi. north of the Delaware Water Gap bridge and about 1 mi. northeast of the presumed early Dutch copper mines at Pahaquarra. The site is ideally located. A silted knoll, having an average elevation of 9 ft. about the surrounding terrace and 20 ft. above the normal flow level of the river, extends across the field in a north-south direction. Van Campen's Brook, meandering through a forest on the eastern edge of the site, is easily accessible and must have provided the Indians with cool, clear, potable water. The Delaware River, flowing about 800 ft. to the west, undoubtedly furnished a variety of freshwater fish and mussels. It probably also served as an important means of canoe travel to north and south. Nearby forests provided firewood and materials for the construction of houses and tools. Edible nuts, such as butternut and hickory, wild grapes and berries, and numerous herbs, roots and tubers, could seasonally be gathered here. Food and fur-bearing animals were probably hunted or trapped in the immediate environment.

Some 2000 ft. east of the site the land rises sharply into the Kittatinny Mountains. Outcroppings of black flint are found in the Kittatinny limestones, and this flint was extensively exploited to provide materials for tool manufacture. These same mountains, known as the Shawanqunk Mountains in New York State, extend almost to the Hudson River at Kingston. Together with the Catskill Mountains further west, they may have been sufficiently confining to influence trade and cultural contact. Pottery styles and artifact types suggest that the Indians in the area above the Delaware Water Gap interacted more intensively with the people in New York State than with the people down-river, at least in Late Woodland times.

The Miller Field has been known as an archaeological site for more than 30 years. The New Jersey Museum conducted two limited excavations on the site in 1959 and 1965, but no reports have ever been issued. The most intensive and prolonged excavations on this site have been carried on by F. Dayton Staats, an amateur archaeologist from Oxford, New Jersey. In eight years he has dug more than 500 features. He has recorded the configuration and stratigraphy of each feature and has numbered, catalogued and preserved all artifactual and dietary evidence. Likewise, in his removal of the overburden in search of pits, he has been careful to record whatever post-molds appeared.

Mr. Staats and I became acquainted in the summer of 1965. At that time he gave me permission to examine his collection and his records. Three significant facts manifested themselves during this preliminary investigation. First, there were post-molds in abundance, and some suggested patterns. The significance of these subsurface features rested in the fact that postmolds and settlement patterns had consistently eluded archaeologists in New Jersey; the literature at least makes scant reference to them (Cross 1941:43, 138; 1956:197). Second, there was Contact Period trade material in some of the pits and burials together with artifacts of Indian manufacture. Such trade material as had been found in New Jersey heretofore was located, for the most part, in the plow zone or under circumstances that were less than ideal. The glass bottle and beads, iron hoes and nails, copper sheet artifacts and gun flints found by Mr. Staats promised to shed important new light on this critical trade period. Third, the ceramic remains, both vessels and tobacco pipes, indicated a temporal range from early Point Peninsula to Late Munsee. Spatially, the ceramic influence embraced an area from the Mohawk Valley in New York to the Overpeck region in Bucks County, Pennsylvania, and the Abbott Farm below Trenton. Distinctive tulip bowl pipes and diagnostic high collar vessels also pointed to the Susquehanna Valley in the west while Bowman's Brook pottery suggested an eastward extension to the Atlantic Ocean. Numerous diagnostic sherds promised a fair evaluation and identification of pottery types, and a correlation of such types with known ceramic tradition in New York State and Pennsylvania.

The site is owned by Mr. Edgar A. Miller, a gentleman farmer and industrialist from Cranford, New Jersey. He gave the author and a Seton Hall University Museum team permission to investigate a sizeable section of the field that was still unexcavated and undisturbed except for minor plow damage. A proposal for a grant to excavate the site was subsequently prepared and submitted to Dr. John L. Cotter and the National Park Service. The grant was issued, and in June 1967 the author and a crew of 18 students and faculty members from Seton Hall University began systematic excavations on the southwestern end of the knoll. A bulldozer was employed to remove a dense growth of weeds and about 4 in. of root-bearing topsoil. However, the remaining 4 to 6 in. of humus above the plow sole was cleared by hand and screened. This soil proved to be the repository of Early-to-Late Woodland artifacts. The plow sole was carefully troweled in order to ascertain the presence of postmolds, pits, or other evidence of cultural disturbance. Suspected postmolds were sectioned to determine their shape and to eliminate rodent burrows. Storage and refuse-filled pits were similarly sectioned to expose leafmold layers, lenses, and other types of stratigraphic detail. Good stratigraphy was not evident and acid soil conditions prevailed throughout the excavation with pH values ranging from 4.7 to 6.0. This negative soil condition helped to account for the poor preservation of organic materials.

After two weeks of work the excavation had produced the first complete house patterns ever discovered in New Jersey. Three longhouses were found. These were similar to those from the Maxon-Derby and Bates sites of early to middle Owasco provenience in central New York (Ritchie 1965, 1969:281-6). The postmold patterns indicated that the structures had rounded ends and an entrance on the long side. One house measuring 60 ft. long by 20 ft. wide had three internal partitions and deep, silo-shaped storage pits at each end, indicating year-round occupancy.

The Late Woodland and proto-historic components on the site are of great interest when compared with similar cultures in New York and Pennsylvania. However, it is not my purpose to discuss these Late Woodland discoveries here. This material is still under study and will be the subject of a separate report, although an Eastern States Archeological Federation *Bulletin* abstract is published (Kraft 1969: 12-3).

What I do wish to present in this paper is a discussion of three components that underlay the Late Woodland manifestations alluded to above. These are a Terminal Archaic (Koens-Crispin) component and two Transitional stage components: the Perkiomen, Miller Field phase, and the Orient fishtail phase. These components from the Miller Field site, and evidence from other sites in Upper Delaware River Valley, have necessitated a re-evaluation of the "Susquehanna Soapstone Culture" (Witthoft 1949:171; 1953:4-31), the "Frost Island Phase" (Ritchie 1965:155-63; 1969:156-64) and the "Orient Phase" (Ritchie 1959; 1965:163-77; 1969:164-78). The majority of the evidence for these determinations came out of the 1968 excavations of the Miller Field site which were a continuation, in depth, of the 1967 excavations referred to above.

Before embarking upon a description of these cultures or traditions I would like to clarify my position concerning the Transitional stage. The term "Transitional" was introduced into archaeological literature by John Witthoft (1953), but it has not received wholehearted acceptance because technically all cultures are in a state of transition. Some scholars prefer instead to recognize a subtle metamorphosis of the Archaic stage into the Woodland stage

(Willey and Phillips 1958; Willey 1966: 265-7). Others, like James Griffin (Jennings and Norbeck, ed. 1964:235) use the term, but see it linked with some sort of burial complex. I find the term to be useful and will, therefore, employ "Transitional stage" in the same way that Witthoft and Ritchie have used it, *i.e.* as a cultural and temporal bridge that spans Late Archaic to Early Woodland times as these stages are defined in the Northeast. There is a very obvious change between the Late Archaic and the Early Woodland. The problem is how and where to draw the line across this cultural shatterbelt. Because the problem on the Miller Field site, and in the Upper Delaware Valley generally, is somewhat different from that in central New York State, Long Island, or even southern New Jersey, an attempt will be made to present the situation as it manifests itself in terms of cultural affinities and radiocarbon dates.

The relatively early C-14 dates (1720-1640 B.C.) that we have obtained for our Koens-Crispin and Perkiomen components suggest two alternatives: (1) on the basis of early dates, absence of pottery, and presumed continuance of the hunting-gathering way of life, we might attribute these cultures, and the related Lehigh, Snook Kill, Perkiomen, and Susquehanna cultures to the Late Archaic stage; or (2) we can use the presence of steatite cooking pots as an important criterion and (a) retain the Koens-Crispin and related Lehigh and Snook Kill cultures in a terminal Archaic stage, because there is as yet no demonstrable stone bowl association with these cultures in New Jersey, New York, or Pennsylvania, and (b) assign the Perkiomen culture to a Transitional stage, since stone cooking pots are an important diagnostic trait for this culture. At the present time I prefer the second alternative.

The Orient fishtail tradition in our area provides similar problems. Our C-14 dates of 1220 B.C. $\pm$ 120 years and similarly early dates from other sites in the Upper Delaware River Valley show that this component is earlier than previously reported, although it is half a millennium later than the Perkiomen and related broadspear cultures (see Table 1). Because of this later date and the occasional associations of early pottery vessels with artifacts of the late fishtail tradition, some archaeologists favor an Early Woodland attribution. I will, however, regard the Orient Fishtail component, at least on the Miller Field site and in northwestern New Jersey, as belonging to the Transitional Stage. My reasons for doing so stem from the realization that despite the more recent dates, and the more gracile projectile points, the general mode of living had not changed significantly from that practiced by the people responsible for the Perkiomen, Susquehanna Soapstone and Frost Island cultures. Hunting and gathering were still the primary forms of subsistence, and the steatite bowl continued to play an important culinary role throughout the Orient phase. We recognize, and herein document the fact, that pottery vessels were introduced in upper Orient times, but we cannot at this time draw that fine line which separates the ceramic-using people of the late Orient tradition from their nonceramic antecedents. Undoubtedly the earliest pottery vessels continued to co-exist with the steatite kettle prototypes and, until we can clearly demonstrate the threshold separating the pre-ceramic phase from the pottery phase representative of the Early Woodland stage, I find it more reasonable to regard the Orient fishtail tradition as belonging to the Late Transitional stage.

The Terminal Archaic Koens-Crispin Component
(probably earlier than 1720 B.C. ± 120 years)

The Koens-Crispin point derives its name from the type site located in Medford, Burlington County, New Jersey, which was excavated by Hawkes and Linton in 1916, and in the late 1930's by Dorothy Cross. The Koens-Crispin point is common on Late Archaic sites in central and southern New Jersey; Joffre Coe and others see affinities between it and the "Savannah River Stemmed" point found in the Carolina Piedmont and other Middle Atlantic and Southern states. Important though the Koens-Crispin point is in New Jersey archaeology, it was never formally described (but see Kraft 1970:55-8) nor are there any C-14 dates for this projectile type, except from the Miller Field site. Joffre Coe (1964:45, 118) does have a date of 1944 B.C ± 250 years (M-524)* for the related Savannah River Stemmed Point.

The significance of this projectile point lies in the fact that the specimens excavated from the Miller Field site indicate the presence of such artifacts farther to the north than was previously supposed. The author has recently seen such Koens-Crispin points from Orange County, New York, and some of the points illustrated by Ritchie from the Weir site appear to be of this type (Ritchie 1965 and 1969 Pl. 49 #3, 4, 12, 13).

The Koens-Crispin point (PL. 1, Figs. A-E) has a large, broad blade, triangular in shape, with slightly excurvate sides. A few specimens have incurvate sides, but these suggest resharpening. Although large and heavy these boldly flaked blades are relatively thin and possess a slightly biconvex or nearly flat cross section in our sample. The shoulders are more or less angular, some being acute, others obtuse, depending upon the degree and type of curvature on the blade edge and the degree to which the shoulders project from the stem. The majority of specimens present an obtuse angle between shoulder and stem, rarely a right angle.

The stems of the Koens-Crispin points excavated by us were tapered and trapezoidal, rarely square or rectangular, and never constricted. Bases are straight to slightly convex and form rounded corners with the sides. The complete specimens range from 2 in. to 2.9 in. long, 1.25 in. to 1.6 in. wide

---

*The notations in parentheses beginning with letters are the C-14 laboratory designations and sample numbers; for example, M-524 means that the sample was the 524th run by the University of Michigan lab.

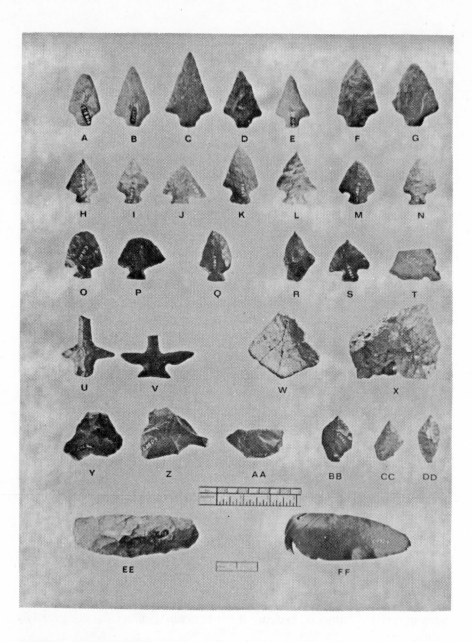

PLATE 1. KOENS-CRISPIN (A-E AND F,G) AND PERKIOMEN—MILLER FIELD PHASE COMPONENT (H-FF)

A-E Koens-Crispin points of argillite; *F-G* Snook Kill and/or Lehigh Broad points of flint; *H-N* Perkiomen Broad spearpoints of jasper; *O,P* Perkiomen Broad points bifacially rechipped into scrapers; *Q* Perkiomen type knife; *R,S* Perkiomen Broad spearpoints rechipped into gravers; *T* blade of a Perkiomen Broad point with tip and base broken off and with one wing bilaterally notched for indeterminate use; *U,V* cruciform drills with broken bits; *W* ladle or scoop made from the side and bottom portion of a steatite bowl sherd; *X* soapstone sherd showing corrugations or chisel-marks typical of the Perkiomen and later Frost Island phase stone bowls; *Y* utilized flake convex scraper; *Z* utilized flake with concave scraper and fine graver tip in center of the projection on the right; *AA* utilized flake knife or side scraper; *BB-DD* unifacially chipped utilized flakes; *EE* chipped celt or adze (6.2 in. long); *FF* polished, pointed poll celt or adze (6.15 in. long). This celt or adze was heat shattered and is here shown reassembled. It was found in a pit with 5 Perkiomen Broad points and a Koens-Crispin point. The pit and its contents are dated at 1720 B.C. ± 120 years (Y-2587).

and .25 in. thick. The majority are 2 in.-2.15 in. long and 1.25 in.-1.5 in. wide. The length-width ratio is 1.5:1 to 1.8:1.

All such projectiles from the Miller Field site are made of purple argillite. The majority of these points found in the Koens-Crispin site were also made of argillite (Cross 1941:86). Probably earlier than 1720 B.C. ± 120 years (Y-2587). (See explanation below), it is related to the Savannah River Stemmed point of the south and is, I believe, ancestral to the Lehigh Broad and Snook Kill points.

Thirteen Koens-Crispin points were excavated on the Miller Field site in 1968. Additional specimens were excavated by us at the Harry's Farm site directly north of Tocks Island in 1969. Of particular interest is the fact that the majority of specimens from the Miller Field site came from a rather concentrated area at and below the Perkiomen component. One undoubted Koens-Crispin point was found in a refuse-filled pit (Feature C-F42 in our records)* together with five Perkiomen Broad points, a polished pointed-pool celt or adze (PL 1, Fig. FF) and hickory nuts. The charcoal from this feature provided a C-14 date of 1720 B.C. ± 120 years (Y-2587). Given the preponderence of Perkiomen Broad points in this one small feature, I find it reasonable to suppose that the Koens-Crispin point had been included with the old dirt at the time the pit was back-filled. If this hypothesis is valid the Koens-Crispin point could conceivably be even older than the C-14 date would indicate. Even if it were no older than 1720 B.C., it would still be as old as the date obtained by Kinsey on a Lehigh Broad point, *i.e.* 1720 B.C. ± 100 years (Kinsey 1968:245-7). Furthermore, this date is 250 years older than that attributed to the stylistically similar Snook Kill point, which has been dated to 1470 B.C. ± 100 years (Ritchie 1965:135; 1969:136). This is, however, to be expected, considering the much more northerly position of the Snook Kill site. Apropos of this latter judgment I feel very strongly that the Lehigh Broad and Snook Kill points are really nothing more than slight variations of, or translations of, Koens-Crispin points into jasper or flint. The design configuration of these three point types is essentially the same, although the contour details on the flint and jasper Lehigh and Snook Kill Points are usually more crisp than those of the normally argillaceous Koens-Crispin points described above. This is especially true where the argillite has deteriorated because of soil conditions. (Compare PL 1, Figs. A-E with F-G).

Both John Witthoft and William A. Ritchie (1961:47; 1965:152; 1969:153) state that the Lehigh Broad and the Snook Kill points are probably related to the broad stemmed points of the Savannah River forms (Claflin 1931; Caldwell 1952:312-4), and Joffre L. Coe also identifies the Savannah

---

* Kraft used a special numbering system to designate features. In this case, C is the section of the site (Kraft divided the very large site into sections designated by letters) and F42 means the forty-second feature found in Section C.

River stemmed point with the Koens-Crispin point (Coe 1964:45). In view of these beliefs I prefer to associate the Lehigh Broad and Snook Kill point with the Koens-Crispin type, since it is the type of priority in the New Jersey-Pennsylvania area (Hawkes and Linton 1916; Cross 1941:81-90).

The Miller Field site, incidentally, yielded four Lehigh Broad spearpoints of fire-reddened jasper and two Snook Kill points of typically New York State chert. Ritchie relates the Snook Kill culture to the terminal Archaic stage in New York State because, except for a single stone potsherd, there is no demonstrable association of steatite pots on any Snook Kill phase site (Ritchie 1965:137; 1969:138). It is for the same reason that I also view the Koens-Crispin and Lehigh cultures as terminal Archaic.

The Transitional Stage
Perkiomen Component - Miller Field Phase (Pl 1, Figs. H-FF)

When Ritchie elucidated the Frost Island phase after his 1961-62 excavations on the O'Neil site in Cayuga County, New York he concluded that this phase, C-14 dated at 1250 B.C. ± 100 years, was "essentially a central New York manifestation" (Ritchie 1965:155, 1969:156). The genesis of this Frost Island phase was, he thought, in a "still unrecognized complex in New York, and a very poorly defined one in Pennsylvania, containing the Perkiomen Broad point" (Ritchie 1965:162; 1969:163). The Miller Field site contained a well defined Perkiomen component that is ancestral to the Frost Island phase by more than 400 years. The dates for this component: 1720 B.C. ± 120 years (Y-2587) and 1640 B.C. ± 100 years (Y-2588) are, incidentally, the oldest recorded dates for the Perkiomen complex.

Because of the comprehensiveness of our Perkiomen component, because of the striking similarities of artifact types with those of the Frost Island phase (excluding only the Susquehanna Broad spearpoint characteristic of the latter phase), and because that Perkiomen component is temporally antecedent to the Frost Island phase, I have postulated this Perkiomen component as the Miller Field phase (Kraft 1970: 62, 130). The people associated with the Perkiomen culture were apparently quite at home in the Upper Delaware River Valley, and for a considerable radius around. The origin of this culture is obscure, although it has been suggested that it developed regionally out of a wide-spread eastern Late Archaic broad-blade tradition such as the Savannah River tradition. More specifically the point type appears to have evolved from the more local Koens-Crispin and Lehigh Broad type antecedents.

The Perkiomen people had a predilection for fine stone, especially Pennsylvania jaspers. Every Perkiomen point found on the Miller Field site was made from brown jasper, except one, which is of high-grade chalcedony. (PL 1, Figs. H-N). The spears or knives were apparently quite large to begin with, and were frequently resharpened and reformed. Broken points were seldom discarded as long as their bases were intact. The points or ends were frequently re-touched bifacially to form different tools; knives, scrapers, and at times even a fine graver tip was isolated from the blade. (PL 1, Figs. O-S). Drills or reamers were sometimes made from broken or excessively resharpened blades, but the exquisite cruciform drills (PL 1, Figs. U, V) appear to have been separately conceived. Aside from repair holes drilled into steatite pots and into steatite beads, nothing has survived to indicate the purpose for which these elongated drills were employed.

Witthoft (1953:11) has stated that "no utilized flakes of any type, or any tools based on flakes" are associated with these broadspear traditions. This belief is also set forth by Ritchie (1965:150; 1969:151) who cites no evidence of such implements in his Frost Island phase. This may quite possibly have been the case on their respective sites, but we have found ample evidence to indicate that naturally sharp percussion flakes removed in the process of point manufacture were often used as knives without further modification. This is evident from the crushed edges found on some flakes. The Miller Field site was especially productive of deliberately modified utilized flake tools; numerous snub-nosed scrapers, side scrapers, concave scrapers, scraper-graver combination tools, and knives were found. Such utilized tools had not been reported with the Perkiomen complex heretofore. Their discovery on the Miller Field site consequently gives these people a considerably embellished tool kit. (PL 1, Figs. Y-DD).

Milling stones and mullers are associated with the Perkiomen component. An unusual feature of such Transitional stage milling stones is that they have their bottom side boldly flaked off. I have the feeling that this practice not only reduced the carrying weight of the milling stone considerably, a decided advantage for migratory people, but at the same time gave the milling stone a "grab" on the floor while food was being ground. Several simple mullers, as well as pitted mullers, were found in the excavation. Anvil stones and hammerstones were relatively common.

Table 1

Some radiocarbon dates from the Upper Delaware River Valley
compared with similar sites in Central New York and Long Island

Upper Delaware River Valley Sites

Lehigh Broad Points:	
Peters-Albrecht Site (Kinsey)	1720 B.C. ± 100
Koens-Crispin Points:	
Miller Field Site (Kraft)	ca. 1720 B.C. ± 120*
Perkiomen Broad Component (Miller Field Phase)	
Miller Field Site (Kraft)	1720 B.C. ± 120
	1640 B.C. ± 100

*This Koens-Crispin point may have been intrusive and hence even earlier than this date.

Table I (cont.)

Orient Fishtail Components:
Miller Field Site (Kraft)   1220 B.C. ± 120

Pennsylvania sites in the area of the Miller
Field site yielded comparable dates.

New York State and Long Island Sites

Snook Kill Points:
Weir Site (Ritchie)   1470 B.C. ± 100

Frost Island Phase:
O'Neil Site (Ritchie)   1250 B.C. ± 100

Orient Phase Sites on Long Island:
Sugar Loaf Hill Site (Ritchie)   1043 B.C. ± 300
Stony Brook Site (Ritchie)   974 B.C. ± 250
                                                       944 B.C. ± 250
Orient No. 2 Site (Ritchie)   950 B.C. ± 250
Jamesport Site (Ritchie)   763 B.C. ± 220

Cooking was presumably carried out in two ways: with pebble-potboilers and with steatite or talc kettles. Several areas of the excavation produced clusters of river pebbles with scaled-off surfaces, and many showed heat discoloration. Some of the stones still had adherent charred organic matter, thus supporting this contention. The Perkiomen people also had fireproof pots made from steatite or soapstone. Most of these pots are flat-bottomed and are corrugated, or show chisel marks on the outside (PL 1, Fig. X). Ritchie found similar steatite vessels associated with his later Frost Island phase. As a matter of fact, the steatite pot sherds from the Miller Field site are scarcely distinguishable from those which Ritchie illustrates on Plate 52 of his *The Archaeology of New York State*. A ladle made from the sherd of a side-and-bottom portion of a soapstone vessel with chisel-marked exterior was also found (PL 1, Fig. W).

A number of refuse-filled pits and hearths were associated with the Perkiomen component on the Miller Field site. Most important of these was pit C-F42, already alluded to. This feature measured 42 in. long, 32 in. wide and 16 in. deep. It was first encountered 7 in. below the plow sole. The fill was very dark and heavily laden with charcoal. Portions of twigs, and almost two dozen pignut hickory nuts (*Hicoria glabra*) were found. Artifacts within this feature included the Koens-Crispin point already mentioned, 5 complete Perkiomen Broad spearpoints all of brown jasper, a polished, pointed-poll celt or adze, numerous jasper flakes, and small lumps of red ochre and calcined bone too small for identification. The celt must have been introduced into the pit at the time that a roaring fire blazed within it, since it was heat-shattered and bits of it had exploded to every corner of the enclosure. All but a few fragments of this celt or bi-convex adze were found, and the implement is now restored (PL 1, Fig. FF). Charcoal from this hearth was submitted to Dr. Minze Stuiver at the Yale Radiocarbon Laboratory and was subsequently dated at 1720 B.C. ± 120 yrs. (Y-2587). Another pit (feature C-F60), located in the same stratigraphic level and less than 10 ft. distant, also had Perkiomen points in the adjacent environment. Charcoal from this feature assayed at 1640 B.C. ± 100 years (Y-2588). These two C-14 dates and others from the Upper Delaware River Valley not only provide the earliest dates for the Perkiomen complex, but also indicate the need for revising and moving the Transitional stage chronology back, at least in New Jersey, to something like 1700 to 1800 B.C. to 1000 B.C., rather than the 1300-1000 B.C. span that Ritchie ascribes to this stage.

Eight additional celts or adzes were excavated in a rather circumscribed area associated with Perkiomen points. Most of these are chipped and a few have their bits honed as well. Many of the remaining stone tools are indistinguishable from those which Ritchie illustrates from the Frost Island phase (Ritchie 1965, 1969: Pl. 53).

Three atlatl, or spear-thrower weights, were found on the site, although I am not certain whether to attribute them to the Perkiomen or to the Orient component, since points of both types were in the immediate environment. Two of these atlatl weights were of the notched, simple-winged types. These were presumably lashed across the centrum. One had an expanded centrum and was drilled (PL 2, Fig. X, Y).

The spearpoints and atlatl weights attest to a hunting and gathering economy, while the steatite bowls and milling stones give insight into food preparation. What was eaten is moot. Except for charred hickory nuts nothing has survived the consuming acidity of the soil.

Life on a campsite located between the Delaware River and Van Campen's Brook must have been based on the utilization of some sort of food derived from the river: sturgeon, shad, eel or the like, and mussel, but we found only two net sinkers that we can confidently assign to the Transitional stage. This does not rule out the possibility that these people made fish weirs or used nets; the net sinkers may have been deposited closer to the river or outside our area of excavation. Then too, Van Campen's Brook may at that time have presented a different ecological environment from the present. Even today beaver occasionally dam up the brook, causing it to back up and flood out the lowlands around the knoll. A considerable lake or marsh would have resulted from such an effort, and numerous species of animals, turtles, frogs, marsh birds, as well as beaver, might have been attracted to such an ecological niche.

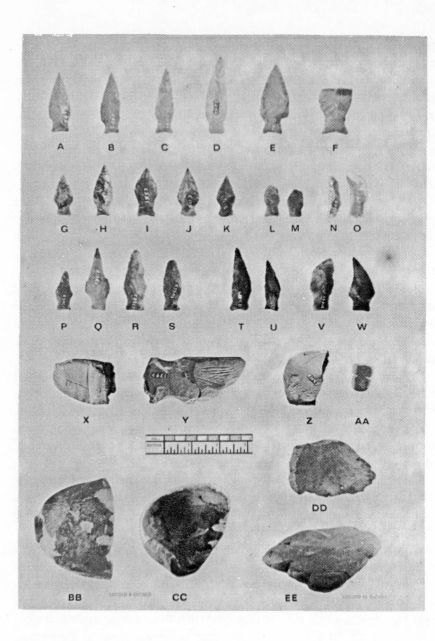

PLATE 2. ORIENT PHASE

A-F elongated Orient fishtail points; *G-K* shortened Orient fishtail points; *L,M* scrapers made from fishtail points; *N,O* utilized flakes associated with the Orient component; *P,Q* fishtail points reshaped as drills; *R,S* unmodified fishtail points with ends worn from use as drills or reamers; *T,U* fishtail knives, Type 1; *V,W* fishtail knives, Type 2; *X* broken wing of a drilled spearthrower weight; *Y* notched spearthrower weight of Perkiomen or Orient phase provenience; *Z* ground bit of chipped celt; *AA* notched soapstone bead; *BB* bottom view of a reused half of a soapstone bowl showing small lug; *CC* upper view of same reused half of a steatite bowl; note that the broken edges have been ground smooth. (This half bowl measures 6.5 in. in length, 7.75 in. in width and 4 in. in height); *DD* broken sherd of an Orient type steatite bowl with drilled repair holes; *EE* milling stone (length 12 in.)

The Orient phase, or fishtail point complex, is best known through the writings of William A. Ritchie (1959, 1965:149-77, 1969:150-78). John Witthoft first described the distinctive fishtail point as a Transitional stage projectile (Witthoft 1953:23), but in *The Stony Brook Site and its relation to Archaic and Transitional Cultures on Long Island,* Ritchie redefined the culture as an essentially Long Island manifestation, with some spill-over into adjacent states. The Miller Field site excavated by the author, and others in the Delaware River Valley, specifically W. Fred Kinsey and David Werner, have shown this complex to be more extensive than was once believed. It now appears that Long Island was not the source of innovation, but was instead the recipient of an already mature and fully developed Orient culture that came by way of New Jersey. Almost everything associated with the Orient phase on Long Island sites has been found on the Miller Field site, and some of the artifacts we excavated were not previously reported for the Orient phase. Most importantly, C-14 date for charcoal associated with a feature attributable to the Orient component on the Miller Field site provided us with a date of 1220 B.C. $\pm$ 120 yrs. (Y-2589). This date, and others from the Upper Delaware River Valley, are several hundred years older (Table 1) than those reported from the Long Island sites.

One hundred and forty-one classic Orient fishtail points were found in the excavation of the Miller Field site, and such points have been collected from many sites on the Upper Delaware River. We were able to separate statistically two types of fishtail points: an elongated fishtail point and a shortened fishtail point (Kraft 1970:66-9). Both types were present on Long Island as well (Ritchie 1969: November 3, personal correspondence). Whether this distinction existed in the mind of the aboriginal flint knapper is a moot point. However, the former is decidedly more gracile and may have represented the ideal construct (PL 2, Figs. A-F). The shortened fishtail form may represent points that have been resharpened or repointed (PL 2, Figs. G-K). We collected 70 of the former and 35 of the latter, and consider the remainder to be intergrades. Every point was made either from Pennsylvania jaspers or from local black flint. Not one point was fabricated out of quartz or quartzite, the prevailing material on Long Island.

The Miller Field site provided a fine assortment of artifacts which were made from broken fishtail points, or which were deliberately developed with fishtail-like bases. In this respect we see the continuance of a tradition already well established during earlier Perkiomen times, as noted previously.

The various tools derived from these fishtail points are of great interest in assessing the lifeways of these people. Except for an occasional fishtail-based drill and strike-a-lights, such derivative implements were unreported heretofore. The fishtail knife, Type 1 (PL 2, Fig. T, U) has many of the characteristics of a paring knife: a keen point, a flat back upon which thumb pressure might be exerted, and a blade set at a very acute angle. The more or less excurvate fishtail knife, Type 2, has similar characteristics, but appears to be less well designed (PL 2, Figs. V, W).

Fishtail-based drills were quite numerous on the Miller Field site and fall into two separate categories: those in which an actual projectile point was pressed into service, the evidence of wear being a thorough polishing and rounding of the point, and those in which the sides were deliberately constricted to produce a narrower bit (PL 2, Figs. P-S). We have evidence of the use of such drills in the perforation of steatite bowls (PL 2, Fig. DD). Gorgets and steatite beads were similarly drilled. However, it seems reasonable to expect that such drills were used for many other purposes as well. The finding of 10 fishtail drills in a relatively small excavated area suggests a rather intensive use. Wooden implements must have had wide use among such people, and holes might have been drilled into these for purposes of suspension, or in order to join one piece to another. Regrettably, nothing has survived to substantiate such conjecture.

Two fishtail scrapers have come from our excavations. These, like the Perkiomen scrapers, were bifacially trimmed across the blade in one case, and very delicately across the base in the second case (PL 2, Figs. L, M). Such artifacts might simply represent instances of broken points pressed into scraper service. Of great interest, too, is the fact that almost three dozen utilized flakes were found in this excavation. These are of convex, concave, and of specialized design (PL 2, Figs. N, O). Such utilized flake implements have not been reported from Long Island, with possibly one exception (Ritchie 1959:47).

The people who made and used the fishtail spearpoint cooked their food in much the same way as did the Perkiomen people. They seem, however, to have favored a more or less oval, round-bottom steatite vessel from which all traces of the quarry pick or chisel were smoothed away. Lugs at the ends of the pot facilitated the carrying of the pot and its contents. These soapstone bowls were probably highly prized and when a crack developed in such a vessel holes were drilled on opposite sides of the fracture in order to lace the pieces together and thereby prevent further cracking. Occasionally, however, a bowl would fracture completely. At such time a section would be saved, the severed ends would be rounded, and the scoop-like remnant would continue in use. Such reused partial steatite bowls were found at the Jamesport site and Sugar Loaf Hill site on Long Island, at the Raccoon Creek site in Salem County, New Jersey (Kier and Calverly 1967:85) and at the Miller Field site (PL 2, Figs. BB, CC). That such bowls continued in use for cooking is attested by the fact that charred organic matter still adheres to the bottom and edges of the reused half pot from the Miller Field site excavation. When such steatite bowls were beyond repair the resultant fragments were occasionally formed into gorgets or beads. One unusual steatite bead (PL 2, Fig. AA), notched instead of drilled, was found in association with fishtail points. A similar bead type was found on the Lackawaxen site in Pike County, Pennsylvania, by Vernon Leslie.

Steatite pots appear to have been part of a mortuary complex on Long Island. On the Miller Field site we uncovered some evidence of a possible mortuary complex consisting of four horseshoe-shaped ovals of fire-cracked stone. (Kraft 1970:47). However, no evidence of bone remained, although it must be noted that the soil within the stone crescents had higher traces of phosphate than surrounding soils. There was no evidence of grave offerings in the immediate surroundings. A postmold pattern emanating from about 9 in. above the horseshoe-shaped configurations suggested a superstructure, possibly a charnel house or memorial structure, but the evidence is tenuous. Such a situation would be unique in the Orient phase if our postulated reconstructions are valid.

Numerous small fire pits and refuse-filled pits can be associated with the fishtail component on the Miller Field site. Hearths are also an important part of this culture. Some of the hearths consisted of a massing of river cobbles atop the living floor. These hearths might be from 2 ft. up to 6 ft. in diameter, although one hearth was 15 ft. long and over 8 ft. wide. This may have been a food-drying or food-smoking area. Other hearths appear to have been superimposed upon shallow pits. In most of these fire places the combustion was so complete that little in the way of charred wood, bone, or vegetal matter survived. Possible strike-a-lights in the form of flint spalls, often of exotic Onandaga chert, were found, but neither pyrite nor limonite was found.

A number of milling stones (PL 2, Fig. EE) were discovered together with mullers, both simple and pitted. Anvil stones, hammerstones and possible teshoas were also found, the latter in the upper level, though well below the plow sole that distinguished the Transitional stage from the Woodland stage components.

On the basis of what we have excavated on the Miller Field site it is evident that many of the interpretations set forth by Ritchie and others concerning the Orient phase are no longer adequate. For example, the statement that the Orient fishtail point occurs only "sporadically in eastern New Jersey" (Ritchie 1959:10, 49, 90; 1965:165; 1969:166), needs to be revised in view of the large numbers of these points occurring in northwestern New Jersey and northeastern Pennsylvania. I can agree with the statement that the "Orient phase conveys the distinct impression of having achieved its climax on Long Island" (Ritchie 1965:173; 1969:174) if by "climax" is meant the final flowering and demise. It is no longer "unequivocal that the Orient culture was native to Long Island" (Ritchie 1965:164, 1969:165). It has not been demonstrated that there were any antecedent cultures on Long Island from which the Orient focus could have developed, nor is there any such evidence from southern New England (Rouse, 1969 November 18, personal correspondence). It is, however, possible to demonstrate such antecedent traditions in the Upper Delaware River Valley, where the Perkiomen-Miller Field phase has similar tool forms and steatite bowl prototypes for the later culture and vessels. Furthermore, the Miller Field site C-14 date of 1220 B.C. ± 120 years (Y-2589), and other C-14 dates from the Upper Delaware River Valley, are at least 200 years earlier than those from Long Island. I would like to suggest that our present evidence shows a derivation of the Orient phase culture from the Perkiomen (Miller Field phase) complex and/or Susquehanna Soapstone culture (Frost Island phase) of the New Jersey-Pennsylvania areas.

The Introduction of Pottery

Long before the steatite bowl fell into disuse a new cultural innovation, pottery, made its appearance on the Miller Field site, on many sites from the Potomac Valley and from Virginia north into central New York, and throughout the Susquehanna Valley. How or where pottery was first introduced into the Northeast is still being investigated and discussed. It is known that the earliest ceramic pottery in our area imitates the general form of the steatite bowls. Even more interesting is the fact that this pottery, called Marcey Creek Plain, is tempered with crushed pieces of broken steatite bowls.

Steatite might have recommended itself quite naturally as temper for this early pottery. It is heat conducting, and most of the crushed steatite so employed was itself once part of a stone cooking vessel. Pottery makers undoubtedly experimented with many forms of tempering material, and once it was discovered that crushed quartz, granite, limestone, or even coarse sand, produce as good or better results, the technological break with the soapstone prototype vessel was complete. Henceforth all vessels would be fabricated from local clays and harder grits. The form of the vessels, however, continued in use for some time after grit temper was substituted for steatite. Lugged, flat-bottomed vessels made with grit-tempered paste and having plain surfaces (Ware Plain Pottery) or cord-marked surfaces were also found on the Miller Field site in an environment containing Orient fishtail points. A similar association of Orient fishtail points with both Marcey Creek Plain and Ware Plain Pottery has been recognized by Fred Ashman on a site in the Millstone River near Rocky Hill in Somerset County, New Jersey. (Kraft 1970:113-9).

As the archaeology in New Jersey matures, and as more sensitive excavations are carried out, I am confident that still closer archaeological affinities will manifest themselves at least between northern New Jersey and New York State and Long Island.

Caldwell, Joseph R.
1952.   "The Archaeology of Eastern Georgia and South Carolina",
          In *Archaeology of Eastern United States*. James B. Griffin (ed.)
          pp. 312-321. University of Chicago Press, Chicago.

Claflin, W. H. Jr.
1931.   "The Stalling's Island Mound, Columbia County, Georgia."
          Papers of the Peabody Museum, Vol. 14, No. 1 Harvard Univer-
          sity, Cambridge.

Coe, Joffrey L.
1964.   "The Formative Cultures of the Carolina Piedmont." *Trans-
          actions of American Philosophical Society* Vol. 54, Part 3,
          Philadelphia.

Cross, Dorothy
1941.   *Archaeology of New Jersey,* Vol. 1, Archeological Society of
          New Jersey and New Jersey State Museum, Trenton.

_____

1956.   *Archaeology of New Jersey,* Vol. 2, Archeological Society of
          New Jersey and New Jersey State Museum, Trenton.

Griffin, James B.
1964.   "The Northeast Woodlands Area." In *Prehistoric Man in the
          New World*, Jesse D. Jennings and Edward Norbeck (ed.), pp.
          223-58. Rice University Semicentennial Publications, The Uni-
          versity of Chicago Press, Chicago.

Hawkes, E. W. and Linton, Ralph
1916.   "A Pre-Lenape Site in New Jersey", *The University Museum,
          Anthropological Publications*, Vol. VI, No. 3, University of
          Pennsylvania, Philadelphia.

Kier, Charles F., Jr. and Calverley, Fred
1957.   "The Raccoon Point, An Early Hunting and Fishing Station in
          the Lower Delaware Valley." *Pennsylvania Archaeologist*
          Vol. 27, No. 2, pp. 61-118, Aliquippa.

Kinsey, W. Fred III
1968.   "A Pennsylvania Transitional Period Radiocarbon Date."
          American Antiquity, Vol. 33, No. 2, pp. 245-7. University of
          Utah Printing Service, Salt Lake City.

Kraft, Herbert C.
  1969.   The Miller Field Site: Warren County, New Jersey, *Eastern States Archeological Federation Bulletin* No. 27 and 28 pp. 12-3. Attleboro.

  1970.   *The Miller Field Site, Warren County, New Jersey. Part I. The Archaic and Transitional Stages.* Seton Hall University Museum Publication. South Orange.

Ritchie, William A.
  1959.   *"The Stony Brook Site and its Relation to Archaic and Transitional Cultures on Long Island,"* New York State Museum and Science, Service, Bulletin, No. 372, Albany.

  1961.   *"A Typology and Nomenclature for New York Projectile Points,"* New York State Museum and Science Service, Bulletin No. 384, Albany.

  1965.   *The Archaeology of New York State*, Natural History Press, Garden City, N.Y.

  1969.   *The Archaeology of New York State* (Revised Edition), Natural History Press, Garden City, N.Y.

Willey, Gordon R.
  1966.   *An Introduction to American Archaeology, Vol. 1, North and Middle America,* Prentice-Hall, Inc. Englewood Cliffs, New Jersey.

Willey and Phillips, Philip
  1959.   *Method and Theory in American Archaeology,* University of Chicago Press, Chicago.

Witthoft, John
  1949.   "An Outline of Pennsylvania Indian History," *Quarterly Journal of the Pennsylvania Historical Association*, Vol. 16, No. 3, pp. 3-15, Harrisburg.

  1953.   "Broad Spearpoints and the Transitional Period Cultures", *Pennsylvania Archaeologists,* Vol. 23, No. 1, pp. 4-31, Milton.

It is with no intent to discourage the citizen archaeologist that it is pointed out that one report on a site may not be enough. The Weinman report is preliminary in tone and effect, a kind of abstract concerned with the arithmetic and primary identifications. Many sites much richer in yield are reported within this limited format to get them quickly into the record. The Miller Field report, on the other hand, deals with summaries and syntheses, and several preliminary reports, made to various recipients, preceded it. There are two sound reasons for writing a preliminary report on a site and following it somewhat later with a fuller treatment of the archaeology-anthropology. Study-analysis is a two-step process. The preliminary report covers step one, the data assembly and description; it is not procrastination to allow these data to simmer, marinate, or mature before attempting the synthesis, the shaping of them into an intelligent and intelligible whole. But the really practical reason for writing two reports is that it is easier to get two shorter reports published than one long one.

The publications most likely to be receptive to a site report from a citizen archaeologist are the state and regional archaeological journals; it is their principal reason for being, though professionals are quite content to appear in the more prestigious ones. These are periodicals, not monograph series, and set limits on the length of contributions. The Kraft submission is about as lengthy as most journal editors are prepared to go. For all practical purposes the only publishers of monograph and book-length manuscripts in archaeology are the university presses which, not unnaturally, use the funds allotted to them to print the dissertations of their graduate students. Archaeological reports are not the stuff of best sellers and commercial publication is out of the question; so also is private publication, unless the archaeologist is in a high income bracket and can write the cost off his taxes. Even duplicating a report can be expensive.

The author can testify from experience that there are all too many unmanageable manuscripts of importance in the files of both authors and editors. The latter can do nothing but attempt to sectionalize them into publishable parts, which cannot always be done. In those cases where nothing can be done, all that work, from site survey to the typing of the report, is another arrow shot into the air. It cannot be emphasized too strongly: *the archaeological dig is not complete until the report is published in some form that makes it available to those to whom the information it contains is what they have been looking for.* The only alternative to publication is the reading of the report as a paper at an archaeological conference where, like the sower's seed, it may fall on barren ground.

To list here the publications for which a site report might be eligible would be of little avail. Such publications change editors without notice, and editors change addresses; things happen to the administration of societies sponsoring publications and journals don't appear for a year, while contributions back up for three or four years. Sometimes journals disappear altogether; many of them are "n.s.," which means nonscheduled, like certain air flights. The situation is, to say the least, fluid. But the collective influence of these publications grows stronger every year as the editorial bias of the field's principal organ, *American Antiquity*, veers more and more decisively toward the anthropological and theoretical preoccupations of the "new" archaeology. State society and regional publications now carry the burden of archaeology as prehistory. The neophyte citizen archaeologist will have to seek advice from a knowledgeable colleague about which are most flourishing and most likely to be interested in his contribution. The fact is that state and regional journals are just that, limited in what they will accept by geographical pertinence; there are never more than two or three journals that will find a submission appropriate.

There is a certain preliminary strategy which the citizen archaeologist may well pursue in advance of submission of a report to a journal editor. On the whole, diggers are close-mouthed about what they are encountering on their sites, but hints dropped within earshot of an editor that what is coming out of a site is new, different, or significant will very often elicit from him a commitment to publish, with some suggestions which, if followed, bind the contract. Editors like to keep their journals in the van of discovery and there is every reason for them to collaborate with the amateur. The opportunity to talk with editors is not the least of the reasons why the citizen archaeologist will attend every conference within his scope of travel.

When the digger sees his report in print he will realize, in a moment of truth, why he dug and why he spent hours under a lamp putting it all together again. The report is the major artifact that comes out of all digs, the artifact into which all other artifacts and data are subsumed. It is a work of man and man's arts and it increases the digger's own stature as a man to have produced it. Anybody, including six-year-old children, can dig creditably, and most literate adults can do the research, once their curiosity is aroused; but to bring a dig to the fruition of a sound, honest, and intelligent report is to create—to manufacture a value for what had no value before, to give meaning to the meaningless and importance to the random. It is to precipitate out of the amorphous the hard gems of reality and truth.

E P I L O G U E:

Where to Dig for More Information

WHENEVER THE OCCASION has arisen in these pages the necessity of consulting the literature and of resort to the library has been stressed, even sermonized on. For the most part the directions given have been about the research of specific data and particularized, site-related problems. But there is a considerable body of general literature that the reader owes it to himself to sample, if he is to appreciate fully and understand pleasurably what he is doing as a prober of anthropological antiquity. To excavate a site or two or three is to know only a battle or a campaign; it is not to know the whole war or the succession of wars. Prehistory nowhere breaks into discrete, unimpinging or unimpinged upon elements. The human race has inhabited the Western Hemisphere for at least 30,000 years; it can be traced culturally to beginnings in Africa at least 2 million years ago.

Recommending a reading list is something more than copying down titles. By reason of the winds of new information, attitudes, and interpretations, books that might have been assessed as important and authoritative five years ago now appear diminished in effectiveness as references. To read them without knowing what has gone stale or sour in them is to drink deep from a slightly brackish

Pierian spring. But there remains some basic books that it is hard to see how an archaeologist can grow in knowledge and in the ability to think about, interpret, and enjoy his work without having gone into seriously. Some of these books are listed below.

WORLD BACKGROUND

Frameworks for Dating Fossil Man, Kenneth Oakley, Aldine Press, Chicago, Ill. The most concise and best organized summary and taxonomy of Old World human fossils and Stone Age industries to be had. Kept up to date by revisions and additions in later editions. The text is in the current English language, not scientific jargon.

The Origin of Races, Carleton S. Coon, Alfred A. Knopf, New York. Even its enemies admit that this book is the best record and analysis of fossil human material available in English. It is entertainingly readable. Some scientists object to its premise that there is a descriptive basis for assigning peoples to races. The nonspecialist will more likely be persuaded by Coon than by his critics.

History of Mankind, Vol. 1, Prehistory and the Beginnings of Civilization, Jackquetta Hawkes and Sir Leonard Woolley, Harper and Row, New York and Evanston. Though published in 1963, this cultural and historical account of the advancement of mankind from pebble tool maker to metallurgy, literacy, and political imperialism is an essential text in any course in world prehistory. The writing is of literary quality.

NEW WORLD BACKGROUND

An Introduction to American Archaeology, Vol. 1, North and Middle America, Gordon R. Willey, Prentice-Hall, Englewood Cliffs, N.J. The illustrations, charts, chronological columns, cultural successions, and, above all, the maps in this handsome volume give it the usefulness of a dictionary, encyclopedia, and road atlas for the territory within which the readers of this book will be working. The beginning archaeologist can orient himself immediately.

Prehistoric Man in the New World, Jesse Jennings and Edward Norbeck, editors, the University of Chicago Press for Rice University. Most colleges with American archaeology courses use this book as the introduction to American prehistoric studies. Each region is summarized and discussed by a regional specialist. The book supplements the Willey volume with much more detailed descriptions and discussions. The papers of which it is comprised were delivered at a symposium in 1962 and consequently no discoveries since then have been taken into account. Nevertheless, these papers present the consolidation and ordering of knowledge made possible by the revolutionary absolute dating technique of radioactive C-14 analysis from the release of the first C-14 dates on

January 1, 1950, to the end of the decade. By 1960, archaeologists, at first wary of this laboratory-generated chronology, had accepted it as their most useful time-determining tool and had reassessed and reassembled the data for all pre-1950 work. Thus the papers read at Rice University, Houston, Texas, on November 9 and 10, 1962 and later edited by Jennings and Norbeck mark the beginning of time-tested synthesis of American prehistory. Read with this background in mind, *Prehistoric Man in the New World* is American prehistory's primer.

No Stone Unturned: An Almanac of North American Prehistory, Louis A. Brennan, Random House, New York. This book, published in 1959, covers approximately the same decade as the above. It presents the argument from evidence and dates then in the literature for the migration of Asiatic peoples into America via a land bridge between Alaska and Chukchi Peninsula before the last advance of the Wisconsin glacier. The periods of existence of this land bridge have been established in *The Bering Land Bridge*, a symposium of papers edited by D. M. Hopkins, Stanford University Press, Stanford, California, 1967.

American Dawn: A New Model of American Prehistory, Louis A. Brennan, Macmillan Co., New York. The evidence that turned up during the 1960s for the pre-Wisconsin III occupation of the Western Hemisphere by chopper-flake people who did not make stone projectile points was developed into a totally new synthesis and schema for an American prehistory of at least 30,000 years in duration. The book was published in the fall of 1970, only six months before MacNeish reported the discovery of the Ayacucho Valley chopper-flake industry that corroborates the schema of *American Dawn*. This schema is likely to prevail and expand, though with alterations.

America's Ancient Treasures, Guide to Archaeological Sites and Museums, Franklin Folsom, Rand McNally and Co., Skokie, Ill. The tourist's guide to American archaeology. It is not a mere list of museums but a selective directory of only those museums, archaeological monuments, and sites open to the public which offer something of interest to the amateur. It is also full of entertaining and informative paragraphs that illuminate the whole subject.

The North American Indians, edited by Roger C. Owen, J. J. F. Deetz, and Anthony D. Fisher, Macmillan Co., New York. This is an anthology of excerpts, more anthropological than archaeological, from papers and monographs on the customs, religions, behavior, and social organizations of American Indians. It provides a basis for analogies with prehistoric Amerinds.

Comparative Studies of North American Indians, Harold E. Driver and William C. Massey, The American Philosophical Society, Philadelphia. This is a compendious collection of information on the tools, equipment, food, subsistence strategies, and kinship-political organizations of Indians. It is absorbing enough for reading in bed.

The Archaeologist at Work, Robert F. Heizer, editor, Harper and Bros., New York. The subtitle of this book, *A Source Book in Archaeological Method and Interpretation*, describes it neatly. It is an anthology of papers and excerpts for the digging archaeologist arranged under such section headings as "stratigraphy and stratification," "seriation," "reconstruction of specific events," "prehistoric ecology," etc.

By contrast with the broadly general literature above is the following list of references which the practical excavator will find enlightening but which he may never chance upon without this mention.

"On the Recovery of Burial Number Two at the Sasqua Hill Site, East Norwalk, Connecticut," Bernard W. Powell, *Pennsylvania Archaeologist*, April, 1965, Washington Boro, Pa. The stabilization and removal *en bloc* for exhibition of a flexed burial.

"Aboriginal Butchering Techniques at the Eschelman Site (36 LA 12), Lancaster Co., Pa.," John Guilday, Paul Parmalee, and Donald P. Tanner, *Pennsylvania Archaeologist*, September, 1962, Washington Boro, Pa. An analysis of 58,000 bone fragments found at a late prehistoric site for evidence of dismembering techniques and procedures. Guilday and Parmalee are two of the foremost zoologists in the field of American fauna, while Tanner is a citizen archaeologist.

"Experiments with the Spear Thrower," Clayton Mau, *Bulletin*, New York State Archaeological Association, Rochester, N.Y. Perhaps the only report on experiments with the ballistics of the atlatl both with and without bannerstones or weights.

"The Teshoa, A Shoshonean Woman's Knife: A Study of American Indian Chopper Industries," Frances Eyman, *Pennsylvania Archaeologist*, October, 1968, Washington Boro, Pa. Man's oldest tool as it persisted into and through all American prehistory.

"Figures in the Rock," James Swauger, *Pennsylvania Archaeologist*, August, 1961, Washington Boro, Pa. How to record petroglyphs (rock carvings) by Dr. Swauger of Carnegie Museum, a specialist in petroglyphs, who has also directed excavations in the Middle East.

"The Utilization of Flakes for Cleaning Fish," Christopher B. Donnam and M. Edward Moseley, *American Antiquity*, October, 1968, Washington, D.C. Archaeological evidence for one of the multifarious uses of simple flakes.

"Techniques of Making Plastic Casts of Artifacts from Permanent Molds," John R. Rohner, *American Antiquity*, April, 1970, Washington, D.C. How to reproduce artifacts.

"A Suggested Terminology and Classification for Burial Description," Roderick Sprague, *American Antiquity*, October, 1968, Washington, D.C. The title is the subject.

"Approaches to Faunal Analysis in Archaeology," Patricia Daly, *American Antiquity*, April, 1969, Washington, D.C. The sense and nonsense in the study of animal bone recovered from sites.

"Ammonium Chloride Powder Used in the Photography of Artifacts," David L. Weide and Gary D. Webster, *American Antiquity*, January, 1967, Washington, D.C. A hint to the photographer of artifacts.

"A Functional Analysis of Certain Chipped Stone Tools," George C. Frison, *American Antiquity*, April, 1968, Washington, D.C. About flaking and the use of flakes.

"Flotation Techniques for the Recovery of Small-Scale Archaeological Remains," Stuart Struever, *American Antiquity*, July, 1968, Washington, D.C. An amazing amount of minute plant and animal material can be recovered by flotation.

"Soil pH as a Tool in Archaeological Site Investigation," James Deetz and Edward Dethlefsen, *American Antiquity*, October, 1963. Soil profiles without visible stratigraphy can be drawn from variability in soil acidity.

"Stratigraphy and Seriation," John Howland Rowe, *American Antiquity*, January, 1961, Washington, D.C. The two kinds of seriation and their correlative use with stratigraphic information.

"The Desert Culture of the Western Great Basin: A Lifeway of Season Transhumance," Emma Lou Davis, *American Antiquity*, October, 1963, Washington, D.C. How Amerinds adapted their subsistence habits to a very difficult environment.

"Archaeological Field Sampling," S. Rottenberg, *American Antiquity*, October, 1964, Washington, D.C. Sampling is not a random process, if it is the intent to discover the nature of a site by testing alone.

"Flaking Stone With Wooden Implements," Don Crabtree, *Science*, July 10, 1970, Washington, D.C. Lithic technology by an expert in experimental methods.

The special techniques and problems of historical archaeology in America have been extensively discussed in the literature of Ivor Noel Hume, who is in charge of the excavation and reconstruction of Colonial Williamsburg. His contributions are:

Historical Archaeology, Alfred A. Knopf, New York. The jacket reads: "A comprehensive guide for both amateurs and professionals to the techniques and methods of excavating historical sites." That says it, except to point out that the book is as readable as it is comprehensive.

Artifacts of Early America, Alfred A. Knopf, New York. A book for the archaeologist, the antiquarian, the antiques dealer, the collector, and the general reader.

While it is a pleasure to make recommendations for reading and to acquaint the newcomer to archaeology with the resources that he can call on (thirty years ago there was not a tenth of the current volume and coverage), there is a point beyond which it becomes auctorial self-indulgence. The citizen archaeologist who reads half the above references will thereafter be able to chart his own course through the library of archaeology and anthropology, following whatever specialty catches his fancy, be it lithic technology or mortuary practices. When he has reached that level of self-sufficiency, he is where it has been the concern of this book to guide him.

This book has tried to achieve something beyond a grammar of methodology. To engage in archaeology as it has been described in these pages is to order one's life in a certain way—a highly satisfactory way, for those temperamentally suited to it. Those who have persevered up to now will know whether they are suited to it and how much they want to give to it of themselves and their time. To men of the author's acquaintance it has been of such absorbing interest that retirement from business was only an opportunity to expand an archaeological avocation into a full-time productive activity, not an end but a beginning. There is a great deal more to it than the mechanics of treasure hunting, as the reader should know.

Why dig? There is no better answer than the following quotation from *The Testimony of the Spade* by Geoffrey Bibby, a field archaeologist (*Searching For Dilmun*, Alfred A. Knopf, is an account of his work in the Middle East) and a writer of charm and force. He says: "Every archaeologist knows in his heart why he digs. He digs . . . that the dead may live again, that what is past may not be forever lost, that something may be salvaged from the wrack of ages, that the past may color the present and give heart to the future."

Whoever digs in this spirit will never regret a minute spent on it; it pays as you go.

Guide to Sites

Kinishba Pueblo, Whiteriver; partly restored Mogollon-Anasazi pueblo.

Kinlichi Tribal Park, Cross Canyon Trading Post; Anasazi houses.

Montezuma Castle National Monument, Flagstaff; a cliff dwelling in pristine condition and Montezuma Well, a spring-fed lake.

Navajo National Monument, Tuba City; cliff villages, three separate ruins.

Old Oraibi, Tuba City; an ancient village still inhabited by the Hopi, open by permission of Hopi elders.

Painted Rocks, Gila Bend; petroglyphs.

Petrified Forest National Monument, 70 miles from Gallup; two Anasazi sites.

Pueblo Grande Museum, Phoenix; a large Hohokam site with associated museum.

Tonto National Monument, 30 miles from Globe; two cliff dwelling ruins.

Toozigoot National Monument, Cottonwood; hilltop village.

Walnut Canyon National Monument, 10 miles from Flagstaff; cliff dwelling complexes.

Walpi, 70 miles from Tuba City; a still inhabited Hopi village where the Snake Dance Ceremony is held in odd-numbered years.

Wupatki National Monument, 45 miles from Flagstaff; 800 ruins.

Arkansas

Caddo Burial Mounds, Murphreesboro; a privately owned, commercially operated tourist enterprise with museum and souvenir shop.

California

Calico Mountains Archaeological Project, near Barstow; a controversial Early Man site in process of excavation.

Chalfont Valley Petroglyphs, Bishop; petroglyphs.

Clear Lake State Park, Lakeport; pre-Pomo Indian settlement.

Coyote Hills Regional Park, Alvarado; shell mounds, museum.

Indian Grinding Rock State Historical Monument, Pine Grove; 363 petroglyphs and 1185 bedrock mortars.

Joshua Tree National Monument, Twentynine Palms; petroglyphs, sites of Pinto Basin culture and others, museum.

Lava Beds Monument, Tule Lake; petroglyphs.

Sequoia and Kings Canyon National Parks, reached from Bakersfield or Fresno; petroglyphs and village site.

Colorado

Great Sand Dunes National Monument, about 30 miles from Alamosa; two archaeological sites with materials dating from 10,000 B.P. to late prehistoric times.

Mesa Verde National Park, reached from Cortez or Mancos; more archaeology than anybody can take in on one visit. In 1972 the great Wetherill Mesa ruins and restoration were added to Mesa Verde.

Delaware

Island Fields, directions available from Delaware State Museum, Dover; a working site, with a village and an extensive cemetery.

Florida

Crystal River Historic Memorial, Crystal River; burial and ceremonial mounds, museum.

Madira Bickel Mound Historic Memorial, reached from Bradenton; a settlement occupied for about 1500 years, with shell, temple mounds on Terra Ceia Island.

Safety Harbor Site, Safety Harbor; temple mound.

Temple Mound Museum and Park, Fort Walton Beach; restored temple mound and museum.

Turtle Mound Historic Memorial, reached from New Smyrna Beach; a huge shell refuse mound, mostly oysters.

Georgia

Etowah Mounds Archaeological Area, Cartersville; a working archaeological project, museum, and mounds restoration project.

Kolomoki Mounds State Park, Blakely; largest mound group in the Gulf Coast region, probable ceremonial and administrative center.

Ocmulgee National Monument, Macon; temple mounds, a restored ceremonial center and museum.

Rock Eagle Effigy Mound, reached from Eatonton; an eagle effigy mound.

Track Rock Archaeological Area, Chattahoochee National Forest, Blairsville; petroglyphs.

Idaho

Alpha Rockshelter, reached from Salmon; cave site, occupied from 8000 B.P., with pictographs.

McCammon Petroglyphs, reached from Pocatello; petroglyphs on roadside boulders.

Nez Perce National Historical Park, Spalding; the Weis Rockshelter, where occupation began 8000 B.P., has been prepared for public viewing.

Illinois

Cahokia Mounds State Park, reached from East St. Louis; a mound group including the largest earthen mound in the United States, so large that an auto road has been built up it.

Dickinson Mounds Museum of the Illinois Indian, Havana; a Hopewellian burial mound and prehistoric village site, museum.

Koster Site, Kampsville; a must-see working site with exposed stratification.

Mississippi Palisades State Park, Savanna; mounds and Indian trails.

Père Marquette State Park, Grafton; 18 known sites.

Starved Rock State Park, Ottawa; Indian trails, cave and open sites.

Indiana

Angel Mounds State Park, Evansville; a mounds and village site so extensive that work has been going on for 20 years.

Mounds State Park, Anderson; nine Hopewellian mounds, chiefly burial tumuli.

Wyandotte Cave, Wyandotte; a calcite and flint mine, privately owned.

Iowa

Effigy Mounds National Monument, Marquette; 200 effigy and geometric figure mounds.

Fish Farm Mounds, New Albin; another group of about 30 mounds spanning the Woodland period.

Pikes Peak State Park, McGregor; a mound group including a spectacular one of a bear.

· Kansas

Indian Burial Pit National Historic Landmark, Niles; a privately operated working site, at which the excavation of a late Woodland village has been competently done and the remains preserved.

Inscription Rock, Lake Kanapolis State Park, reached from Ellsworth; petroglyphs.

Pawnee Indian Village Museum, near Belleville; displays of materials recovered from excavation of a Pawnee village, of which many exposed features can be seen.

Kentucky

Adena Park, near Lexington; circular earthwork ceremonial center of Adena culture.

Ancient Burial City, Wickliffe (reached from Cairo, Illinois); a private commercial exhibit with mound groups and village patterns. The archaeological interpretations are questionable, but the material is rich.

Blue Licks Battlefield State Park, Blue Licks (reached from Lexington); a salt spring used by Paleo-hunters and a Fort Ancient culture village site.

Mammoth Cave, Cave City; a cave site the archaeology of which has been explored only recently.

Louisiana

Marksville Prehistoric Indian Park State Monument, Marksville; 40 acres of burial and temple mounds, museum.

Poverty Point, Bayou Macon; Poverty Point culture earthworks and mound group, on private property.

Maine

Damariscotta Shell Mounds, Damariscotta; not a formal site or excavation, though there has been some excavation. These shell heaps are an example of shell refuse accumulations at habitation locations.

Maryland

Piscataway Park, reached from Alexandria, Virginia; an area heavily occupied by Indians for up to 10,000 years which has been excavated. Excavation may or may not be underway.

Massachusetts

Dighton Rock State Park, Fall River; the Indian petroglyphs on the rock that gives this site its name are much confused by non-Indian additions. The inscribed rock has been more important as a subject of controversy than as archaeology.

Plimoth Plantation Inc., Plymouth; an Indian "farmstead" of mild interest is associated with the Colonial exhibits.

Michigan

Fort Michilimackinac National Historic Landmark, Mackinaw City; a working site during July and August, with museum.

Isle Royale National Park, reached by boat only, from Houghton, Michigan or Grand Portage, Minnesota; an aboriginal mining center for native copper widely used throughout several cultures beginning about 7000 B.P.

Norton Mounds National Historic Landmark, Grand Rapids; a Hopewell mound group on which no official excavation has been done, though some work may begin soon.

Minnesota

Mille Lacs State Park, Lake Mille Lacs; museum, with demonstrations by Ojibway Indians of rice gathering and processing. University of Minnesota field parties are usually at work in the park in season.

Pipestone National Monument, Pipestone; quarry for catlinite or Indian pipestone, museum.

Mississippi

Bynum Mounds, Natchez Trace (reached from Tupelo); burial mound group.

Emerald Mound, Natchez Trace; third largest temple mound in the United States.

Natchez Trace, runs from Nashville, Tennessee to Natchez, Mississippi, with a visitors' center at Tupelo, Miss. The Trace passes many mound groups and excavated sites the records of which are on file at the center.

Owl Creek Indian Mounds, Tombigbee National Forest, Davis Lake; five mounds including two restored ceremonial mounds.

Missouri

Graham Cave State Park, reached from Danville or Montgomery City; a working site showing 10,000 years of human habitation.

Towosahgy State Park, reached from East Prairie; a working site on a 30-acre Mississippian culture village.

Utz Site, Van Meter State Park, reached from Marshall; a working site, a cooperative project of the University of Missouri and the Missouri State Park Board, through the Lyman Archaeological Research Center and the Hamilton Field School.

Washington State Park, De Soto; two petroglyph sites, museum.

Montana

Madison Buffalo Jump, reached from Logan; the complete site plan where buffalo were driven over a bluff to slaughter plus the tepees where the hunters lived during the drive and butchering.

Pictograph Cave State Monument, reached from Billings; a deep-deposit cave with pictographs, or wall paintings.

Nevada

Lake Mead National Recreation Area, reached from Las Vegas or Glendale; petroglyphs and other sites.

Rocky Gap Recreation Area, reached from Las Vegas; petroglyphs and a settlement pattern.

New Jersey

Abbott Farm Site, Trenton; one of the most famous sites in the United States, this site is maintained as part of the Watson House restoration, headquarters and museum for the New Jersey Daughters of the American Revolution; it is apparently inexhaustible and excavation may or may not be going on at any given time.

New Mexico

Acoma Pueblo, reached from Albuquerque; an ancient pueblo still being lived in. Permission must be obtained from village authorities to take photos or do drawings.

Aztec Ruins National Monument, Aztec; a huge ruined town-size settlement with the great kiva, or ceremonial apartment, restored.

Bandelier National Monument, reached from Santa Fe; dwelling ruins running for two miles along the side of a gorge with manmade caves in the cliffs behind them.

Chaco Canyon National Monument, Crownpoint; location of the famous Pueblo Bonito, a masonry apartment building of 800 rooms; several hundred other sites on the grounds.

Coronado State Monument, Albuquerque; the location of the huge Kuaua Pueblo, with over 1200 rooms, built of adobe.

El Morro National Monument, El Morro; partially excavated and preserved pueblo Indian village; other village ruins and petroglyphs.

Gila Cliff Dwellings National Monument, near Silver City; ruins of a village settlement built in a huge cave.

Gran Quivira National Monument, reached from Mountainair; a Spanish mission and excavated and unexcavated Pueblo Indian ruins.

Jemez State Monument, Los Alamos; the partially excavated ruins of a very large pueblo.

Kwilleylekia Ruins Monument, reached from Silver City; a privately owned site under continuous professionally directed excavation. Tours and lectures are conducted by informed personnel.

Laguna Pueblo, reached from Albuquerque; a still inhabited archaeological site.

Pecos National Monument, reached from Santa Fe; ruins of a pueblo that was probably the most populous in the present United States at the time of Spanish contact.

Picuris Pueblo, reached from Riverside; a partially excavated settlement.

Puye Cliff Ruins, on Santa Clara Reservation, reached from Espanola; a huge ruin in three levels, on cliffs, in cliffs, and at base of cliffs; some sections excavated and restored or preserved.

Quarai State Monument, reached from Mountainair; an unexcavated pueblo ruin and a Spanish mission of the 17th century.

Sandia Cave National Historic Landmark, reached from Albuquerque; a strenuous climb to an important Early Man site.

San Juan Pueblo, Espanola; a Spanish-contact period pueblo ruin.

Santa Clara Pueblo, reached from Santa Fe; a relatively modern pueblo dating from the early 16th century.

Taos Pueblo, Taos; still occupied pueblo dating from pre-contact times.

Three Rivers Petroglyphs, reached from Carrizozo; some 500 petroglyphs along a half-mile stretch of trail.

Zia Pueblo, reached from Santa Ana; partially excavated ruins and still inhabited dwellings; may be under excavation.

New York
Owasco Village, Auburn; reconstruction of a village of the ancestral Iroquois Owasco culture which cast a wide net of influence over New York and Pennsylvania aborigines about A.D. 1000.

North Carolina
Oconaluftee Indian Village, Cherokee; reconstructed Cherokee village on a site dating back some 5000 years.

Town Creek Indian Mound, Mount Gilead; a palisaded village site, with plaza and temple mound of the late prehistoric period as reconstructed; museum.

North Dakota
Crowley Flint Quarry, Hebron; an aboriginal flint mine.

Double Ditch Site, Bismarck; remains of a large Mandan Indian village.

Fort Clark Site, Fort Clark; a contact period Mandan village.

Huff Village Site, Huff; remains of a palisaded Mandan village.

Menoken Site, Menoken; remains of a Mandan village.

Molander Site, Price; Mandan earth lodge village site.

Slant Village Site, Fort Lincoln State Park, Mandan; restored Mandan earth lodges of prehistoric period.

Writing Rock Boulder, Fortuna; a glacier boulder covered with petroglyphs.

Ohio

Campbell Mound, Columbus; a pre-Hopewell Adena culture mound.

Flint Ridge Quarry, Zanesville; the most famous aboriginal flint source in the eastern United States; the variegated flints and chalcedonies are very distinctive. Museum at site near Brownsville.

Fort Ancient, near Lebanon; Hopewellian earthworks, apparently fortifications, and a later settlement by the quite different Fort Ancient people. Museum.

Fort Hill State Memorial, reached from Hillsboro or Chillicothe; Hopewellian ceremonial and defensive earthworks. Museum.

Inscription Rock, Kelleys Island in Lake Erie off Sandusky; a petroglyph-covered boulder.

Leo Rock, Leo, near Coalton; a boulder used for petroglyphs.

Miamisburg Mound, Miamisburg; a large Adena mound.

Mound City Group National Monument, Chillicothe; apparently a burial mound and ceremonial center for the Ohio Hopewell people. Materials taken from these mounds are the most spectacular of prehistoric provenience found in the present United States. Museum.

Newark Earthworks, Newark; another large Hopewellian earthworks complex. Unfortunately not much of the complex remains; it once comprised burial tumuli and "geometric" earthworks, apparently enclosing sacred precincts. Included in the Newark complex are the Wright Earthworks and the Octagon Mound.

Seip Mound, Bainbridge; a group of Hopewellian burial mounds, with a circular earthwork over a mile in circumference. Museum.

Serpent Mound, Locust Grove; a quarter-mile-long effigy mound of a snake with an egg in its mouth, thought to be Adena. One of the greatest prehistoric wonders within the present United States.

Story Mound, Chillicothe; a reconstructed Adena mound visible from the street.

Tarlton Cross Mound, Tarlton; an effigy or geometric mound in the shape of a Greek cross, with conical mounds in association.

Oklahoma

Indian City, Andarko; an outdoor museum operated by an Indian-managed corporation consisting of reconstructions of house patterns for Indians of the southern plains and Southwest. The reconstructions are authentic.

Oregon

Collier State Park Pit-House, reached from Klamath Falls; an excavated and partially restored pit-house.

South Carolina

Seewee Mound, Francis Marion National Forest, reached from Charleston; a shell mound and associated living area.

Tennessee

Chucalissa Town, Memphis; a very interesting Mississippian culture town in two parts: the ceremonial, temple mound precincts and the inhabited section. Partly reconstructed and restored; some excavation may be going on. Museum.

Old Stone Fort State Park, Manchester; sections of stone wall, possibly built under Hopewellian influence, along a high bluff of the Little Duck River.

Shiloh Mounds, Shiloh National Military Park, reached from Savannah; a collection of about 33 mounds, some burial, some dwelling mounds.

Texas

Alibates Flint Quarry and Texas Panhandle Pueblo Culture National Monument, Sanford; this site may not yet be open to general visitation but may be viewed by special appointment. Alibates flint is as famous in the West as Flint Ridge stone is in the East. Both were used at least 10,000 years ago. A Pueblo Indian-related people later built a village near the quarry, about a mile in length along the outcrop.

Utah

Anasazi Indian Village State Historic Site, Escalante; an excavated Anasazi village with museum.

Arch Canyon Indian Ruin, reached from Blanding; Anasazi dwelling remains.

Calf Creek Recreation Site, reached from Boulder or Escalante; ruins of two Anasazi villages.

Canyonlands National Park, reached from Moab or Monticello; an area rich in Anasazi remains, pictographs, and petroglyphs.

Danger Cave State Historic Site, Wendover; a key site of the Desert Culture with a time depth of 11,000 years.

Grand Gulch, reached from Blanding; a rugged canyon traversible only afoot or on horseback but affording a rich display of Anasazi culture.

Hovenweep National Monument, reached from Cortez; an unexcavated series of ruins which are being preserved for future archaeological work, but the public is admitted.

Natural Bridges National Monument, reached from Blanding; over 200 Anasazi sites.

Newspaper Rock, Indian Creek State Park, reached from Monticello on road to Canyonlands National Park; hundreds of petroglyphs on the face of a cliff.

Parowan Gap Indian Drawings, Parowan; pictographs and petroglyphs that can be seen from the highway.

Washington

Painted Rocks Sites, near Spokane and Yakima; pictographs.

Lake Lenore Caves, reached from Coulee City; seven shelter caves in Lower Grand Coulee canyon.

West Virginia

Grave Creek Mound State Park, Moundsville; the largest known Adena mound in the center of an assemblage of at least 47 mounds, marking this area as a highly important Adena district. Museum.

St. Albans Site, St. Albans; one of the four or five most important sites in America, but not open to the public. It has not even been thoroughly excavated because of lack of financing by governmental or foundation agencies, let alone prepared for public inspection.

Wisconsin

Aztalan State Park, Aztalan; palisaded town, almost a city, of the Mississippian period. The people of this settlement were apparently aliens who maintained themselves in a hostile countryside by strong fortifications and a disciplined military.

Copper Culture State Park, Oconto; the type site for the Old Copper culture. The site, a cemetery, has been excavated and there are plans for preparing it for public viewing. Work may be going on at any time.

Devils Lake State Park, Baraboo; animal effigy mounds.

Durst Rockshelter, Leland; a cave shelter site occupied for 8000 years.

Gullickson's Glen, reached from Black River; cliffs of a narrow valley covered with petroglyphs.

High Cliff State Park, reached from Menasha; a group of 13 effigy mounds within the park on a bluff overlooking Lake Winnebago.

Lizard Mound State Park, West Bend; a group of 31 effigy mounds and geometric shapes.

Man Mound, Baraboo; an unusual anthropomorphic effigy mound.

Menasha Mound, Menasha; a bird effigy mound. There are so many effigy mounds in Wisconsin that an Effigy Mound culture has been postulated. Very few effigy mounds are found elsewhere.

Mendota State Hospital Mound, Madison; a bird effigy mound with a wing span of 625 feet.

Muscoda Mounds, Muscoda; an effigy mound group on private land but open to the public.

Nelson Dewey State Park, Cassville; a group of animal and enigmatic figure effigy mounds.

Panther Intaglio or Pit, Fort Atkinson; effigy mound group with a unique effigy dug out as a pit about a foot deep.

Perrot State Park, Trempealeau; a group of conical mounds.

Sheboygan Mound Park, Sheboygan; animal effigy mounds with geometric mounds that may or may not be of the same culture.

University of Wisconsin Campus Mounds, Madison; four groups of mounds located on the campus.

Wyalusing State Park, Prairie du Chien; a high ridge in the park used by aborigines as the natural feature on which to locate their burial mounds; apparently of a pre-Effigy Mound culture period.

Wyoming

Obsidian Cliff, Yellowstone National Park, near Norris; a quarry site for obsidian, a tool and stone artifact material. The obsidian from this site has been found as far away as Hopewell sites in Ohio.

CANADA

British Columbia

'Ksan Village, Hazelton; a reconstructed Gitskan Indian village where aboriginal crafts are demonstrated by Indians; some prehistoric structures.

Thunderbird Park, Victoria; a full-scale Kwakiutl Indian house and a collection of totem poles of Northwest Indian groups.

Newfoundland

L'Anse Aux Meadows, at northern tip of Great Northern Peninsula; prehistoric, but Norse, not aboriginal. The stabilization of the site of a Viking village of about A.D. 1000 and proof of early European exploration of America.

Ontario

Serpent Mound, Peterboro; an effigy mound that may be related to Hopewellian culture.

Sheguiandah Site, Sheguiandah; an important Early Man site though its age has not been established beyond controversy. The culture was apparently that of chopper-flake makers. Guided tours of site must be arranged ahead of time through the curator of the site museum.

Prince Edward Island

Micmac Village, Rocky Point; a contact period Micmac Indian village reconstructed, with small museum.

The indispensable reference for the citizen archaeologist who plans to visit the above sites or the museums appearing in the following list is Franklin Folsom's *America's Ancient Treasures*, Rand McNally Guide to Archaeological Sites and Museums (New York, Chicago, San Francisco). Explicit directions for traveling to most of the sites and museums listed here are outlined in the Folsom book.

Guide to Museums

In the preceding list of prehistoric Indian sites those sites with museums in association were so noted. Such museums are usually most valuable to the student because they properly identify their materials culturally and place the cultures they represent in the correct sequential context. The value of other museums varies widely. Some museums and collections of material are of almost no value and some, because they mislabel, misidentify, or do not update the information about their materials, should be avoided. The good museums deserve the attention of the citizen archaeologist. Listed here are some of the museums which can be visited with profit.

*   Designates museums with limited or special collections.
**   Designates museums where materials are arranged according to local or area sequences.
#   Designates museums with ethnographic displays or diorama exhibits.

Note: The above designation system is not to be construed as a quality rating system.

UNITED STATES

Alabama
*Alabama Department of Archives and History, Montgomery.
**Alabama Museum of Natural History, University of Alabama, Tuscaloosa.

*Birmingham Museum of Art, Birmingham; Moundville site collections.

**Montgomery Museum of Fine Arts, Montgomery; valuable displays of type artifacts, pottery, and industrial techniques.

Alaska

**Alaska State Museum, Juneau; devoted to Northwest coastal, Athapascan Indian, Aleutian, and Eskimo cultures.

**Anchorage Historical and Fine Arts Museum, Anchorage; the Alaskan sequence as above.

**University Museum, Fairbanks; recoveries from most of the important excavations in Alaska: Cape Denbigh, Iyatayet, Ipiutak, St. Lawrence Island, and the Punuk Islands.

Arizona

**Amerind Foundation Museum, reached from Tucson or Dragoon; very fine collection of Southwest desert area materials.

*Eastern Arizona Museum and Historical Society, Pima.

* #Heard Museum of Anthropology and Primitive Art, Phoenix.

** #Museum of Northern Arizona, Flagstaff; Basketmaker-Pueblo sequence; fine ethnographic displays.

* #Navajo Tribal Museum, Window Rock; dioramas and exhibits of Navajo and Anasazi lifeways.

*Pueblo Grande Museum, Phoenix; the museum houses collections from the excavated site on which it stands.

Arkansas

**Arkansas State University Museum, Jonesboro; special display of the archaeology of a temple mound.

*Henderson State College Museum, Arkadelphia; material mostly of the Caddo culture.

*Henry Clay Hampson II Memorial Museum of Archaeology, Jonesboro; mostly material from a single site, the Nodena mound.

*Museum of Science and Natural History, Little Rock; recoveries from area mounds.

**University of Arkansas Museum, Fayetteville; the Archaic "Bluff Shelter" sequence of Arkansas and materials from the looted Spiro Mound.

California

**Adan Treganza Anthropology Museum, San Francisco State College, San Francisco; northern and central California sequences.

* #Antelope Valley Museum, Lancaster; materials from California from 10,000 B.P., Anasazi and Alaskan displays.

** #Bowers Museum, Santa Ana; local sequence, dioramas of Plains and Alaskan cultures; exhibit of unique West Coast "cogged stones."

* #California State Indian Museum, Sacramento; lifeways of California Indians.

**Catalina Island Museum, Santa Catalina Island; the Canalino sequence as excavated.

*Death Valley National Monument Museum, Furnace Creek; material collected from Death Valley.

*Joshua Tree National Monument Visitors Center, Twentynine Palms; the Pinto Basin sequence.

* #Kern County Museum, Bakersfield; local collections and basket-weaving techniques.

*Lompoc Museum, Lompoc; late prehistoric Chumas Indian materials.

** #Los Angeles County Museum of History and Science, Los Angeles; southern California coastal sequence, from Oak Grove to Canalino.

*Maturango Museum of Indian Wells Valley, China Lake; materials from Pinto Basin to contact Shoshonean times.

*Museum of Early Man, Santa Barbara; the southern California sequence from Milling Stone to Canalino.

* #Oakland Museum, Oakland; exhibits of local materials with emphasis on ethnology and environmental adaptation.

*Palm Springs Desert Museum, Palm Springs.

* #Randall Museum, San Francisco; emphasis on cultural process and evolution, using materials from the vast collections of the Robert Lowie Museum of Anthropology, University of California.

**San Bernardino County Museum, Bloomington; an archaeologist's museum; materials from refined local sequences and the controversial Calico Mountains excavation.

**San Diego Museum of Man, San Diego; two important southern California and Desert Culture patterns: the San Dieguito and the Diegueno, both taking their name from San Diego. This museum has an extensive collection of materials used to show cultural sequence and evolution.

** #Santa Barbara Museum of Natural History, Santa Barbara; extensive displays of California sequence materials; ethnographic dioramas.

** #Southwest Museum, Los Angeles; a panoramic view of American prehistory; Sandia, Clovis, and Folsom Early Man materials; dioramas.

* #Tulare County Museum, Visalia; local materials and the ethnology of the Yokuts Indians.

Colorado

* #Colorado State Museum, Denver; materials from cultures of the region dating from A.D. time; Ute ethnology dioramas.

** #Denver Museum of Natural History, Denver; materials and exhibits ranging widely in time over the Plains and Southwest. This museum sponsored the cardinal excavations of the Folsom Early Man phase.

* #Koshare Indian Museum, Otero Junior College, La Junta.

* #Moraine Park Visitors Center, Rocky Mountain National Park, Estes Park; Plains Indian ethnology.

* #Trinidad State Junior College Museum, Trinidad; prehistoric paleontology, geology, and anthropology coordinated for the Southern Plains and the Texas Panhandle.

** #University of Colorado Museum, Boulder; one of the coming museums for American archaeology; materials include those from the Olsen-Chubbock bison kill site, where the skeletons of about 190 bison of extinct species were recovered with artifacts.

*Ute Indian Museum, Montrose.

Connecticut

* #Bruce Museum, Greenwich; eastern Woodland Indian dioramas.

* #Children's Museum, Hartford; mainly ethnological, with explanation of archaeological techniques.

*Connecticut State Library Museum, Hartford.

**Gunn Memorial Library Museum, Washington; materials covering the period from about 6000 B.P. to Colonial times. (The Connecticut local sequence has not been well established.)

*Mattatuck Museum, Waterbury.

* #New Britain Children's Museum, New Britain.

* #Peabody Museum of Natural History at Yale University, New Haven. The Museum has sponsored many archaeological explorations all over America, and the recovered materials repose here. It is a better museum for the advanced or specializing student than for the beginner, but the exhibits are engrossing.

* #Stamford Museum and Nature Center, Stamford.

Delaware

*Delaware State Museum, Dover.

*Hagley Museum, Wilmington.

** #Iron Hill Museum, near Newark; includes one exhibit tracing the sketchily known Delaware sequence.

* #Zwaanendael Museum, Lewes.

District of Columbia

** #Museum of Natural History, United States National Museum, Smithsonian Institution, Washington; the.complete museum, for beginner and advanced archaeologist from any part of the country.

Florida

** #Florida State Museum, Gainesville. The museum occupied new quarters in 1971 and should soon be Florida's leading museum of archaeology and prehistory.

*St. Petersburg Historical Society, St. Petersburg.

*South Florida Museum and Planetarium, Bradenton.

**Temple Mound Museum, Fort Walton; the Gulf Coast sequence from Paleo Indian to European contact times.

Georgia

* #Albany Area Junior Museum, Albany.

** #Columbus Museum of Arts and Crafts, Columbus; dioramas on how to do site excavation.

Idaho

** #Idaho State University Museum, Pocatello; the state's only museum, up-to-date on Northwest prehistory.

Illinois

*Burpee Natural History Museum, Rockford.

** #Field Museum of Natural History, Chicago; second only to the Smithsonian on the list of America's great museums.

** #Illinois State Museum, Springfield. A party from this museum excavated the Modoc Rockshelter, and the materials are housed here.

*Lakeview Center for the Arts and Sciences, Peoria.

*Madison County Historical Museum, Edwardsville.

**Southern Illinois University Museum, Carbondale. The university has been very active in Midwest and Southwest excavations.

** #University of Illinois Museum of Natural History, Urbana.

Indiana

* #Children's Museum, Indianapolis.
  *Indiana Historical Society, Indianapolis.
  *Indiana State Museum, Indianapolis.
  *Indiana University Museum, Bloomington.
  **Miami County Historical Museum, Peru.
  *Puterbaugh Museum, Peru.

Iowa

  *Davenport Public Museum, Davenport.
  *Iowa State Museum, Des Moines; materials from ceramic times only.
  **Museum of History and Science, Waterloo; the only museum in the state that has even a sketchy cultural sequence display.
* #Sioux City Public Museum, Sioux City.
  *State University of Iowa Museum of Natural History, Iowa City.

Kentucky

  *Behringer Museum of Natural History, Covington.
  *Blue Licks Museum, Blue Licks Battlefield State Park, Blue Licks; spotty but very interesting materials.
* #Western Kentucky University Museum, Bowling Green; a new and growing museum.

Louisiana

* #Louisiana State Exhibit Museum, Shreveport; recommended for its Paleo-hunter and Poverty Point exhibits.

Maine

  *Aroostook Historical and Art Museum, Houlton; materials from Red Paint culture sites.
  *Bangor Historical Society Museum, Bangor.
* #Robert Abbe Museum, Acadia National Park, near Bar Harbor.
  **Wilson Museum, Castine; weak on Archaic and Paleo periods.

Maryland

** #Maryland Academy of Sciences, Baltimore. Occupying a new building in 1973, this should be one of the better museums for the archaeologist of the eastern seaboard to visit.
  *Museum of Natural History, Baltimore.

Massachusetts

** #Bronson Museum, Attleboro; the headquarters of State Archaeologist Dr. Maurice Robbins, who has also excavated extensively in the state.
* #Children's Museum, Boston.
  *Fruitlands Museum, Harvard.
** #Peabody Foundation for Archaeology, Phillips Academy, Andover; indispensable to the worker in New England archaeology; explanation of method and theory in archaeology exemplified (MacNeish is director of the Foundation).
** #Peabody Museum of Archaeology and Ethnology, Harvard University, Cambridge; one of the country's great archaeological museums but of more

value to the advanced amateur than to the beginner looking for information on his local sequences.

*Peabody Museum of Salem, Salem; for the ethnologist rather than the archaeologist.

Michigan
** #Cranbrook Institute of Science, Bloomfield Hills; the Michigan sequence as well as some important site materials.

*Grand Rapids Public Museum, Grand Rapids.

*Kalamazoo Public Museum, Kalamazoo.

*Michigan Historical Commission Museum, Lansing; Old Copper culture and Hopewell displays.

** #Michigan State University Museum, East Lansing; both local and continental sequences and exhibits.

** #University of Michigan Exhibit Museum, Ann Arbor; materials for the archaeologist who wants information on Old World Stone Age. The university of Michigan Department of Anthropology is probably the most influential graduate school for American archaeologists in the country.

Minnesota
*Kathio Indian Museum, Lake Mille Lacs; mostly contact period materials.

*Minnesota Historical Society Museum, St. Paul; mostly late prehistoric and contact period materials.

Mississippi
*Natchez Trace Visitors Center, Tupelo; an information and display center which should be visited before taking the Trace through the mound country of Mississippi.

* #State Historical Museum, Jackson; interesting material on burial mounds.

** #University of Mississippi Anthropological Museum, University; for the specialist in the state of Mississippi and the lower Mississippi Valley.

Missouri
*Clay County Historical Museum, Liberty; materials from the important late Paleo-hunter site of Nebo Hill, among others.

** #Kansas City Museum of History and Science, Kansas City; for the excavator working in the Missouri area; site as well as sequence materials.

**Missouri Historical Society, St. Louis; excavated materials from Missouri and the Mississippi Valley covering the Paleo to protohistoric sequence.

**Museum of Science and Natural History, St. Louis; while the Paleo *et seq.* sequence is represented, the materials are selected from local collections; a good Mississippian display.

*St. Joseph Museum, St. Joseph.

*School of the Ozarks, Foster Museum, Point Lookout.

** #University of Missouri Museum of Anthropology, Columbia. If the specialist in Missouri archaeology can visit only one museum, this is it.

Montana
*Gallatin County Museum, Bozeman.

*Mac's Museum of Natural History, Broadus.

* #Museum of the Plains Indians, Browning.

*Museum of the Rockies, Montana State University, Bozeman; has materials from the important Paleo-hunter MacHaffie site.

Nebraska

* #Fort Robinson Museum, Crawford.

** #University of Nebraska Museum, Lincoln; has materials from several impor- tant sites, including the Scotts Bluff bison kill site and Signal Butte.

Nevada

*Lost City Museum of Archeology, Overton; rich collections of regional cul- ture materials, including some from Gypsum Cave.

**Nevada Historical Society Museum, Reno; materials from several scientif- ically excavated stratified sites, including Fishbone Cave.

* #University Museum of Natural History, University of Nevada, Las Vegas; im- portant for the students of the Desert culture.

New Hampshire

** #Dartmouth College Museum, Hanover; an outline of the New England sequence; other materials from continental America.

*Libby Museum, Wolfeboro.

*Manchester Historical Association, Manchester.

Woodman Institute, Dover; has Red Paint culture materials.

New Jersey

*Cumberland County Historical Museum, Greenwich.

*Morris Museum of Arts and Sciences, Morristown.

*Newark Museum, Newark; has a wide range of chronological and cultural materials.

** #New Jersey State Museum, Trenton; one section is devoted to the total ar- chaeological process, from survey to laboratory; many fine displays and much unique or rare material.

*Princeton University Museum of Natural History, Princeton; has some im- portant materials, including a display of the early bison hunting Cody complex.

** #Seton Hall University Museum, South Orange; an expanding museum and center for investigation of local archaeology.

** #Sussex County Historical Museum, Newton; materials from local Paleo to Woodland sequence.

New York

*American Museum of Natural History, New York City. While this is, in gen- eral, one of America's great museums, its American prehistoric displays have not been updated for two generations; the materials on display are of little help to the citizen archaeologist.

**Bear Mountain Trailside Museum, Bear Mountain State Park just south of West Point; an excellent small museum archaeologically well arranged.

*Brooklyn Children's Museum, Brooklyn; has good collections not on display that may be seen by students on request.

*Brooklyn Museum, Brooklyn.

*Buffalo Museum of Science, Buffalo; important to specialists in the Iroquois.

*Cayuga Museum of History and Art, Auburn; the Iroquois sequence of the Owasco culture.

*Chemung County Historical Society, Elmira; materials from the important Lamoka culture.

**Cooperstown Indian Museum, Cooperstown; materials from the central New York Paleo *et seq.* sequence.

** #Fort Stanwix Museum, Rome; more historic than prehistoric in emphasis, it displays sequence materials.

* #Fort William Henry Restoration and Museum, Lake George; some prehistoric materials and displays.

**Hartwick College Yager Museum, Oneonta; good displays of Upper Susquehanna Valley sequential material.

* #Heye Museum of the American Indian, New York City. Though the material on display is prodigious, it is for the sight-seer rather than the serious worker in archaeology.

**Howe Public Library, Wellsville; a limited collection of sequential materials.

** #Nassau County Historical Museum, Salisbury, Long Island; a new and growing museum with special interest for Long Island specialists.

** #New York State Museum, Albany. Headquarters of New York State archaeologist William Ritchie, one of the leading regional archaeologists (now retired), the State Museum is authoritative on New York and northeastern archaeology.

* #Niagara County Historical Center, Lockport; local materials.

** #Old Fort Johnson, Amsterdam; local materials and materials on loan from the State Museum.

*Ontario County Museum, Canandaigua.

*Ossining Historical Society Museum, Ossining; local collections mostly in storage.

*Oysterponds Historical Society Museum, Orient, Long Island.

*Powell House Museum of Huntington Historical Society, Huntington.

** #Roberson Center for the Arts and Sciences, Binghamton; local recoveries and collections arranged sequentially.

** #Rochester Museum and Science Center, Rochester; with the State Museum, Albany, the best choice for investigators of New York prehistory.

* #Six Nations Indian Museum, Onchiota; devoted exclusively to the Iroquois.

*Suffolk Museum, Stony Brook; materials from the important Stony Brook site.

**Tioga County Historical Society Museum, Oswego.

North Carolina

* #Catawba College Museum, Salisbury; material on the seaboard cultures of the Southeast. Material not on exhibit can be seen on request.

**Charlotte Nature Museum Inc., Charlotte; artifacts arranged by cultures and time periods.

**Greensboro Historical Museum, Greensboro; the Piedmont sequence.

**Morrow Mountain State Park Natural History Museum, near Albemarle; locally collected and excavated materials in sequence.

** #Schiele Museum of Natural History, Gastonia.

**University of North Carolina Research Laboratories of Anthropology; headquarters of Dr. Joffre Coe, delineator of the Piedmont sequence and the eastern Archaic.

North Dakota

**State Historical Society Museum, Bismarck; extensive collections from sites its parties have excavated.

Ohio

**Allen County Museum, Lima; materials from Paleo-hunter to Fort Ancient (late prehistoric) periods. Features glacial Kame culture materials.

* #Cincinnati Museum of Natural History, Cincinnati. Good collections of the cultures for which Ohio is famous: Adena, Hopewell, and Fort Ancient, collected by the museum's teams.

**Dayton Museum of Natural History, Dayton; Ohio sequence materials from Paleo-hunter times. The museum conducts its own digs in which lay archaeologists may take part.

*Firelands Museum, Norwalk; Ohio materials from all periods; some European Paleolithic exhibits.

**Licking County Historical Society Museum, Newark; mainly Hopewellian materials, but an interesting series of panels on the Ohio sequence.

*Miami County Archaeological Museum, Pleasant Hill; locally collected artifacts from several periods.

* #Museum of Health and Natural History, Toledo; much authentic material from a hit-skip Ohio sequence.

*Natural Science Museum, Cleveland; Ohio and North American materials.

** #Ohio Historical Museum, on the campus of Ohio State University, Columbus; overflowing with material from one of the richest states, archaeologically, in the nation.

*Warren County Historical Society, Lebanon; Hopewell and Fort Ancient materials.

* # Western Reserve Historical Society Museum, Cleveland.

*Wyandot County Historical Society Museum, Sandusky; glacial Kame culture and other local materials.

Oklahoma

*Creek Indian Museum, Okmulgee; Mississippian period mound and Caddoan materials.

*East Central Museum, East Central College, Ada; limited time period materials, but one display identifies North American projectile points as to type and age.

*Gilcrease Institute of American History and Art, Tulsa; excellent but eclectic collections. Two good ones are a display of projectile points from well-known cultures and an exhibit of prehistoric bone pathology.

** #Museum of the Great Plains, Lawton; fine collections from Plains sequence.

*No Man's Land Historical Museum, Panhandle State College, Goodwell; Oklahoma Basketmaker and Plains culture artifacts.

Oklahoma Historical Society Museum, Oklahoma City; random area materials, including some from the Spiro Mound, infamously looted by miners during the Depression years.

* #Philbrook Art Center, Tulsa; several priceless collections from Oklahoma and Southwest sites, including Spiro.

** #Stovall Museum, University of Oklahoma, Norman; the most complete and modern archaeological museum in the state.

* #Woolaroc Museum, near Bartlettsville; Oklahoma materials with a rare collection of Oklahoma Hopewell.

Oregon

*Tillamook County Pioneer Museum, Tillamook; random local collections.

** #University of Oregon Museum of Natural History, Eugene; the museum for students of Northwest and Plateau prehistory. It has sponsored many important excavations.

*Winquatt Museum, The Dalles; material salvaged from The Dalles area of the Columbia River before it was inundated by dam impoundment.

Pennsylvania

** #Carnegie Museum, Pittsburgh; the Anthropology Center is in new quarters at Butler. The Museum has been very active in excavations in the Upper Ohio Valley and is very cooperative with nonprofessional archaeologists, to whom it grants fellowships. It is a center for regional archaeological activity.

** #Fort Ligonier Memorial Museum, Ligonier; in addition to the restoration of the French and Indian War fort, one building is reserved for collections from many excavated prehistoric sites.

** #Indian Steps Museum, near Airville; the Pennsylvania succession from Paleo to historic period.

*Mercer Museum, Doylestown; limited collection of Delaware Indian material.

*Monroe County Historical Society Museum, Stroudsburg.

** #North Museum, Franklin and Marshall College, Lancaster; small but very shrewdly arranged, up-to-date collections. Director Fred Kinsey is one of the East's most productive digging archaeologists.

*Parker Indian Museum, Brookville.

** #Pennsylvania State Museum (William Penn Memorial Museum), Harrisburg. This important museum is in a new building, with new exhibits prepared by high-order professionals aware of the growing trend towards archaeology as anthropology.

* #Tioga Point Museum, Athens; worthwhile for its exhibit of the local pottery sequence.

** #University of Pennsylvania Museum, Philadelphia; one of the five finest archaeological museums in the country; lacks nothing the student needs, though he may have to ask for it.

* #Wyoming Historical and Genealogical Society Museum, Wilkes-Barre; Susquehanna River valley materials.

Rhode Island

* #Haffenreffer Museum, Brown University, Bristol; probably the finest museum in the non-Arctic United States on the Arctic because of the work of the late J. L. Giddings. Many displays, very sensitive about cultural-environmental adjustment.

* #Rhode Island Historical Society Museum, Providence; a good range of Rhode Island materials.

* #Roger Williams Park Museum and Planetarium, Providence; illustrative and instructive displays but little material.

South Carolina

* #Nature Museum of York County.

South Dakota

** #Over Dakota Museum, University of South Dakota, Vermillion; the South Dakota Plains sequence, from excavated materials.

** #South Dakota State Historical Museum, Pierre; recently renovated and modernized in arrangement of materials.

Tennessee
* * #Children's Museum, Nashville.
* * #Lookout Mountain Museum, Chattanooga; local collections, some from important sites; a lithic technology display.
* ** #McClung Museum, University of Tennessee, Knoxville; rich collections from the work of noted archaeologists Madeline Kneberg and T. M. N. Lewis, including the important Eva and Hiwasee Island sites.
* * #Traveller's Rest Historic House.

Texas
* * #El Paso Centennial Museum, the University of Texas at El Paso; mainly local ceramic period materials.
* ** #Fort Worth Museum of Science and History, Fort Worth; archaeological and ethnographic materials from all over the continent; a good Texas Paleo to historic period sequence.
* * #Panhandle-Plains Historical Museum, Canyon; authentic Early Hunter and a range of later materials.
* * #Strecker Museum, Baylor University, Waco.
* *Sul Ross University Museum, Alpine.
* ** #Texas Memorial Museum, University of Texas, Austin; archaeological, ethnographic, technological, and culture evolution displays; a must for the Southern Plains student.
* * #Texas Tech University Museum, Lubbock.

Utah
* *Brigham Young Anthropology Museum.
* *Prehistoric Museum, College of Eastern Utah, Price.
* **University of Utah Anthropology Museum, Salt Lake City; well organized, with materials from the key Danger Cave site of the Desert Culture.

Vermont
* *Daniels Museum, on Vermont 73 near Sudbury.
* *Fleming Museum, University of Vermont, Burlington.
* *Vermont Historical Society Museum, Montpelier.
* *Walker Museum, White River Junction.

Virginia
* *Jamestown Festival Park, near Williamsburg.
* * #Norfolk Museum of Arts and Sciences, Norfolk; interesting dioramas.
* ** #Valentine Museum, Richmond; the Virginia sequence from Paleo-hunter to historic times; and exhibit on stratigraphy.

Washington
* *Eastern Washington State Historical Society Museum, Spokane.
* *East Museum, Balsam.
* *Fort Simcoe Museum, Fort Simcoe.
* *Pacific Northwest Indian Center, Yakima.
* *Sakajawea State Park Museum, near Pasco.
* *Seattle Art Museum, Seattle.
* *State Capitol Museum, Olympia.
* *Wanapum Tour Center, Ellensburg.

West Virginia.
    *Department of Archives and History Museum, Charleston.
** # West Virginia Geologic and Economic Survey, Section of Archaeology Museum, Morgantown; very sound on the West Virginia-Upper Ohio Valley sequence; has the materials from the St. Albans site and from other excavations by Bettye Broyles.

Wisconsin
    *Hoard Historical Museum, Fort Atkinson; said to contain 10,000 artifacts from the local area.
    *Lake Mills-Aztalan Historical Society Museum, Lake Mills.
** # Logan Museum of Anthropology, Beloit College, Beloit; wide-ranging world collections along with good local sequence materials and cultural exhibits.
** # Milwaukee Public Museum, Milwaukee; the Wisconsin sequence and a great deal more, all in a building with pervasive archaeological ambiance.
    *Neville Public Museum, Green Bay; Old Copper culture, Red Ocher culture, and local Woodland period materials.
    *Oconto County Historical Society Museum, Oconto; materials from the Old Copper site of Oconto.
    **Oskosh Public Museum, Oskosh; sketchy Wisconsin sequence collected from local excavation.
    *Rahr Civic Center and Public Museum, Manitowac; Old Copper, Hopewell, Mississippian materials.
    *Sheboygan County Museum, Sheboygan.
** # State Historical Society Museum, Madison; significant collections from excavated sites; demonstrations of methodology.
    *Wisconsin State University Museum of Anthropology, Oskosh.

Wyoming
    *Buffalo Bill and Plains Indian Museum, Cody.
    *Gatchell Memorial Museum, Buffalo.
** # Wyoming State Museum, Cheyenne; recent renovation and modernization has made this a sound museum for the student of Plains prehistory.

CANADA

Alberta
  * # Glenbow Museum, Calgary; a growing museum which has recently begun to sponsor significant excavation.
    *Luxton Museum, Banff.
    **University of Alberta Anthropology Exhibits, Edmonton; a sketchy display of local sequence materials.

British Columbia
    #British Columbia Provincial Museum, Victoria; mainly Northwest Coast Indian ethnology.
  * # Campbell River Museum, Campbell River; ethnological Northwest Coast emphasis with some regional prehistoric material.
    #Museum of Northern British Columbia, Prince Rupert; mainly late prehistoric ethnological materials.
    *Penticton Museum and Archives, Penticton; local collections and some excavated materials from inland sites.

University of British Columbia, Vancouver; collections from Northwest Coast, Eskimo, and Plains cultures.

* # Simon Fraser University Museum of Archeology, Burnaby; opened to the public on a limited basis in 1972.

Manitoba

**Manitoba Museum of Man and Nature, Winnipeg; though not arranged sequentially, Canadian cultures through time are represented; emphasis on cultural-environment adjustment. In new quarters.

*University of Winnipeg Anthropology Museum; materials being rearranged to show Boreal Forest and Plains cultures.

New Brunswick

*New Brunswick Museum, St. John; interesting local materials.

Newfoundland

*Newfoundland Museum, St. John's; collections and excavated materials of the unique Beothuck Indians.

Nova Scotia

* # Nova Scotia Museum, Citadel Hill Branch.

**Nova Scotia Museum, Halifax; Paleo-hunter to Late Woodland sequence for the region.

Ontario

*Algonquin Provincial Park Museum, Whitney; excavated materials from local area.

*Assignack Historical Society Museum, Manitowaning; collections from the important Sheguiandah site.

*Brant Museum, Burlington; spotty collections of local material.

**Bruce County Museum, Southampton; good Archaic to Late Woodland sequence materials.

*Campbell Memorial Museum, Perth.

* # Chatham-Kent Museum, Chatham; technological displays of stone tool-making and the evolution of Woodland pottery; stratigraphic display.

*Huronia Museum, Midland.

**Lennox and Addington Historical Society Museum, Napanee; local sequence materials from Middle Archaic to historic periods.

*McMaster University Museum, Hamilton. The museum is to be housed in a new building and enlarged, and its arrangements updated. Local and North American materials.

** # National Museum of Man, Ottawa; covers prehistory of Canada, Plains, and Eskimo, Northwest Coast, and Iroquois cultures.

* # Royal Ontario Museum, Toronto; while this museum is not arranged by culture sequence, its ethnological approach and its range and richness of materials give it highest rating.

**Simcoe County Museum and Archives, Barrie; materials mostly from scientifically excavated sites; a must for the Ontario student.

*Thunder Bay Historical Society Museum, Thunder Bay; Cummins site materials, including Paleo-hunter and Old Copper materials; also Woodland and late prehistoric collections.

*United Counties Museum, Cornwall.

*University of Western Ontario Museum of Indian Archaeology and Pioneer Life, London.

*Woodwinds Historical Museum, Barlochan.

Quebec

McCord Museum, McGill University; not yet open at this writing.

Saskatchewan

** # Saskatchewan Museum of Natural History, Regina; many locally collected and excavated materials from all periods; ethnological and culture-environment adaptation emphasis.

Yukon Territory

MacBride Centennial Museum, Whitehorse.

Guide to Resources

This section consists of a précis of useful information on archaeological facilities and activities state by state. The information is directive rather than exhaustive, with the intention of indicating to those interested where they can address their inquiries. Names are not used in places where they would seem to be appropriate because officeholders—state archaeologists, editors, directors—can change without notice. Addresses of state societies and their publications are given unless the current address is in doubt. The reader should be cautioned that these addresses change rapidly too.

One of the items under each state is the name of a publication which the author recommends that the beginner use to initiate his acquaintance with the archaeology of the state or region. It is not necessarily the "best" book or reference but it is deemed the one most likely to prove stimulating.

"Colleges and universities" means those that have done work and offered courses in American prehistoric archaeology.

Alabama
State archaeologist: none; contact University of Alabama Department of Sociology and Anthropology, University.
State society: Alabama Archaeological Society (14 chapters); contact University of Alabama, University.

Society publication: *Journal of Alabama Archaeology*, semiannual; contact University of Alabama, University.

Colleges, universities: University of Alabama, University.

State legislation: all excavation, survey reserved to the state; excavation by nonresidents and removal of materials from the state prohibited. Such legislation is impossible to enforce.

Recommended: "Stanfield-Worley Bluff Shelter Excavations," David L. DeJarnette, Edward B. Kurjack, and James Cambron, *Journal of Alabama Archaeology*, Vol. VIII, No. 182, University, Alabama.

Alaska

State archaeologist: none; contact Alaska Division of Parks, Historic Preservation and Archaeology Unit, Anchorage.

State society: none.

State publications: *Anthropological Papers of the University of Alaska*, College, nonscheduled.

Colleges, universities: University of Alaska, College.

State legislation: a permit from the commissioner of natural resources is required to excavate, remove, or disturb archaeological materials; permits are granted only to qualified investigators.

Recommended: *Early Man in the Arctic*, J. L. Giddings, Alfred Knopf, New York.

Arizona

State archaeologist: none; contact University of Arizona, Department of Anthropology, Tucson, or Arizona State University, Department of Anthropology, Tempe.

State society: Arizona Archaeological and Historical Society; contact Arizona State Museum, University of Arizona, Tucson.

Society publication: *The Kiva*, quarterly; contact Arizona State Museum, University of Arizona, Tucson.

Colleges, universities: University of Arizona, Tucson; Arizona State University, Tempe.

State legislation: permits from the director of the Arizona State Museum, Tucson, are required for excavation on state controlled lands; permits are issued only to scientific and educational institutions.

Recommended: *Bat Cave*, Herbert W. Dick, The School of American Research, Santa Fe.

Arkansas

State archaeologist: yes; contact at Arkansas Archeological Survey, University of Arkansas Museum, Fayetteville 72701.

State society: Arkansas Archeological Society, University of Arkansas Museum, Fayetteville.

Society publication: *The Arkansas Archeologist*, University of Arkansas Museum, Fayetteville.

Colleges, universities: University of Arkansas, Fayetteville.

State legislation: Arkansas has the most comprehensive legally established archaeological program in the country. See *Public Archeology* by Charles McGimsey, director of the Arkansas Archeological Survey, Seminar Press (subsidiary of Academic Press), New York. Special programs for nonprofessionals.

Recommended: "The Ozark Bluff Dwellers," M. R. Harrington, *Indiana Notes and Monographs*, Vol. XII, Museum of the American Indian, Heye Foundation, New York, N.Y. 10032.

California

State archaeologist: none; contact State Department of Parks, Sacramento; University of California at Berkeley, Archeological Research Facility, Berkeley; University of California at Los Angeles, Los Angeles Archeological Survey, Los Angeles.

State society: California Archeological Society.

Society publication: *The California Archeologist*, quarterly.

Colleges, universities: University of California at Los Angeles and at Berkeley and State Colleges at Chico, Long Beach, Sacramento, San Diego, and San Francisco.

State legislation: excavation and removal of archaeological materials from state lands is prohibited except by permit from the Director of the Division of Beaches and Parks. Disturbance of remains on private lands is restricted to the owner thereof. Marin and Inyo Counties have special ordinances.

Recommended: Robert Heizer, "The Western Coast of North America" in *Prehistoric Man in the New World*, edited by Jesse Jennings and E. Norbeck, University of Chicago Press, Chicago.

Colorado

State archaeologist: none; contact University of Colorado Department of Anthropology, Boulder 80302.

State society: Colorado Archaeological Society, Department of Anthropology, University of Colorado.

Society publication: *Southwestern Lore*, quarterly; Department of Anthropology, University of Colorado.

Colleges, universities: University of Colorado, Boulder.

State legislation: all materials of scientific value, historic, prehistoric, fossil, and pertaining to natural history, occurring on state lands, belong to the state. Permits for survey, excavation, and removal of materials are issued by the State Historical Society (State Museum, Denver 80203) at the request of a state agency or municipal authority.

Recommended: *Excavations in the LoDaisKa Site in the Denver, Colorado, Area*, H. J. and C. C. Irwin, Denver Museum of Natural History, Denver.

Connecticut

State archaeologist: yes; contact at University of Connecticut, Office of the State Archeologist, Storrs 06268.

State society: Archeological Society of Connecticut; contact Office of the State Archeologist, University of Connecticut, Storrs.

Society publication: *The Bulletin*, annual; contact Office of the State Archeologist, University of Connecticut, Storrs.

Colleges, universities: University of Connecticut, Storrs; Yale University, New Haven.

State legislation: no restrictive legislation; the state archeologist is directed to do excavation and research but is given no funds to do so.

Recommended: *An Introduction to the Archaeology and History of the Connecticut Valley Indian*, edited by William R. Young, the Springfield Museum of Science, Springfield.

Delaware

State archaeologist: yes; contact at State Archaeologist, Department of State, Archaeological Society of Delaware; Hall of Records, Dover 19901.

State society: Division of Historical and Cultural Affairs, address varies; contact state archaeologist, above.

Society publication: *The Bulletin,* nonscheduled; contact state archaeologist.

Colleges, universities: University of Delaware, Newark.

State legislation: survey, excavation, disturbance of archaeological remains on state lands prohibited except by permit from the office of the governor; excavation on private lands is "discouraged" except for scientific purposes and under scientific direction. Nonprofessionals are well received by state archaeologist.

Recommended: "Time-Depth and Early Man in the Delaware Valley," Ronald J. Mason, in *Bulletin of the Archaeological Society of Delaware,* Vol. IX, No. 1; contact state archaeologist.

Florida

State archaeologist: yes; contact at Bureau of Historic Sites and Properties, Tallahassee 32300.

State society: Florida Anthropological Society; contact Department of Anthropology, University of Florida, Gainesville 32601.

Society publication: *The Florida Anthropologist,* quarterly; contact Department of Anthropology, University of Florida, Gainesville.

Colleges, universities: University of Florida, Gainesville; Florida Atlantic University, Boca Raton; Florida State University, Tallahassee.

State legislation: a comprehensive act not only declares all archaeological sites and a broad range of materials of historic, scientific, and public interest located on state lands to belong to the state but sets up several agencies for researching them; there is no mention of investigation on private lands.

Recommended: *The Florida Indian and His Neighbors,* edited by J. W. Griffin, Rollins College, Winter Park.

Georgia

State archaeologist: no; contact Georgia Historical Commission, Atlanta 30303. The Commission is empowered to appoint a state archaeologist.

State society: Society for the Preservation of Early Georgia History; this society appears to be dormant.

Society publication: none.

Colleges, universities: University of Georgia, Athens; Georgia State College, Atlanta.

State legislation: excavation and removal of materials from state lands is prohibited except by permit from the Historical Commission. The Commission is authorized to pay a finder's fee to those who report archaeological sites, treasure trove, or sunken ships.

Recommended: *Archaeological Survey of Northern Georgia,* Robert Wauchope, Memoir of the Society for American Archaeology, 1703 New Hampshire Ave., N.W., Washington, D.C. 20009.

Idaho

State archaeologist: no; contact Idaho Historical Society, Boise 83706.

State society: none.

Colleges, universities: Idaho State University, Pocatello; University of Idaho, Moscow.

State legislation: the Historical Society issues permits for excavation on state lands only to qualified persons; excavation or disturbance of remains without permit is prohibited.

Recommended: *The Old Cordilleran Culture in the Pacific Northwest,* B. R. Butler, Idaho State University Museum, Pocatello.

Illinois

State archaeologist: no single such officeholder but the Illinois Archeological Survey is an organization of all working archaeologists in the state which coordinates investigation and research activity; contact Illinois Archeological Survey, University of Illinois, Urbana 61801.

State society: no society for nonprofessionals; contact Illinois Archeological Survey for current research information.

Publication: *The Bulletin*, nonscheduled, a publication of the Survey; contact Illinois Archeological Survey.

Colleges, universities: University of Illinois, Urbana; Southern Illinois University, Carbondale.

State legislation: permits are issued to "competent persons" to excavate on state lands by the state department controlling the specific area. No regulations on private lands excavation.

Recommended: *Illinois Archaeology*, edited by Elaine A. Bluhm, Illinois Archeological Survey, University of Illinois, Urbana.

Indiana

State archaeologist: none; contact Indiana University, Glen A. Black Laboratory of Archaeology, Bloomington 47401.

State society: State Historical Society, State Museum, Indianapolis 46304.

Society publication: *Prehistory Research Series*, nonscheduled, State Historical Society, State Museum, Indianapolis.

Colleges, universities: Indiana University, Bloomington; Ball State University, Muncie.

State legislation: none.

Recommended: *Angel Site, Vanderburgh County, Indiana*, Glenn L. Black, Indiana Historical Society, Indianapolis.

Iowa

State archaeologist: yes; contact at State University of Iowa, Department of Sociology and Anthropology, Iowa City 52240.

State society: Iowa Archaeological Society, State University of Iowa, Iowa City.

Society publication: *The Journal*, quarterly, State University of Iowa, Iowa City.

Colleges, universities: State University of Iowa, Iowa City; Iowa State University, Ames.

State legislation: a weak and confused law prohibits "natural attractions" which may or may not include archaeological materials, from being removed from lands under the jurisdiction of the State Conservation Commission; no provision for archaeological excavation permits. No mention of excavation on private lands.

Recommended: *Men of Ancient Iowa*, Marshall McKusick, Iowa State University Press, Ames.

Kansas

State archaeologist: none; contact Kansas State Historical Society, Topeka 66612.

State society: Kansas Anthropological Association; contact Kansas State Historical Society, Topeka.

Society publication: *Newsletter*, monthly; Kansas State Historical Society, Topeka.

Colleges, universities: University of Kansas, Lawrenceville.

State legislation: standard restriction on excavating or disturbing sites on state lands except by permit; permits are issued by the Antiquities Commission, the chairman of which is the secretary of the Historical Society. No private lands excavation mentioned.

Recommended: *An Introduction to Kansas Archeology*, Waldo Wedel, Bureau of American Ethnology, Smithsonian Institution, Washington, D.C.

Kentucky

State archaeologist: none; contact Department of Anthropology, University of Kentucky, Lexington 40506.

State society: a state society is, at this writing, in the process of formation and acceptance by the Eastern States Archaeological Federation; for information contact Ronald A. Thomas, Secretary of ESAF, State Archaeologist, Hall of Records, Dover, Delaware 19901.

Society publication: none.

Colleges, universities: University of Kentucky, Lexington; University of Louisville, Louisville; University of Western Kentucky, Bowling Green.

State legislation: the Department of Anthropology of the University of Kentucky, Lexington, is empowered to grant permits to excavate on state lands; in actuality the University of Kentucky, the University of Louisville, and the University of Western Kentucky are informally coordinated into the Kentucky Archaeological Survey, modeled on the Illinois Survey, with the members holding "open permits" for survey and excavation. Permits are granted only to professional archaeologists and institutions. No mention of digging on private lands.

Recommended: *Late Paleo-Indian and Early Archaic Manifestations in Western Kentucky*, Martha Ann Rolingson and Douglas W. Schwartz, University of Kentucky Press, Lexington.

Louisiana

State archaeologist: none; contact Louisiana State University, Department of Geography and Anthropology, Baton Rouge 70803.

State society: none.

Colleges, universities: Louisiana State University, Baton Rouge; University of Louisiana at New Orleans; University of Southwestern Louisiana, LaFayette; Northeast Louisiana University, Monroe.

State legislation: none stipulating restrictions on survey or excavation.

Recommended: *Prehistoric Indian Settlements of the Changing Mississippi River Delta*, William G. McIntire, Louisiana State University, Baton Rouge.

Maine

State archaeologist: none; contact Department of Sociology and Anthropology, University of Maine, Orono 04473.

State societies: (1) Maine Archaeological Society, Wilson Museum, Castine; (2) Robert Abbe Museum Archeological Society, Robert Abbe Museum of Stone Age Antiquities, Bar Harbor.

Society publications: (1) Maine Archaeological Society (no title) quarterly, Wilson Museum, Castine; (2) *Bulletin*, nonscheduled, Robert Abbe Museum of Stone Age Antiquities, Bar Harbor.

Colleges, universities: University of Maine, Orono.

State legislation: sites may be dug on state lands, in coastal waters, and in lakes over 10 acres only by permit from the director of the Maine State Museum, Augusta, and the senior archaeologist at the University of Maine. All materials belong to the state. No digging restrictions for private lands.

Recommended: *Prehistoric Cultural Relations Between the Arctic and Temperate Zones of North America*, edited by J. M. Campbell, Arctic Institute of North America, Montreal.

Maryland
State archaeologist: yes; contact at State Archaeologist, Maryland Geological Survey, Johns Hopkins University, Baltimore 21218.

State societies: (1) Archaeological Society of Maryland; for information contact John P. O'Hehir, 4436 Ambler Dr., Kensington 20795; (2) Archaeological Society of Maryland Inc.; for information contact Mrs. Iris McGillivray, 17 East Branch Lane, Baltimore 21202.

Society publications: (1) *Archaeological Society of Maryland Newsletter*, monthly, 2944 Knoll Circle, Ellicott City 21043; (2) *Maryland Archeology*, quarterly; R.D. 1, Box 322, Abington 21009.

Colleges, universities: Johns Hopkins University, Baltimore; University of Maryland, College Park.

State legislation: standard restriction on excavation except by permit, granted only to qualified persons by the Maryland Geological Survey. Nonprofessionals are urged by the legislation to participate under professional guidance, and the state archaeologist works closely with nonprofessional groups.

Recommended: "An Hypothesis Concerning Archaic Period Settlement of Zekiah Swamp," Reginald Looker, Jr. and William A. Tidwell, *Miscellaneous Papers, Archeological Society of Maryland*, No. 5, Maryland Academy of Sciences, Baltimore.

"The Accokeek Creek Site," Robert L. Stephenson and Alice Ferguson, *Anthropological Papers*, University of Michigan, Ann Arbor.

Massachusetts
State archaeologist: yes; contact at Bronson Museum, Attleboro 02703.

State society: Massachusetts Archaeological Society Inc., Bronson Museum, Attleboro.

Society publication: *Bulletin*, quarterly, Bronson Museum, Attleboro.

Colleges, universities: University of Massachusetts, Amherst; Harvard University, Cambridge; Boston University, Boston; Stonehill College, North Easton.

State legislation: the Massachusetts Historical Commission has broad powers to inspect and certify sites, buildings, etc. as of historic interest and significance. Once certified as a "historic landmark," the site comes under the Commission's jurisdiction for preservation; hence only the Commission can grant permits for excavation or other alteration. Certification applies to private lands but the right of eminent domain may not be used except through court order. Nonprofessionals do most of the work in the state.

Recommended: *Wapanucket # 6, an Archaic Village in Middleboro, Massachusetts*, Maurice Robbins, Massachusetts Archaeological Society, Bronson Museum, Attleboro.

The Archaeology of Martha's Vineyard: A Framework for the Prehistory of Southern New England, William A. Ritchie, Natural History Press, Garden City, New York.

Michigan
State archaeologist: none; contact Department of Anthropology, University of Michigan, Ann Arbor 48104.

State society: Michigan Archaeological Association, Department of Anthropology, Western Michigan State University, Kalamazoo 49001.

State publication: *Michigan Archaeologist*, quarterly, Anthropology Department, Michigan State University, East Lansing.

Colleges, universities: University of Michigan, Ann Arbor; Michigan State University, East Lansing; Western Michigan State University, Kalamazoo; Wayne State University, Detroit.

State legislation: the state reserves to itself the right to explore and excavate on state-owned or controlled lands, including Great Lakes underwater lands, but the Department of Natural Resources, Lansing, grants permits to institutions or persons deemed qualified. Permission of the owner is required by law before excavation on private lands.

Recommended: *The Archaeology of Michigan*, James Fitting, Natural History Press, Garden City, New York.

Minnesota

State archaeologist: yes; contact at Department of Anthropology, University of Minnesota, Minneapolis 55455.

State society: Minnesota State Archaeological Society, Department of Anthropology, University of Minnesota, Minneapolis.

Society publications: *Minnesota Archaeologist*, quarterly, and *Newsletter*, nonscheduled, Department of Anthropology, University of Minnesota, Minneapolis.

Colleges, universities: University of Minnesota, Minneapolis.

State legislation: like Michigan, Minnesota reserves to the state the right to excavate on state-owned and controlled lands, with permits being issued to qualified persons by the director of the Minnesota Historical Society, St. Paul 55101. Excavation on private lands is to be "discouraged" and all sites are to be reported to the state archaeologist.

Recommended: *The Prehistoric Peoples of Minnesota*, Elden Johnson, Minnesota Historical Society, St. Paul.

Mississippi

State archaeologist: no; contact State Department of Archives and History, Jackson 39533.

State society: Mississippi Archaeological Association; 919 Bridge St., Gulfport 39501.

Society publication: none.

Colleges, universities: University of Mississippi, University; Mississippi State University, State College.

State legislation: the state declares all sites, sunken ships, buildings, artifacts, and localities of historical interest on state lands to be under its jurisdiction and control as archaeological landmarks. Permits for work, alteration, removal, or destruction are issued by the Board of Trustees of the Department of Archives and History. A site on private land may be declared a landmark with the consent of the owner.

Recommended: "The Jaketown Site in West-Central Mississippi," James A. Ford, Philip Phillips, and William G. Haag, *Anthropological Papers,* The American Museum of Natural History, New York.

Missouri

State archaeologist: no; contact Director of American Archaeology, University of Missouri, Columbia 65201.

State society: Missouri Archaeological Society; contact Department of Anthropology, University of Missouri, Columbia.

Society publication: *The Missouri Archaeologist,* nonscheduled; contact Lyman Center for Archaeological Research, University of Missouri, Miami, Missouri 65344.

Colleges, universities: University of Missouri, Columbia; University of Missouri, Miami.

State legislation: minimal; destruction of archaeological material on state park lands is prohibited. The state program is vigorous, however, and cordial towards nonprofessionals.

Recommended: *Graham Cave, An Archaic Site in Montgomery County, Missouri,* Wilfred D. Logan, Missouri Archaeological Society, Columbia.

Montana

State archaeologist: no; contact Department of Anthropology, University of Montana, Missoula 59801.

State society: Montana Archaeological Society, Department of Anthropology, University of Montana, Missoula.

Society publication: *Archaeology in Montana,* Department of Anthropology, University of Montana, Missoula.

Colleges, universities: University of Montana, Missoula; Montana State University, Bozeman.

State legislation: excavation permits, issued by the commissioner of public lands on recommendation of the Board of Trustees of the State Historical Society, are required, but the act does not specify whether for public or private lands. There is, however, no way of enforcing prohibition on excavation on private lands.

Recommended: "Archaeology of the Lower Bighorn Canyon, Montana," Lionel A. Brown, *Archaeology in Montana,* Vol. IX, No. 4, Department of Anthropology, University of Montana, Missoula.

Nebraska

State archaeologist: no; contact Nebraska State Historical Society, 1500 R St., Lincoln 68508.

State society: Nebraska State Historical Society, Lincoln.

Society publication: *Nebraska History,* quarterly.

Colleges, universities: University of Nebraska, Lincoln.

State legislation: none.

Recommended: *Chapters in Nebraska Archaeology,* edited by E. H. Bell, University of Nebraska, Lincoln.

Nevada

State archaeologist: no; contact Nevada Archeological Survey, University of Nevada, Reno.

State society: Nevada Historical Society, Nevada State Museum, Reno.

Society publication: none.

Colleges, universities: University of Nevada, Reno; University of Nevada, Las Vegas.

State legislation: A permit for survey or excavation is required from the directors of the Nevada State Museum, Reno. Work must be done by qualified persons from scientific institutions for public benefit.

Recommended: "The Culture History of Lovelock Cave, Nevada," Gordon L. Grosscup, *Reports,* The University of California Archaeological Survey, Berkeley.

New Hampshire

State archaeologist: no.

State society: New Hampshire Archeological Society, Department of Anthropology, Franklin Pierce College, Rindge.

Society publication: *New Hampshire Archeologist,* Franklin Pierce College, Rindge.

Colleges, Universities: Franklin Pierce College, Rindge; Dartmouth College, Hanover.

State legislation: none.

Recommended: *Prehistoric Cultural Relations Between the Arctic and Temperate Zones of North America,* edited by J. M. Campbell, Arctic Institute of North America, Montreal.

New Jersey

State archaeologist: none; contact Bureau of Research-Archeology, State Museum, Trenton 08625.

State society: Archeological Society of New Jersey; contact Janet Pollak, Department of Anthropology, Rutgers University, New Brunswick 08903.

Society publication: *Newsletter,* quarterly; contact Edward Rutsch, Fairleigh Dickinson University, Madison.

Colleges, universities: Rutgers University, New Brunswick; Fairleigh Dickinson, Madison; Seton Hall University, South Orange.

State legislation: none.

Recommended: *The Abbott Farm,* The Archaeology of New Jersey, Vol. II, Dorothy Cross, New Jersey State Museum, Trenton.

The Miller Field Site, Part I, Herbert C. Kraft, Seton Hall University Press, South Orange, New Jersey.

New Mexico

State archaeologist: yes; he is curator-in-charge at the Laboratory of Anthropology of the Museum of New Mexico, Santa Fe 87501.

State society: Archaeological Society of New Mexico, Museum of New Mexico, Santa Fe.

State publication: *El Palacio,* Museum of New Mexico, Santa Fe.

Colleges, universities: University of New Mexico, Albuquerque; Eastern New Mexico University, Portales.

State legislation: permits to excavate or engage in other archaeological activities are given only to institutions or recognized societies with historical and prehistoric interests. The permits are issued by the Cultural Properties Review Committee, which designates sites or "cultural properties" on state lands and, in certain instances, on private lands. A landowner may receive a property tax reduction for the preservation, restoration, or maintenance of a "cultural property."

Recommended: *Southwestern Archaeology,* 2nd edition, John C. McGregor, University of Illinois Press, Urbana.

New York

State archaeologist: yes; contact at New York State Museum and Science Service, State Education Building, Albany 12210.

State society: New York State Archeological Association; contact Rochester Museum and Science Center, Rochester 14607.

Society publication: *The Bulletin,* three times a year, Rochester Museum and Science Center, Rochester.

Colleges, universities: Columbia University, New York City; New York University, New York City; Queens College, Flushing; University of Buffalo, Buffalo; Ithaca

College, Ithaca; State University of New York at Binghamton; State University of New York at Albany.

State legislation: permits for excavation on state lands are issued by the commissioner of education. No mention of excavation on private lands. State archaeologist cooperates regularly with nonprofessionals.

Recommended: *The Archaeology of New York State*, William A. Ritchie, Natural History Press, Garden City, New York.

North Carolina

State archaeologist: yes; contact at Research Laboratory of Anthropology, University of North Carolina, Chapel Hill 27514.

State society: The Archaeological Society of North Carolina; contact at Research Laboratory of Anthropology, University of North Carolina, Chapel Hill.

Society publication: *Southern Indian Studies*, Research Laboratory of Anthropology, University of North Carolina, Chapel Hill.

Colleges, universities: University of North Carolina, Chapel Hill.

State legislation: excavation on state lands is by permit from the director of the State Museum, Raleigh, or the State Department of Archives and History, Raleigh. Private landowners are asked to refrain from permitting excavation and to seek professional help when sites are discovered on their property.

Recommended: *The Formative Cultures of the Carolina Piedmont*, Joffre L. Coe, American Philosophical Society, Philadelphia, Pennsylvania.

North Dakota

State archaeologist: no; contact State Historical Society of North Dakota, Bismarck 58501.

State society: State Historical Society of North Dakota, Bismarck.

Society publication: *North Dakota History*, quarterly.

Colleges, universities: University of North Dakota, Grand Forks.

State legislation: permits to excavate on state land are required; they are issued by the state Historical Society Board for one year to qualified persons. Private landowners may excavate on their property and issue permits to excavate.

Recommended: *Prehistoric Man on the Great Plains*, Waldo R. Wedel, University of Oklahoma Press, Norman.

Ohio

State archaeologist: no; contact Ohio Historical Society, Columbus 43211.

State society: (1) Ohio Academy of Science, Anthropology Section, State Museum, Columbus (this is the society recognized by the Eastern States Archaeological Federation); (2) The Archaeological Society of Ohio.

Society publications: (1) *Ohio History*, quarterly, Columbus; (2) *Ohio Archaeologist*.

Colleges, universities: Ohio State University, Columbus; Case-Western Reserve College, Cleveland; Miami University, Oxford.

Recommended: *The Fort Ancient Aspect*, James B. Griffin, University of Michigan Press, Ann Arbor.

Prehistory of the Upper Ohio Valley, William J. Mayer-Oakes, Carnegie Museum, Pittsburgh, Pennsylvania.

Oklahoma

State archaeologist: yes; contact at Department of Anthropology, University of Oklahoma, Norman 73069.

State society: Oklahoma Anthropological Society, Department of Anthropology, University of Oklahoma, Norman.

Society publication: *The Bulletin*, annual.

Colleges, universities: University of Oklahoma, Norman.

State legislation: a license is required for all excavation, whether on public or private lands, and 50 percent of the material recovered must be handed over to the state. Licenses, only to qualified persons, are $50 for one year, $25 for renewals. The legislation is probably unworkable, especially as to private lands.

Recommended: *The Cultural Sequence at the Packard Site, Mayes County, Oklahoma*, Don G. Wyckoff, Oklahoma River Basin Survey Project, University of Oklahoma, Norman.

A Survey of Oklahoma Archaeology, Texas Archaeological and Paleontological Society, Lubbock.

Oregon

State archaeologist: no; contact Oregon State Museum of Anthropology, Eugene 97403.

State society: Oregon Archaeological Society; contact Department of Anthropology, University of Oregon, Eugene.

Society publication: *Screenings*, monthly; contact Department of Anthropology, University of Oregon, Eugene.

Colleges, universities: University of Oregon, Eugene; Oregon State University, Corvallis.

State legislation: excavation permits for public lands must be obtained from the Division of Public Lands in Salem and the president of the University of Oregon. Individuals may excavate on public-owned beaches. No other mention of excavation on private lands.

Recommended: *Cultural Sequences at The Dalles, Oregon*, L. S. Cressman, The American Philosophical Society, Philadelphia, Pennsylvania.

Pennsylvania

State archaeologist: yes; contact at William Penn Memorial Museum, Harrisburg 17108.

State society: Society for Pennsylvania Archaeology; contact North Museum, Franklin and Marshall College, Lancaster 17604.

Society publication: *Pennsylvania Archaeologist*, three times a year; contact Society Archives Repository, Carnegie Museum, Pittsburgh 15213.

Colleges, universities: Franklin and Marshall College, Lancaster; University of Pennsylvania, Philadelphia; Pennsylvania State University, University Park.

State legislation: minimal; the Pennsylvania Historical and Museum Commission is charged with historic and prehistoric sites excavation, but there is no provision for permits on either private or public lands. Nonprofessionals receive help and direction from the state archaeologist and other Pennsylvania professionals.

Recommended: *Foundations of Pennsylvania Prehistory*, edited by Barry Kent, Ira F. Smith III, and Catherine McCann, The Pennsylvania Historical and Museum Commission, Harrisburg.

Rhode Island

State archaeologist: no.

State society: Narragansett Archaeological Society of Rhode Island; contact William S. Fowler, Bronson Museum, Attleboro, Massachusetts, or at 67 Primrose Hill Rd., Barrington, Rhode Island 02806.

State publication: none.

Colleges, universities: Brown University, Providence.

State legislation: none.

Recommended: *The Archaeology of Martha's Vineyard: A Framework for the Prehistory of Southern New England,* William A. Ritchie, Natural History Press, Garden City, New York.

South Carolina

State archaeologist: yes; contact at University of South Carolina, Institute of Archaeology and Anthropology, Columbia 29208.

State society: South Carolina Archeology Society, 1601 St. Anthony Dr., Florence 29501.

Society publication: none.

Colleges, universities: University of South Carolina.

State legislation: none directly relating to either state or public lands, except for lands under coastal waters. Permits are required for search of these underwater lands.

Recommended: *The Formative Cultures of the Carolina Piedmont,* Joffre L. Coe, The American Philosophical Society, Philadelphia, Pennsylvania.

South Dakota

State archaeologist: no; contact W. H. Over Museum, University of South Dakota, Vermillion 57069.

State society: South Dakota State Historical Society, Pierre 57501.

Society publication: none.

Colleges, universities: University of South Dakota, Vermillion.

State legislation: the Archaeological Commission is directed to study the prehistory and history of the state on private and public lands, with permits from the State Historical Society being required. Permits granted only to qualified persons. Digging on private lands, however, is specifically exempt from interference or regulation.

Recommended: *Prehistoric Man on the Great Plains,* Waldo R. Wedel, University of Oklahoma Press, Norman.

Tennessee

State archaeologist: yes; contact at Department of Conservation, Division of Archaeology, Nashville.

State society: Tennessee Archaeological Society; contact Alfred K. Guthe, McClung Museum, University of Tennessee, Knoxville 37916.

Society publication: *Tennessee Archaeologist,* McClung Museum, University of Tennessee, Knoxville.

Colleges, universities: University of Tennessee, Knoxville; Memphis State University, Memphis; Vanderbilt University, Nashville.

State legislation: the Division of Archaeology controls archaeology in the state, initiating and maintaining research. Permits to excavate on state lands are issued by the Division only on condition that all materials become the property of the state, to be kept in state custody. Excavation on private land is forbidden without the permission of the landowner, a tacit admission that the landowner may excavate himself as well as give permission. Further, the state archaeologist is required to issue a permit to any citizen or group of citizens to excavate or surface hunt. The citizen or citizens may retain the materials recovered. The latter provision almost negates the intent of the legislation.

Recommended: *Tribes That Slumber: Indian Tribes in the Tennessee Region,* T. M. N. Lewis and Madeline Kneberg, University of Tennessee Press, Knoxville.

Texas

State archaeologist: yes; contact at Texas Historical Survey Committee, Austin 12276.

State society: Texas Archeological Society; contact Department of Anthropology, University of Texas, Austin.

Society publication: *Bulletin,* annual; Department of Anthropology, University of Texas, Austin.

Colleges, universities: University of Texas, Austin; Texas Western College, El Paso; West Texas State University, Canyon; Texas Technological College, Lubbock.

State legislation: the Antiquities Committee issues permits for work on state lands. Sites on private lands may be declared landmarks under state control, with the consent of the owner. The state drives a hard bargain on retention of excavated materials, but excavation on private lands is not touched upon.

Recommended: "A Review of Texas Archeology, Part I," edited by Edward B. Jelks, E. Mott Davis, and Henry B. Sturgis, *Bulletin of the Texas Archeological Society,* Texas Memorial Museum, Austin.

Utah

State archaeologist: no; contact director of archaeological research at the Department of Anthropology, University of Utah, Salt Lake City 84122.

State society: Utah Statewide Archaeological Society; for information contact Department of Anthropology, University of Utah, Salt Lake City.

Society publication: *Utah Archaeology,* quarterly; for information contact Department of Anthropology, University of Utah, Salt Lake City.

Colleges, universities: University of Utah, Salt Lake City; Brigham Young University, Provo 84601.

State legislation: permit power for excavation on state lands is vested in the Division of Parks and Recreation, Salt Lake City. No regulation of excavation on private lands.

Recommended: *Danger Cave,* Jesse D. Jennings, Memoirs of the Society for American Archaeology, 1703 New Hampshire Ave., N.W., Washington, D.C. 20009.

Vermont

State archaeologist: no; contact Department of Sociology and Anthropology, University of Vermont, Burlington 05401.

State society: Vermont Archaeological Society Inc.; contact Director of Libraries, St. Michael's College, Winooski.

Society publication: VAS Monograph Series, nonscheduled; contact Director of Libraries, St. Michael's College, Winooski.

Colleges, universities: University of Vermont, Burlington; St. Michael's College, Winooski; Lyndon State College, Lyndonville.

State legislation: none.

Recommended: *Archaeology in Vermont: Some Reviews Supplemented by Materials from New England and New York,* John C. Huden, University of Vermont, Burlington.

Virginia

State archaeologist: yes; contact Virginia State Library, Richmond 23219.

State society: Archeological Society of Virginia, contact state archaeologist, Virginia State Library, Richmond.

Society publication: *Quarterly Bulletin*; for information contact Virginia State Library, Richmond.

Colleges, universities: College of William and Mary, Williamsburg; University of Virginia, Charlottesville.

State legislation: The Landmarks Committee, within the executive department, is given the responsibility of surveying the state for historic and prehistoric sites. Tax assessments may be reduced on properties declared landmarks by the Committee. There is no provision for the issuance of permits nor mention of excavation on private lands. Much of the extensive archaeological work in Virginia is done by nonprofessionals cooperating with the state archaeologist.

Recommended: "The Accokeek Creek Site," Robert L. Stephenson and Alice L. Ferguson, *Anthropological Papers*, University of Michigan, Ann Arbor.

Washington

State archaeologist: no; contact either Department of Anthropology, University of Washington, Seattle 98105, or Department of Anthropology, Washington State University, Pullman 99163.

State society: Washington Archaeological Society; contact Department of Anthropology, University of Washington, Seattle.

Society publication: *The Washington Archaeologist*; contact Department of Anthropology, University of Washington, Seattle.

Colleges, universities: University of Washington, Seattle; Washington State University, Pullman.

State legislation: destruction of prehistoric remains is prohibited except by permission granted by the president of the University of Washington or Washington State University. The prohibition apparently covers both public and private lands, but is weak.

Recommended: *Early Man in Washington*, Richard D. Daugherty, Department of Conservation, Olympia.

West Virginia

State archaeologist: yes; contact at West Virginia Geological and Economic Survey, Morgantown 26505.

State society: West Virginia Archeological Society Inc; contact West Virginia Geological Survey, Morgantown.

Society publication: *The West Virginia Archeologist*; West Virginia Geological Survey, Morgantown.

Colleges, universities: University of West Virginia, Morgantown.

State legislation: the West Virginia Antiquities Commission is directed and empowered to locate sites, direct archaeological research, and determine priorities for state lands and for private lands when rights have been acquired.

Recommended: *Introduction to West Virginia Archeology*, Edward V. McMichael, West Virginia Geological and Economic Survey, Morgantown.

Wisconsin

State archaeologist: yes; contact at State Historical Society of Wisconsin, Madison 53706.

State society: Wisconsin Archeological Society, Milwaukee Public Museum, Milwaukee 53201.

Society publication: *The Wisconsin Archeologist*; Milwaukee Public Museum, Milwaukee.

Colleges, universities: University of Wisconsin—Milwaukee, Milwaukee; University of Wisconsin, Madison.

State legislation: Only the state archaeologist or persons granted permits by the State Historical Society of Wisconsin may excavate on state lands. Excavation on private lands is discouraged, but may be done with the written permission of the landowner.

Recommended: *Indian Life in the Upper Great Lakes: 11,000 B.C. to A.D. 1800*, George I. Quimby, University of Chicago Press, Chicago, Illinois.

Prehistoric Indians of Wisconsin, Robert E. Ritzenthaler, Milwaukee Public Museum, Milwaukee.

Wyoming

State archaeologist: yes; contact at Department of Anthropology, University of Wyoming, Laramie 82070.

State society: none.

Society publication: none.

Colleges, universities: University of Wyoming, Laramie.

State legislation: a permit from the State Board of Land Commissioners is required for excavation on state lands. No mention of private lands excavation.

Recommended: "The McKean Site in Northeastern Wyoming," William Mulloy, *Southwestern Journal of Anthropology*, Albuquerque, New Mexico.

CANADA

Miscellaneous information for Canadian beginners

Alberta

Society: Archaeological Society of Alberta; contact Department of Sociology and Anthropology, University of Alberta, Edmonton.

Society publication: *Archaeological Society of Alberta Newsletter*, quarterly; contact Department of Sociology and Anthropology, University of Alberta, Edmonton.

Manitoba

Society: Manitoba Archaeological Society; contact Publications Committee, Box 1171, Winnipeg 1.

Society publication: *Manitoba Archaeological Newsletter*; contact Publications Committee, Box 1171, Winnipeg 1.

Ontario

Society: Ontario Archaeological Society; contact Royal Ontario Museum, Toronto.

Society publication: *Ontario Archaeology*; contact editor, Department of Anthropology, University of Toronto, Toronto.

Saskatchewan

Periodical publication: *Napao, A Saskatchewan Anthropology Journal*; Department of Anthropology and Archaeology, University of Saskatchewan, Saskatoon.

Helpful Periodicals

American Antiquity, the quarterly journal of the Society for American Archaeology; contact *American Antiquity*, 1703 New Hampshire Ave., N.W., Washington, D.C. 20009. Policy emphasis on archaeology as anthropology.

Science, American Association for the Advancement of Science, weekly, 50 weeks per year; 1515 Massachusetts Ave., N.W., Washington, D.C. 20005. Occasional but important and timely pieces on archaeology.

Scientific American, monthly; Scientific American Inc., 415 Madison Ave., New York, N.Y. 10017. Occasional important and current articles, written for the general reader, on archaeology.

Archaeology, quarterly; Archaeological Institute of America, 100 Washington Square East, New York, N.Y. 10003.

American Journal of Archaeology, quarterly; Archaeological Institute of America, Princeton University, Princeton, N.J. 08540.

Bulletin, Eastern States Archaeological Association, annual; Office of State Archeologist, Hall of Records, Dover, Del. Abstracts of papers delivered at the ESAF annual meeting.

Index